Exclusive Online Resou⋯

As our valued reader, your purchase of this book includes access to exclusive online resources designed to enhance your learning experience. These resources can be downloaded from our website, www.vibrantpublishers.com, and are created to help you turn data into insights effectively, with Microsoft® Power BI.

Online resources for this book include the following essential components:

1. HR Dataset Template
2. Power BI Report Template
3. Power BI Visualization Guide for Managers
4. Creating a Power BI Template Using HR_Dataset
5. Case Study: People Analytics Dashboard
6. People Analytics KPI Dashboard Template
7. Employee Productivity Report Template
8. Engagement & Well-Being Survey Visualization Template
9. Attrition Risk Forecasting Template

Kindly note: All images included in this book are also accessible through the Online Resources section.

Why are these online resources valuable?

- **Practical learning:** These resources will allow you to experiment with real-world datasets to sharpen your Power BI skills and improve data interpretation.
- **Readily usable structures:** They provide pre-built layouts, saving time and effort for you to quickly start building your reports.

- **Best practices in design:** The templates are structured using best practices of Power BI, helping you understand report design and visualization principles.
- **Step-by-step learning:** They guide you through creating your Power BI template from scratch, building a deep understanding of the tool's capabilities.

How to access your online resources:

1. Visit the website: Go to www.vibrantpublishers.com
2. Find your book: Navigate to the book's product page via the "Shop" menu or by searching for the book title in the search bar.
3. Request the resources: Scroll down to the "Request Sample Book/ Online Resource" section.
4. Enter your details: Enter your preferred email ID and select "Online Resource" as the resource type. Lastly, select "user type" and submit the request.
5. Check your inbox: The resources will be delivered directly to your email.

https://bit.ly/mpbi-slm

Alternatively, for quick access, simply scan the QR code below to go directly to the product page and request the online resources by filling in the required details.

Happy learning!

VIBRANT
PUBLISHERS ™

SELF-LEARNING MANAGEMENT SERIES

MICROSOFT®
POWER BI
ESSENTIALS
YOU ALWAYS WANTED TO KNOW

Transform data into actionable insights, harnessing the potential of Power BI for organizational success.

DR. SINI V. PILLAI

MICROSOFT® POWER BI ESSENTIALS YOU ALWAYS WANTED TO KNOW

First Edition

Published by Vibrant Publishers LLC, USA, www.vibrantpublishers.com

Paperback: 978-1-63651-571-7
Ebook: 978-1-63651-572-4
Hardback: 978-1-63651-573-1

Library of Congress Control Number: 2025942512

This publication is designed to provide accurate and authoritative information regarding the subject matter covered. The Author has made every effort in the preparation of this book to ensure the accuracy of the information. However, information in this book is sold without warranty, either expressed or implied. The Author or the Publisher will not be liable for any damages caused or alleged to be caused either directly or indirectly by this book.

All trademarks and registered trademarks mentioned in this publication are the property of their respective owners. These trademarks are used for editorial and educational purposes only, without intent to infringe upon any trademark rights. This publication is independent and has not been authorized, endorsed, or approved by any trademark owner.

Vibrant Publishers' books are available at special quantity discounts for sales promotions, or for use in corporate training programs. For more information, please write to bulkorders@vibrantpublishers.com

Please email feedback/corrections (technical, grammatical, or spelling) to spellerrors@vibrantpublishers.com

Vibrant publishes in a variety of print and electronic formats and by print-on-demand. Some material included with standard print versions of this book may not be included in e-books or in print-on-demand. To access the complete catalog of Vibrant Publishers, visit www.vibrantpublishers.com

SELF-LEARNING MANAGEMENT SERIES

TITLE	PAPERBACK* ISBN
BUSINESS AND ENTREPRENEURSHIP	
BUSINESS COMMUNICATION ESSENTIALS	9781636511634
BUSINESS ETHICS ESSENTIALS	9781636513324
BUSINESS LAW ESSENTIALS	9781636511702
BUSINESS PLAN ESSENTIALS	9781636511214
BUSINESS STRATEGY ESSENTIALS	9781949395778
ENTREPRENEURSHIP ESSENTIALS	9781636511603
INTERNATIONAL BUSINESS ESSENTIALS	9781636513294
PRINCIPLES OF MANAGEMENT ESSENTIALS	9781636511542
COMPUTER SCIENCE AND TECHNOLOGY	
BLOCKCHAIN ESSENTIALS	9781636513003
MACHINE LEARNING ESSENTIALS	9781636513775
PYTHON ESSENTIALS	9781636512938
DATA SCIENCE FOR BUSINESS	
BUSINESS INTELLIGENCE ESSENTIALS	9781636513362
DATA ANALYTICS ESSENTIALS	9781636511184
FINANCIAL LITERACY AND ECONOMICS	
COST ACCOUNTING & MANAGEMENT ESSENTIALS	9781636511030
FINANCIAL ACCOUNTING ESSENTIALS	9781636510972
FINANCIAL MANAGEMENT ESSENTIALS	9781636511009
MACROECONOMICS ESSENTIALS	9781636511818
MICROECONOMICS ESSENTIALS	9781636511153
PERSONAL FINANCE ESSENTIALS	9781636511849
PRINCIPLES OF ECONOMICS ESSENTIALS	9781636512334

*Also available in Hardback & Ebook formats

SELF-LEARNING MANAGEMENT SERIES

TITLE	PAPERBACK* ISBN

HR, DIVERSITY, AND ORGANIZATIONAL SUCCESS

DIVERSITY, EQUITY, AND INCLUSION ESSENTIALS	9781636512976
DIVERSITY IN THE WORKPLACE ESSENTIALS	9781636511122
HR ANALYTICS ESSENTIALS	9781636510347
HUMAN RESOURCE MANAGEMENT ESSENTIALS	9781949395839
ORGANIZATIONAL BEHAVIOR ESSENTIALS	9781636512303
ORGANIZATIONAL DEVELOPMENT ESSENTIALS	9781636511481

LEADERSHIP AND PERSONAL DEVELOPMENT

DECISION MAKING ESSENTIALS	9781636510026
INDIA'S ROAD TO TRANSFORMATION: WHY LEADERSHIP MATTERS	9781636512273
LEADERSHIP ESSENTIALS	9781636510316
TIME MANAGEMENT ESSENTIALS	9781636511665

MODERN MARKETING AND SALES

CONSUMER BEHAVIOR ESSENTIALS	9781636513263
DIGITAL MARKETING ESSENTIALS	9781949395747
MARKETING MANAGEMENT ESSENTIALS	9781636511788
MARKET RESEARCH ESSENTIALS	9781636513744
SALES MANAGEMENT ESSENTIALS	9781636510743
SERVICES MARKETING ESSENTIALS	9781636511733
SOCIAL MEDIA MARKETING ESSENTIALS	9781636512181

*Also available in Hardback & Ebook formats

SELF-LEARNING MANAGEMENT SERIES

TITLE	PAPERBACK* ISBN
OPERATIONS MANAGEMENT	
AGILE ESSENTIALS	9781636510057
OPERATIONS & SUPPLY CHAIN MANAGEMENT ESSENTIALS	9781949395242
PROJECT MANAGEMENT ESSENTIALS	9781636510712
STAKEHOLDER ENGAGEMENT ESSENTIALS	9781636511511
CURRENT AFFAIRS	
DIGITAL SHOCK	9781636513805

*Also available in Hardback & Ebook formats

About the Author

Dr. Sini V. Pillai is a researcher and an academician at Digital University Kerala with a profound passion for data analytics and business intelligence. She brings over 15 years of academic and practical insight into how technology can be harnessed to advance business goals. Her expertise in Power BI and its application in managerial decision-making has made her a trusted advisor to professionals and entrepreneurs seeking to unlock the power of data within their organizations.

Dr. Pillai holds a Ph.D. in management, specializing in the intersection of technology and business strategy. Her research has been published in top-tier journals, focusing on digital transformation, technology-enabled product development, and strategic management. Outside academia, she consults with organizations, translating technical expertise into practical strategies that foster organizational growth.

With *Microsoft Power BI Essentials You Always Wanted to Know (Microsoft Power BI Essentials)*, Dr. Pillai empowers leaders and professionals to fully utilize the power of data analytics. She aims to inspire a shift in how organizations operate and grow in today's fast-paced, data-driven world.

What Experts Say About This Book!

"Microsoft Power BI Essentials" by Dr. Sini V. Pillai is primarily meant for practitioners who want to upgrade their technology skills in "digital storytelling," but can also be used by teachers, students, and professionals. In this era of data and data-driven systems across areas ranging from business and economics to politics, this book serves as a guide to understanding, analyzing, and presenting data and making recommendations.

The book is relatively brief, spanning seven chapters, yet comprehensive enough to equip the reader with the essential knowledge on all the relevant topics. Meaningful illustrations and use cases are provided in each chapter to guide the reader hands-on, so immediate application is possible in the area of interest to the reader. The author has attempted to provide adequate conceptual depth on the topics, keeping in mind a wide range of user backgrounds, and at the same time ensuring effective skill development for diverse applications.

– Prof. K G Satheesh Kumar, PhD,
Emeritus Visiting Professor and Chair, Digital University Kerala

The topics covered in the book, including data storytelling, importing and transforming data, data modeling, exploring visuals, formatting visuals, digital storytelling, and lastly deploying reports, illustrate a cascade of information about Business Intelligence. Each chapter highlights targeted 'key learning objectives,' fun facts, practical tips, activities, chapter summaries, discussion questions, a 10-point quiz, and case studies for two chapters together, with all types of eye-catching representations; precisely a "self learning book." Indeed, the book transformed 'ideas into actionable insights.' It truly turned 'data' into insight and insight into 'action.'

– Dr. A.V.V. Prasada Raju,
FIIIE, FIIM, FIE, FMTC, FCAE, SMAE, SMISE Chairman,
IIIE National Council

This book by Dr. Sini V. Pillai offers a concise, detailed tutorial on how to become proficient with Power BI. Its lesson format, which includes knowledge-testing quizzes at the conclusion of each chapter, is what I enjoy most about it. It goes into great detail while remaining practical, demonstrating how Power BI may be used in a variety of actual business scenarios. It's a great resource for both novices and experts, full of examples and simple to follow.

– Bianca Szasz, Ph.D.,
Space Systems Engineer

Table of Contents

4   Exploring Visuals and Charts   137

5   KPI and Formatting Visuals   203

Acknowledgement

I extend my heartfelt gratitude to all those who supported and inspired me throughout the journey of writing *Microsoft Power BI Essentials*. Most importantly, I am deeply thankful to my university librarian, Dr. Gopakumar V., whose motivation and unwavering belief in my abilities gave me the confidence to take up this writing endeavor. His insightful input and timely facilitation of access to valuable resources played a crucial role in shaping the content of this book.

I am especially grateful to Dr. Saji Gopinath, former Vice Chancellor, Digital University Kerala, for his visionary leadership and inspiration, which have always motivated me to pursue impactful academic work. I would also like to express sincere appreciation to my family for their unconditional support, patience, and encouragement throughout the writing process. A special note of thanks to my husband, Vinu P. Nair, and to my dear sons, Asvin and Ayaan, whose smiles, love, and energy have been my greatest source of joy and balance during this journey. Their understanding and faith in me kept me grounded and focused.

My students have been a continual source of inspiration—your curiosity and enthusiasm for learning have guided the practical direction of this book. I also thank my colleagues and friends, whose collaboration, insightful discussions, and words of encouragement contributed immensely to the completion of this work.

I dedicate this book to each one of you with gratitude.

Preface

Making data-driven decisions has become essential in today's fast-paced business environment. As someone who has worked in both industry and academia, I have seen how data can transform decision-making into a calculated risk-taking process, leading to better outcomes for manufacturing and service organizations. I have also witnessed the challenges confronted by various complex data analytics tools. This is where *Microsoft Power BI* (Power BI) comes into play, bridging the gap between raw data and actionable insights and empowering managers to lead confidently.

My inspiration for writing this book has emerged from the drive to learn and master Power BI. Through trial and error and countless hours of self-study using real-world applications, I learned how to tap into the highest potential of Power BI. The self-study experience fueled my passion for sharing this knowledge with others.

Throughout the seven chapters of this book, I have distilled my professional experience and insights into practical guidance with step-by-step instructions that you can apply directly. *Microsoft Power BI* Essentials will guide you in making data-driven decisions, streamlining business processes, and enhancing performance using Power BI applications. My ultimate goal is to equip you with the tools and confidence to turn data into a strategic asset for you and your organization.

The journey of writing this book has been deeply fulfilling, and I'm thrilled to be able to share it with you.

Introduction to the Book

Microsoft Power BI Essentials is an introductory guide for entrepreneurs, leaders, and professionals to understand the capabilities of Power BI for effective data analysis and storytelling. Power BI facilitates data visualizations by seamlessly transforming complex datasets into visual formats with rich, interactive experiences.

The book comprises seven chapters, each focusing on various aspects of the Power BI application. The First Chapter details data and sources of data. It highlights the need to transform data into visualizations for digital storytelling, which is inevitable for managers dealing with complex data volumes. The Second Chapter deals with understanding how to connect with various data sources, Excel, SQL Server, and the Web. It explains how to use Power BI Query Editor, a powerful tool in Power BI to perform transformations and data cleaning. Various transformation processes, such as filtering, sorting, and merging, are also illustrated with examples.

Chapter Three explores the principles of data modeling, introducing how to create data models that are scalable and flexible. The chapter also covers identifying, editing relationships, and exploring new relationships in data tables. It addresses summarization, categorization, hiding, renaming, deleting columns, and other operations in creating data models. The Fourth Chapter highlights different forms of data visualizations available; about 27 visualization tools are represented with data and examples. Readers can evaluate various options and choose the best visualization tool to plot and represent their data, meeting reporting requirements.

The Fifth Chapter offers insight into key performance indicators and various formatting options in visualizations. Learning about them will enable readers to enrich business stories to track performances, measures, and indicators. Chapter Six explores how to customize visualizations for larger plots and scales in a geographical context, using spatial analysis and precise map-based visualizations.

Lastly, Chapter Seven will introduce Power BI Desktop, which focuses on creating Power BI datasets, reports, and dashboards. It applies a managerial perspective to craft data storytelling with business acumen. The book follows a structured approach that serves as the right starting point for beginners. It helps them use data to make informed decisions through effective visualizations and the power of digital storytelling.

Who Can Benefit From This Book?

Business leaders, analysts, and professionals are expected to derive meaningful insights from data to drive innovation, optimize performance, and influence high-level decisions. *Microsoft Power BI* Essentials shall serve as a comprehensive guide to bridge the gap between data and insights through effective visualizations and interactive storytelling.

This book is designed to support a wide range of learners and professionals, including:

- **Early-career professionals:** aiming to upskill and stand out in roles involving data interpretation and reporting.

- **Data enthusiasts and analysts:** seeking a beginner-friendly guide to strengthen their knowledge of Power BI fundamentals and interactivity.

- **Trainers and educators:** who wish to use a reliable resource to introduce Power BI in classrooms and training programs.

- **Managers and decision makers:** who are looking to use Power BI for building dashboards that support strategic decisions and performance tracking.

- **IT and MIS Professionals:** interested in integrating business intelligence tools into enterprise-level solutions and driving system-wide improvements.

How to Use This Book?

We live in a world powered by data. The success of any business manager depends on their ability to analyze and interpret that data, not just for making informed decisions or streamlining operations, but for shaping enterprise-level strategy.

This book is a ready-to-act guide to help leaders and professionals enhance data skills, especially for newcomers eager to make data-driven decisions. Each chapter of the book concentrates on a diverse aspect of Power BI. From data preparation and modeling to advanced visualizations and real-world business applications, the book guides readers through key Power BI features in a step-by-step manner.

If you are new to Power BI, start with Chapter One and continue till Chapter Three. These chapters will enable an understanding of the foundations and core functionalities of Power BI. Further, explore the chapters till Chapter Seven.

If you are a manager responsible for data-driven decision-making, focus on Chapters Four, Five, Six, and Seven. These chapters shall help identify visualization components best representing the data, determine the key performance indicators, and aid in spatial data analysis. The last chapter will provide a managerial perspective on using Power BI Desktop to curate data stories and gain actionable insights.

This page is intentionally left blank

CHAPTER 1

Introduction to Power BI, Data, and Storytelling

Key Learning Objectives

- Understand various types of data and data sources.
- Gain familiarity with Power BI, its relevance for professionals, organizations, and its installation process.
- Learn how data analysis works and compare Power BI with other analytic tools.
- Explore the significance of data visualization and storytelling.

Data is everywhere in various forms and formats, such as spreadsheets and databases. Data emerges as an inevitable asset for driving strategic decision-making in any organization that seeks operational efficiency and organizational success. Organizations today have access to this omnipresent data resource from various sources, including traditional systems, social media, customer interactions, and Internet of Things (IoT) devices.

However, for enterprises, the actual power of data lies in converting it to the required information, also known as actionable intelligence. This is where the concept of "business intelligence" comes into the picture. Simply explained, Business Intelligence (BI) is the process of collecting, analyzing, and presenting data to help organizations make informed decisions. BI involves using tools, technologies, and practices to turn raw data into actionable insights. It improves strategic planning, performance, and competitiveness.

To carry out these functions—to set up a robust BI system within an organization and generate valuable insights, one would need a recognized and trustworthy BI tool. Microsoft Power BI is a leading BI transformation tool that aggregates, cleans, and converts data in order to uncover trends and patterns within the data and make data-driven decisions.

In this chapter, you will be introduced to analytical capabilities in Power BI for data-driven decision-making. This will be followed by a step-by-step guide on installing Power BI, enabling you to leverage the benefits of BI in an enterprise setting.

Given that data is central to BI, next, we will delve into an overview of data, including sources and types, and explore the technical aspects of data. We will understand the distinction between structured, semi-structured, and unstructured data, including numerical data. The chapter will also shed light on the various key functions surrounding data, which are fulfilled through Power BI. This includes data analysis, storytelling, and visualization. Further, we will understand the importance of data visualization in BI for business managers.

Before we proceed to understanding all about Power BI, its features, and core components, let's first understand the role of data in BI and the essential terminologies of data that we will come across frequently in the book.

1.1 Data Foundations: Building Blocks for Power BI

Data is a valuable asset when it is properly processed. The following section will outline the role of data in BI. It will equip us to understand how data provides different views when worked on, so let's begin:

- **Decision-making:** Data enables informed decision-making by providing valuable insights and guiding strategic choices in organizations. Analyzing, interpreting, and identifying trends and correlations helps improve overall business performance. Data-driven decision-making also helps to address pressing societal challenges and improve public services.

- **Competitive analysis:** Leveraging data to assess customer preferences and market trends, followed by optimizing internal and external operations, equips organizations to stay ahead of the competition, especially when developing new products and services. Data analysis also helps identify organizational bottlenecks and inefficiencies. It optimizes resource allocation by developing evidence-based policies for higher management to act upon. This leads to enhanced productivity and cost savings for the business.

- **Customization:** Pooling data at a granular level and sorting and analyzing it based on market requirements enables organizations to reflect on customers' behavior and perceptions. Thus, it aids in customizing business solutions and enhances the overall customer experience.

- **Risk mitigation:** Data helps organizations identify emerging opportunities and potential risks by monitoring market and consumer trends. Thereby, businesses can proactively adopt strategies to identify new markets and mitigate risks, well before the time.

- **Innovation:** Data is crucial in scientific research and technological advancements. This includes advancements in healthcare, climate change, space exploration, and similar fields. It is the need of the hour to conduct research and make ground-breaking innovations to shape the future. Ultimately, data becomes crucial in driving positive social change by addressing social issues such as poverty and inequality, and improving the lives of individuals and communities.

Based on its characteristics, data can be classified into several types. We will look into the various types of data in the upcoming section.

1.1.1 Types of data

Data varies from structured formats to unstructured formats like multimedia files. When processed effectively, these data formats can reveal patterns and insights critical for decision-making and drive strategic growth. Let's understand the different types of data:

Structured data

A highly organized data structure follows a predefined format, typically stored in relational databases or spreadsheets. Structured data is organized into rows and columns with well-defined relationships. Examples of structured data are sales data, customer data, financial records, and inventory data.

Unstructured data

Unstructured data does not have a predefined format. It is often generated in large volumes and cannot be processed using traditional methods. Unstructured data includes data from emails, social media posts, audio and video files, and images. This type of data demands advanced techniques like natural language processing, machine learning, and computer vision to be processed and analyzed for meaningful insights.

Semi-structured data

Semi-structured data does not conform exactly to a structured or an unstructured type of data format. These data models fall somewhere between structured and unstructured types. Semi-structured data has some form of organizational properties, but they do not adhere to a specific, rigid, pre-defined format.

This type of data often contains tags, labels, or metadata. Examples of semi-structured data include Extensible Markup Language (XML) files, JavaScript Object Notation (JSON) data, weblogs, and emails with specific formatting.

Time-series data

Time-series data represents measurements or observations collected over a specific time interval. Typically, it includes a timestamp associated with each data point. It is commonly used in weather forecasting and stock market analysis.

Geospatial data

Geospatial data refers to data associated with specific geographic locations on the Earth. This includes maps, satellite imagery, Global Positioning System (GPS) data, and spatial boundaries. Geospatial data is used in urban planning, transportation, environmental monitoring, and location-based services.

Categorical data

Categorical data does not have a numerical value; rather, it represents qualities, characteristics, or attributes. Examples include gender (male, female), product categories, segments, and customer segments with predefined options.

Numerical data

Numerical data represents quantitative values that can be measured or expressed as numbers and categorized into discrete or continuous data. Discrete data represents counts, such as the number of customers and units sold. Continuous data represents measurements on a continuous scale, such as temperature, height, weight, or revenue.

The data types mentioned above are not mutually exclusive. A dataset often contains a combination of different data types. Such raw datasets require proper analysis as they reveal no meaningful story or insights by themselves. Data analysis and visualization techniques must incorporate the characteristics and requirements of the specific data type, extract meaningful insights, and derive conclusions.

Figure 1.1	Types of Data

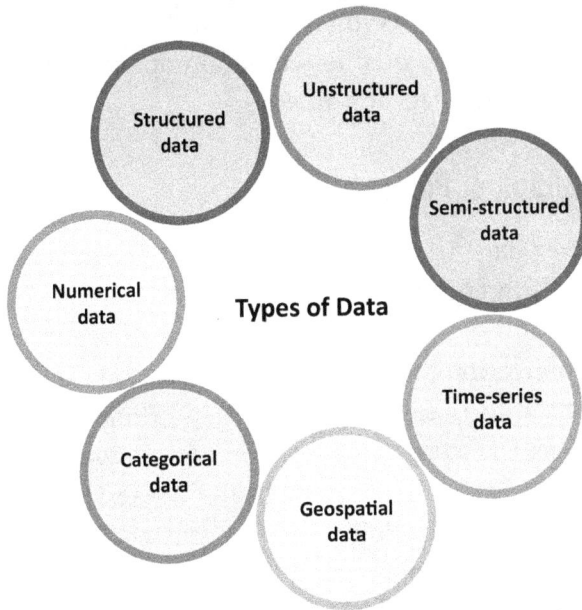

Now that we have equipped ourselves with the foundations of data for business intelligence, let's begin by exploring the star of the show, "Power BI," in the upcoming section.

1.2 What Is Power BI?

Power BI, developed by Microsoft, is a powerful tool for managing datasets and creating intelligent visualizations, all within a single platform. Power BI has massive applications as a corporate BI solution. It helps to generate reliable outcomes within just a few hours.

It is a robust data analytics tool that bridges raw data and business intelligence. It empowers businesses to model and visualize data with visually engaging, actionable, and clear insights. These visualization capabilities enable managers to convert data and represent it as customizable dashboards and reports. Visualizing data allows us to unveil the story behind large volumes of data. This capability is indispensable for any business to attain operational efficiency through impactful decision-making.

1.2.1 Evolution of Power BI

Over the years, the increasing demand for an accessible business intelligence tool has driven Power BI to evolve into a versatile solution. The journey of Power BI began in 2010 as a data visualization tool by Microsoft, built on the Microsoft Silverlight platform for a project named "Project Crescent." Later, Project Crescent was rebranded as "Power View" when it was released in 2013. It offered data visualization within Excel and SharePoint; however, its accessibility was limited only to those platforms. With time, the increasing demand for an impactful BI tool drove Microsoft to develop Power BI as a standalone platform.

In 2015, Power BI was officially launched. At this point, it was more of a versatile, cloud-based tool with interactive data visualization abilities, providing business intelligence solutions. The new Power BI version is a combined capability version incorporating Power View, Power Query, and Power Pivot. This version was more user-friendly with a drag-and-drop interface. It made data analysis accessible to all types of users, both technical and non-technical. It provided a suite of dashboards with real-time analytics sourced from Excel, SQL databases, and web services.

As it evolved further, Power BI offered custom visuals, and in 2016, it added Power BI Desktop, allowing more complex data modeling. Over time, Power BI Premium was introduced by presenting dedicated cloud resources with enhanced capacity for scaling it at an enterprise level.

Artificial Intelligence (AI), machine learning integrations, and advanced AI capabilities for sentiment analysis have made it a more robust tool for data modeling. Organizations of all sizes, from small to medium to large enterprises, can now leverage data for informed decision-making thanks to Power BI.

Table 1.1   Evolution of Power BI

Year	Milestone
2010	Power BI was kick-started as a data visualization tool by Microsoft for a project named "Project Crescent."
2013	Power BI Office 365 was released as an add-on to Excel, featuring tools like Power Pivot.
2015	Power BI Desktop was launched with Power BI Cloud as a standalone service.
2016	Power BI custom visuals were introduced.
2017	Power BI Embedded was released primarily to allow users to integrate visual analytics capabilities of Power BI directly into their applications.
2018	AI and Natural Language Query capabilities were introduced in Power BI.
2020	Enhanced collaboration features were added to Power BI.
2021	A premium per-user licensing for accessing advanced features was introduced.
2022	Hybrid data connectivity was enhanced for better integration and performance.
2023	AI-powered copilot features were introduced in Power BI to assist with data analysis and report creation.
2024	Additional features were added, such as a path layer for Azure Maps, text slicer, Copilot in Power BI mobile apps, visual cards update, and more.

1.3 Why Power BI Is Beneficial for Professionals and Businesses

For professionals, especially managers, Power BI is a promising tool that assists in monitoring operations and deriving answers quickly using rich visualizations in dashboards. It hosts a series of features for effective project management, especially when multiple projects are ongoing simultaneously. Let's explore some of its key benefits, detailed below:

Effective project management

Managers who want to succeed should be aware of essential metrics and trends within and outside their organization. Power BI helps identify trends and seize new opportunities by delivering valuable insights through interactive reports and dashboards.

Diverse Power BI dashboards can be created for different stakeholders with role-based credentials for interaction with reports. Dashboards also enable users to gain substantial insights into project performance and track everything centrally. Power BI also facilitates functions like monitoring the status of multiple projects, managing engagement across various teams, managing resources, and prioritizing tasks by managing an entire project portfolio for managers.

Data transformation

Built-in custom visualizations can be enabled to get deeper insights, enrich project data, and transform it in a way the manager would like to view. Various projects and their performance over different metrics can be visualized in Power BI for better and prompt decision-making.

Tailor-made reports

One of the significant benefits of Power BI for businesses and professionals is that it helps generate reports with meaningful insights, tailor-made for each requirement. For example, total project costs can be displayed against overall completion days, plotted in column charts; table reports can be automatically generated in various styles based on the type of data.

Unified performance reporting

Multiple measures can be presented visually within the same grid in a Power BI report for managers, across departments like finance, marketing, sales, human resources, Information Technology (IT), and operations. Thus, Power BI is considered a self-service tool by various branches of business as they rely on it to source, transform, and model data, and derive insights about the performance of resources in the organization.

Power BI mobile app

Today, many BI tools are available for managers, but most may not be as efficient, fast, interactive, and user-friendly as Power BI. In some cases, other tools may not process real-time data effectively, and reports generated by them may not be compatible with mobile devices.

Decision-makers and managers require quick access to accurate data and information at their fingertips and in a secure manner. The Power BI mobile app addresses this issue by being available across all versions. It is also easy to set up.

Through these key functionalities, Power BI turns data into actionable analytics and improves productivity across multiple projects.

1.3.1 Key features of Power BI

Let's cover a few key features of Power BI for enterprises and professionals:

- In Power BI, data can be accessed from various sources, including large datasets. It can connect to many databases and integrate with corporate systems, making it easier to import, export, and share data using Power Query.
- Power BI equips users to generate real-time reports with interactive and insightful data visualizations.
- The user interface of Power BI enables data exploration with interactive elements and dynamic features, allowing users to ask questions about the data.
- Power BI provides the current status of data to all stakeholders simultaneously.
- It delivers personalized and curated content for professionals and management.
- It generates quick solutions with reports and visualizations.

1.4 Power BI and Data

To derive reliable insights for accurate decision-making, the Power BI tool combines data from various sources and formats, including structured, semi-structured, and unstructured data. By transforming this diverse data into digestible visuals, Power BI helps identify trends and patterns and enables managers to create interactive dashboards and reports.

However, the effectiveness of Power BI is dependent on the quality of data it processes. High-quality data is essential to ensure error-free, holistic analysis and actionable insights, making it a critical factor for informed decisions. In the next section, we will explore how Power BI carries out a vast array of important data functions to ensure that the data used for analysis is homogeneous and precise.

1.4.1 Power BI: One-stop shop for data modeling, visualization, and reporting

Power BI uses Power Query for data transformation, including filtering, cleaning, and standardizing functions. Data transformation and modeling make data more consistent and reliable for analysis. These capabilities of Power Query enable establishing relationships between various datasets to analyze patterns from different perspectives. Further, it identifies underlying connections for multidimensional analysis.

Key capabilities:

In addition to these data functions, Power BI also offers other solutions for strategic analysis, such as visualization tools, including bar charts, line graphs, maps, and custom visuals to present key metrics and trends. Power BI dashboards facilitate real-time data updates with interactive visuals. Managers can drill down for more granular insights about the data trends and evaluate various scenarios using the "what-if" analysis feature.

Power BI also leverages AI to generate deeper insights and uncover patterns that may not be immediately apparent. This feature of Power BI enables predictive analytics for proactive decision-making, allowing businesses to overcome risks effectively.

The following sections will guide us through the fundamentals of Power BI, followed by an introduction to

Power BI Desktop View, and storytelling in Power BI with data analysis and visualization.

1.5 Core Elements of Power BI

In this section, we'll dive into the primary elements that make Power BI a versatile and indispensable tool for data analytics and business intelligence:

1. Visualization

Visualization is the process of representing data through engaging visuals such as charts, graphs, maps, or other interactive graphics. Power BI has a good number of visualizations that represent data in creative ways; a few of them are shown in Figure 1.2 below.

Figure 1.2 Sample Visualizations Generated in Power BI

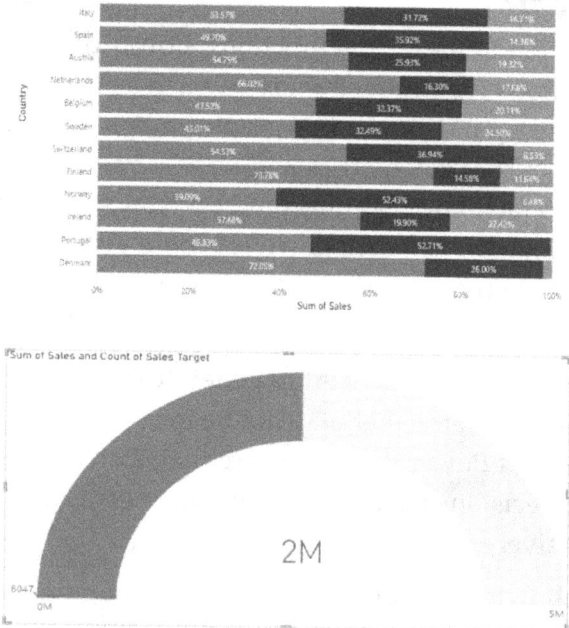

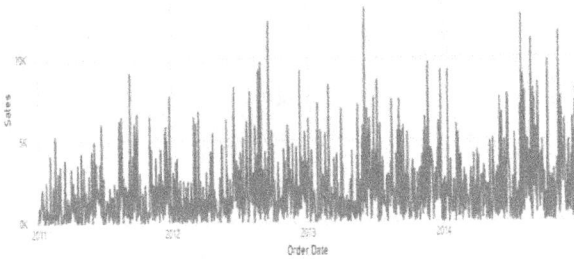

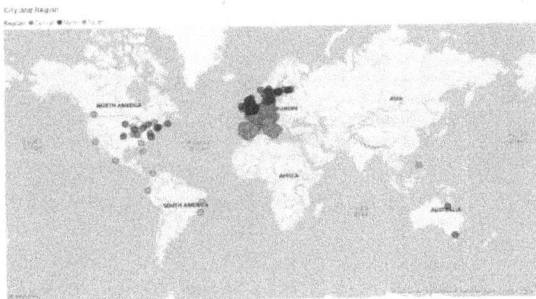

2. Datasets

A dataset is a collection of data used by Power BI to create visualizations such as charts, graphs, or maps. In other words, the data powering a report's visuals is referred to as the dataset. A dataset does not need to originate from a single source and can be a filtered collection of data from multiple sources. Figure 1.3 shows a sample dataset in Power BI, which uses Excel.

Figure 1.3 Example of a Dataset

Order ID	Order Date	Customer Name	Country	State	City	Region	Segment	Ship Mode
AZ-2011-6674500	04 January 2011	Devin Huddleston	France	Auvergne-Rhône-Alpes	Valence	Central	Consumer	Economy
AZ-2011-2002251	20 January 2011	Nathan Iqbal	France	Ile-de-France	Villiers-sur-Marne	Central	Consumer	Economy
AZ-2011-5010109	25 January 2011	Walter Coley	France	Ile-de-France	Maisons-Alfort	Central	Consumer	Economy
AZ-2011-2397035	07 February 2011	Millie Newman	France	Nord-Pas-de-Calais-Picardie	Boulogne-sur-Mer	Central	Consumer	Economy
AZ-2011-4069925	01 March 2011	Oscar Clayton	France	Alsace-Champagne-Ardenne-Lorraine	Colmar	Central	Consumer	Economy
AZ-2011-3714764	11 March 2011	Ashton Charles	France	Aquitaine-Limousin-Poitou-Charentes	Pessac	Central	Consumer	Economy
AZ-2011-332801	19 April 2011	Koby Tompson	France	Auvergne-Rhône-Alpes	Riom	Central	Consumer	Economy
BN-2011-5672017	27 April 2011	Louie Knight	France	Alsace-Champagne-Ardenne-Lorraine	Chaumont	Central	Consumer	Economy
AZ-2011-2112563	10 May 2011	Francesca Bowen	France	Ile-de-France	Champigny-sur-Marne	Central	Consumer	Economy
AZ-2011-7005483	13 May 2011	Robert James	France	Ile-de-France	Vincennes	Central	Consumer	Economy
BN-2011-4249147	03 June 2011	Ada Dalton	France	Alsace-Champagne-Ardenne-Lorraine	Strasbourg	Central	Home Office	Economy
AZ-2011-3901505	27 June 2011	Kayla Tearle	France	Aquitaine-Limousin-Poitou-Charentes	Mont-de-Marsan	Central	Corporate	Economy
AZ-2011-6011646	09 July 2011	Nancy Fike	France	Ile-de-France	Vincennes	Central	Corporate	Economy
AZ-2011-3858939	29 September 2011	Julian Mack	France	Ile-de-France	Courbevoie	Central	Consumer	Economy

3. Reports

A report is a structured collection of visualizations spread across a single or multiple pages. It organizes these visual elements to effectively communicate the insights and narratives derived from the input data. A report usually comprises several charts, pie, line, or bar charts, maps, and graphs that convey key information.

4. Dashboards

A dashboard is an assortment of visualizations on a single page. It is similar to a report; however, it can fit on a single page. It can be shared with another user or multiple users, who can then interact with the data offered in the dashboard. Figure 1.4 below shows a sample dashboard in Power BI.

Figure 1.4   Sample Dashboard in Power BI

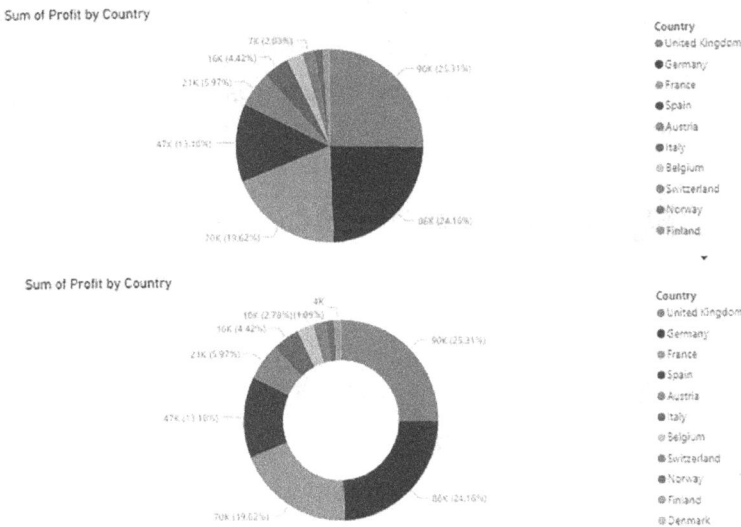

1.6 Power BI Desktop View

Based on the nature and requirements of projects and resources, organizations can use Power BI tools such as "Power BI Desktop" and "Power BI Service" in their everyday workflows for data analysis and subsequent visualizations. While Power BI Desktop is a Windows application installed on a computer, and Power BI Service is a cloud-based platform accessed through a web browser, both are considered two sides of the same coin. We will explore more about the functionalities of Power BI Service towards the end of the book in Chapter Seven. For now, in this section, let's learn the key functionalities of Power BI Desktop.

Power BI Desktop is a Windows desktop application that facilitates building queries, models, and reports from data sources to visualize data. Processing is done in Power BI Desktop, and reports are published in Power BI Service. The ribbon in Power BI Desktop includes groups of commands such as Data, Queries, Insert, Calculations, Sensitivity, and Share. Refer to Figure 1.5 to see the groups of commands on the Home screen.

Figure 1.5 **Power BI Desktop Group of Commands**

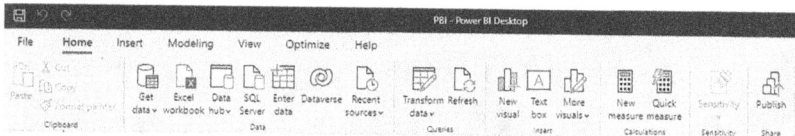

The Data pane includes an option of "Get Data," which leads to multiple sources and helps to select data connectors. Data sources include Excel workbook, Data hub, SQL Server, Dataverse, and Recent sources, which lists previously used connections. Additionally, the option to enter data manually is also available.

Under the Queries group, the "Transform data" option opens the Power Query Editor, allowing you to perform data transformations on the imported data. "New visual, Text box, and More visuals" options allow inserting visuals from app sources and files. "New measure and Quick measure" under Calculations enable enhanced data analysis. Sharing of report pages is done via the Publish button on the Power BI Home screen.

The Power BI Desktop application is easy to use. It simplifies data processing and analysis. It integrates visual analytics with intuitive report authoring, enabling managers to discover patterns quickly. It helps them explore a single, unified view of linked and interactive visualizations.

With this foundational understanding of the features and capabilities of Power BI, let's understand how to install this tool in the upcoming section.

1.6.1 How to install Power BI

Power BI Desktop is a free tool for basic data analysis and visualization, and it is available for download from the Microsoft website. Users can create detailed reports and dashboards using the free version. However, sharing these reports with online collaborators or distributing them as part of a broader report requires a paid Power BI license.

Here's a step-by-step guide on how you can install the Power BI Desktop application:

1. Visit the official website of Microsoft. The link is as follows: https://powerbi.microsoft.com/en-us/downloads/

2. You will see a button to download the Microsoft Power BI Desktop application. Click on it as it takes you to the Microsoft Office Store.

3. You can download the Power BI Desktop version from the Microsoft Store.

4. Double-click the .exe file, start the installation, and follow the instructions displayed.

5. Once it is downloaded, check "Downloads" in your system.

6. Wait until the installation is complete and click on the finish button to end the installation process.
   Power BI is now successfully installed on your system, and a shortcut has been created on the desktop.

Having understood the scope and benefits of Power BI and its installation process, let's proceed to the next section, which will help us understand the scope of Power BI further.

1.7 Data Analysis and Visualization

Data analysis and visualization functionalities are essential components of what Power BI offers. Thus, we will benefit from understanding these processes in detail through this section.

1.7.1 Data analysis

Data analysis is the process of organizing and summarizing data, while transforming it into meaningful information. Various metrics, key performance indicators, and comparisons of diverse measures can be extracted during the transformation by applying statistical tools or algorithms.

Data analysis encompasses statistical analysis, data mining, and machine learning techniques. These techniques examine and explore the data, uncover hidden insights, and identify patterns, trends, and relationships among datasets. This helps in drawing meaningful insights and making informed decisions based on the data.

Numerous tools with unique features are available to handle vast datasets and make strategic decisions. The features of these analytic tools facilitate various types of analysis, including statistical, predictive, and exploratory approaches. Let's compare popular data analytics tools such as Power BI, Microsoft Excel, Tableau, and Python to understand their capabilities and limitations:

1. Power BI

Power BI is preferred by organizations for its strong integration with Microsoft products, its cost-effectiveness, and accessibility. This tool offers native integrations with Excel, Azure, and other Microsoft services, making it ideal for companies already using Microsoft's ecosystem.

Power BI is different from Excel, Tableau, and Python in that it combines robust data analysis with visualizations, providing real-time analytics. This feature makes it valuable for organizations seeking data-driven decision-making. It is also preferred over analytic tools such as Tableau and Python as it tends to be more affordable, especially for small to medium-sized businesses. Moreover, its user-friendly interface is an advantage for non-technical users, simplifying report building without requiring extensive training.

Power BI is also different from the Google Analytics tool, which primarily focuses on analyzing data from websites and providing insights on digital platforms with prebuilt charts and tables. Power BI, on the other hand, excels in providing customizable, interactive, and real-time data visualizations across a business.

2. Microsoft Excel

Excel is one of the most common and widely used data analysis tools. Recent advancements in Excel, such as the statistical analysis capability, data manipulation, and visualization functions, make Excel stand out in handling larger datasets. It offers a variety of statistical functions, such as regression analysis, descriptive statistics, and Analysis of Variance (ANOVA).

PivotTables in Excel facilitate analyzing large datasets, allowing users to filter and compare metrics across various dimensions, and categorize and summarize data. Further, various chart options in Excel convert data to visualizations, making data insights easily understandable.

Use cases of Excel include financial analysis to summarize financial data into easily interpretable dashboards. It also allows users to compare various metrics, such as sales and performance, and represent the data using multiple charts. Additionally, scenario analysis can be performed by using different inputs to predict outcomes with What-If Analysis tools.

Although Excel offers data analysis capabilities with graphs and charts, it lacks the capability to process huge datasets and create dynamically interactive dashboards. Collaboration capabilities are also limited with large files in Excel, making it difficult to manage version control.

3. Tableau

Tableau is a data visualization and analytics platform that transforms datasets to create interactive dashboards. It supports connections to a wide range of data sources, enabling data consolidation across various departments and functions.

Tableau facilitates a holistic view that enables the exploration of data in real-time, even location-based, to uncover deeper insights about geographic patterns and trends. Use cases include tracking sales volume and revenue through interactive dashboards to monitor sales growth; performing customer segmentation, targeting, and positioning for more effective marketing; and conducting location-based analysis for regional marketing strategies.

Tableau excels in highly customizable visualizations but often lacks flexibility in data preparation, sorting, collaboration, and integration with enterprise-wide systems. Tableau can be more complex to learn, demanding a higher time commitment from users to utilize its features fully. Tableau is also relatively expensive in terms of pricing.

4. Python

Python is a leading language tool for data analytics and supports everything from statistical analysis to machine learning and data visualization. Python uses libraries such as Pandas for data manipulation, filtering, and aggregation; NumPy for calculations, Matplotlib and Seaborn for creating customized visualizations, and Scikit-Learn for implementing machine learning algorithms to support advanced analytics tasks.

Python use cases include customer behavior prediction, inventory requirement prediction, sales forecasting, text analysis, and sentiment analysis to understand customer behavior through emotions clearly. However, creating interactive dashboards using Python requires high coding effort, which can be a challenge for non-technical users. Also, connecting to data sources in Python is time-consuming.

FUN FACT

- Power BI is like an automatic coffee machine. It is built for self-service and quick user insights. Power BI shares a lot of DNA with Excel, which is known as the Swiss Army Knife of data analytics.

- Netflix, Instagram, and Google all run on Python scripts. Python's machine learning library lets you predict stock prices, customer churn, and even the weather.

1.7.2 Data visualization

Data represents a collection of facts, figures, and statistics with immense organizational potential for productive decision-making. It originates from various sources such as customer or sales transactions, social media, market research, or IoT devices. However, data alone is often complex to comprehend in its raw form and thus needs to be processed using various data analysis techniques. This is where data visualization comes into play.

Data visualization is the graphical representation of data and information in a way that simplifies their understanding and supports effective strategy development. Under this process, raw data is transformed into visual formats such as charts, graphs, maps, and even dashboards. These visual formats are easier to interpret and analyze. Complex data trends and relationships become apparent by visually presenting data, empowering swift analysis.

Today, data visualization has become a critical tool for managers to interpret and act on huge volumes of data generated in the business landscape. The relevance of data visualization is depicted below using real-world case studies:

1. Ensuring clear communication with data visualization

One of the primary advantages of data visualization is its ability to communicate complex information clearly and concisely to users. With visualization features, managers would not need to move through spreadsheets or extensive reports manually, dedicating their productive time. Visual representations overcome these challenges faced by managers, enabling them to grasp critical insights at a glance.

The ability to visualize data enhances communication within teams and/ or departments, fostering and facilitating effective collaboration. It enables managers to quickly identify new opportunities and uncover potential and hidden risks. Managers will be able to assess performance metrics, leading to more timely and informed decision-making for success.

Example: Airbnb

Airbnb is one of the most trusted global online marketplaces for short-term rental experiences. It deals with vast amounts of data every day and uses this data to make strategic decisions. Initially, teams at Airbnb used spreadsheets to monitor operations. This often delays decision-making and reduces productivity. It impacted teams' ability to remain focused and agile in a highly competitive market.

However, over time, Airbnb overcame the challenge of synthesizing data into actionable insights. It adopted data visualization practices to transform key operational and strategic data into real-time interactive dashboards that provided visual insights at a glance.

Airbnb leveraged these visualizations to analyze host performance, market supply-demand mismatches, customer satisfaction, and preferences. The company's data visualization capabilities enhanced its decision-making process by providing a concise view of the data. This saved managers' time and thus increased productivity with quality. By visualizing critical insights, teams could communicate more efficiently and foster teamwork across departments (Sinthong & Carey, 2021).

2. Leveraging data visualization to improve analytical capabilities

Another powerful function of data visualization is that it enables improved data analysis by allowing managers to delve deep into data in real time. Using platforms like Power BI, managers can drill down, filter, and explore specific aspects. They can uncover hidden relationships, ask better questions, and derive valuable insights on interacting with data.

The drill-down feature in Power BI allows users to break down data into more granular levels. Data can be made country-specific, region-specific, city-specific, and even individual retail chain-specific. This feature also provides detailed reports that aid managers in investigating a particular data segment without cluttering the main dashboard. In Power BI, filters allow users to narrow down data, and slicers create an intuitive, user-friendly interface to filter reports instantly.

Example: Retail chain

For example, let's consider the case of a large retail chain that wants to optimize its store performance by understanding sales figures at different levels. This includes sales data at the company level, individual product category levels, and data based on product categories at specific stores. Earlier, the company could only identify relationships between sales, inventory, and customer demographics by exploring sales figures. They analyzed geographical patterns and product categories based on location to uncover these insights.

However, with time, the retail chain's management team required a tool to examine sales data across diverse regions, stores, and product categories. They adopted Power BI to create interactive dashboards for their managers. This equipped them to break high-level sales data into smaller units based on specific regions, stores, and product categories. Filters and slicers helped managers to filter data by product categories.

Users could now analyze sales trends across different variables, including seasons, so that the performance of each product category could be analyzed. Managers could thus explore relationships between inventory and sales in real time. Based on these data variables, managers created visuals, including heat maps, to identify underperforming stores. They used bar charts to compare product sales across various locations.

Example: Heathrow Airport

The Heathrow Airport in England is another example where data visualization, packed with data analytics capability, revolutionized operational efficiency. The Heathrow Airport is one of the busiest airports in the world. It handles over 80 million passengers a year. Using data visualization dashboards, the airport management can track and manage real-time operational metrics such as flight information and baggage handling. They also track security queue lengths and passenger flow. This improves operational efficiency and customer experience.

These cases demonstrate how real-time data visualization aids organizations in monitoring dynamic systems and improving processes to enhance customer satisfaction. It enables better analytics capability to deep dive into data and explore insights for faster corrective actions (Guo et al., 2020; Mullan, 2019).

3. Compelling storytelling through visualizations

Transforming data into compelling stories and effectively conveying a message to captivate stakeholders is another key application of data visualization. This storytelling approach helps stakeholders identify key insights and patterns. By presenting data in a meaningful context in the background of a story, managers can drive stakeholder engagement and influence decision-makers throughout the organization.

Example: Airbnb

In another instance, Airbnb used a storytelling approach to engage multiple stakeholders and boost its growth when faced with increasing competition. The data team at Airbnb used visualization to transform vast amounts of user data into clear, compelling stories with emotional resonance to the data. In presentations to investors, Airbnb combined visual elements with a clear narrative explaining how the company positioned itself to dominate the short-term rental market.

This blend of data and storytelling helped Airbnb demonstrate its growth potential, which ultimately helped them achieve successful fundraising and fueled their expansion. By contextualizing this data within a broader story about market growth, Airbnb secured additional funding and increased stakeholder engagement, leading to its continued global expansion (von Hoffen et al., 2018; Lu & Wang, 2025).

ACTIVITY

Think of a time when a decision in your organization was made based purely on intuition or limited data. How might that decision have changed if a Power BI dashboard had been used to visualize and analyze relevant data? What insights could have emerged, and how would storytelling through visuals have influenced stakeholders?

1.7.3 Unveiling stories from data: Analysis meets visualization

As seen in Section 1.1 earlier, data holds immense potential in the current world and is the lifeblood of any organization. It flows through every aspect of business operations, offering valuable insights. However, raw data cannot convey any meaningful insights. Raw data must be transformed into actionable information through data analysis and visualization to uncover meaningful patterns. By combining these processes, organizations can unlock the true power of data and drive innovation.

Analyzed data can be visually represented through charts, maps, graphs, and other elements in an engaging format. This helps to simplify the representation of complex information. In this way, when data analysis is combined with data visualization, it helps unveil the story hidden within the data.

Data analysis is the substance, and data visualization helps communicate the substance in a visual form. Visualizations help in highlighting trends and correlations among various variables, enabling users to communicate complex stories behind the data more quickly and precisely. Data visualization thus serves as a powerful tool for storytelling by facilitating a simplified, visual presentation of data analysis findings.

Through this chapter, we explored the key features and benefits of Power BI. The chapter highlighted how visualization and analytics help transform data using tools like Power BI. From interactive dashboards and tailored reports to seamless mobile access, Power BI is a transformative tool that enhances productivity. In the upcoming chapter, we will dive into the more technical aspects of importing and transforming data, which are essential next steps in utilizing Power BI.

Chapter Summary

- Data enables informed decision-making and improves performance by analyzing, interpreting, and identifying patterns and correlations.

- Based on its characteristics, data can be classified as structured, unstructured, semi-structured, time-series, geospatial, categorical, and numerical data.

- Power BI, a leading BI tool, aggregates and visualizes data, enabling businesses to attain operational efficiency. It aids managers in project monitoring and real-time reporting, empowering them to generate data-driven solutions faster.

- Data analysis is the process of organizing and summarizing data, while transforming it into meaningful information. It encompasses techniques such as statistical analysis, data mining, and machine learning.

- Data visualization is the graphical representation of data and information that simplifies the understanding of data and aids in accurate decision-making.

- Visualizing data clarifies complex information, enabling quicker review through charts, graphs, and dashboards.

- Power BI, Excel, Tableau, and Python each offer unique strengths for data analytics.

- Power BI is popular among users for offering real-time, interactive visualizations, integration abilities, and cost-effectiveness.

- When data analysis is combined with data visualization, it unveils and communicates complex stories hidden within data. Data visualization facilitates a simplified, visual presentation of the findings and insights from data analysis.

- Entities like Airbnb and Heathrow Airport leverage visualizations through tools like Power BI to improve productivity and customer satisfaction.

QUIZ

1. **Why is Power BI suitable for managers?**
   a. Free to use
   b. Advanced coding capabilities
   c. Allows real-time data updates and interactive visualizations
   d. Only for IT professionals

2. **Identify which is not a data source.**
   a. Databases
   b. Photographs
   c. PowerPoint Slides
   d. Spreadsheets

3. **What is the primary purpose of data visualization?**
   a. To generate charts without data
   b. To simplify the complexities of data
   c. To stock data
   d. To hide data from audiences

4. **Identify the tool emphasized in the chapter as suitable for data visualization and storytelling.**
   a. Excel
   b. SQL
   c. Power BI
   d. Tableau

5. **Why is digital storytelling imperative for managers?**
    a. It helps in upholding physical records.
    b. It turns data into actionable business visions.
    c. It permits the removal of unnecessary data.
    d. It replaces written reports completely.

6. **What is the key advantage of converting data into visual stories?**
    a. It decreases data accuracy.
    b. It increases the data volume.
    c. It allows easy printing of data.
    d. It makes data more engaging and comprehensible.

7. **What do data visualizations help managers do?**
    a. Increase the size of datasets
    b. Recognize trends and patterns
    c. Decrease data storage requirements
    d. Change data into text reports

8. **What is an example of unstructured data?**
    a. Emails
    b. Excel/ spreadsheets
    c. CSV files
    d. SQL databases

9. **Power BI is best known for its capability to:**
    a. Store large quantities of data.
    b. Convert raw data into compelling visualizations.
    c. Conduct a complex financial investigation.
    d. Generate written reports.

10. **When generating a visualization, it is imperative to:**
    a. Use as many colors as possible.
    b. Focus on the key message to convey.
    c. Include all existing data.
    d. Avoid using labels on the charts.

Answers

1 – c	2 – c	3 – b	4 – c	5 – b
6 – d	7 – b	8 – a	9 – b	10 – b

CHAPTER 2

Importing and Transforming Data in Power BI

Key Learning Objectives

- Learn to import data from Excel, SQL Server, and the Web using Power Query Editor in Power BI.
- Explore the functionalities of Power Query Editor to clean, reshape, and customize data for specific analytical needs.
- Gain insights into advanced data transformation methods, including pivoting, merging, and conditional transformations.
- Understand how to run R scripts for data modeling and leverage AI-driven sentiment analysis within Power BI.

We know that no data is a perfect fit for analysis, as data rarely exists in the format that managers or analysts require. Therefore, it must be refined, cleaned, and structured to remove errors and ensure it serves its intended purpose.

In this chapter, we will explore how to efficiently bring data into Power BI and transform it to meet analytical needs. The chapter provides a detailed walkthrough of sourcing data from Excel, SQL Server, and the Web, utilizing the Power Query Editor to shape and clean the data effectively.

Key functionalities such as data transformation, column modifications, conditional columns, fill up and down operations, pivot/ unpivot transformations, and merging queries are covered in depth.

Additionally, we will understand the integration of R scripts in Power BI for advanced data modeling and conclude with an exploration of AI-driven analytics, including sentiment analysis, to enhance business intelligence capabilities.

2.1 Sources of Data for Managers

The first step in initiating a project in Power BI is to identify the data source and establish a connection with that specified data source. The most common data sources include Excel workbooks, Text/CSV files, Power BI datasets, Dataflows, Dataverse, SQL Servers, Analysis Services, Web sources, OData feeds, Databases, Power Platform tools, Azure services, online services, other web services, and Power BI template apps, among others.

You can connect to a data source in Power BI using three methods: Import, DirectQuery, or Live Connection. In this chapter, we will focus on the "Import" method, which is the most commonly used approach to bring data into Power BI.

Power BI retrieves data from the selected source in the form of rows and stores it using a special technology called xVelocity (part of SQL Server Analysis Services). This engine compresses the data, reducing its size to about one-tenth of the original, making it faster and more efficient for analysis.

The steps for importing data from three primary sources—Excel Workbook, SQL Server, and Web—are described in the upcoming sections.

2.1.1 Sourcing data from Excel

The step-by-step guide for using Excel data in Power BI is as follows:

1. Open Power BI desktop.
2. Select the "Get Data" option from the Home screen.
3. Click the down arrow to view available data connectors. Excel can be found in the list.
4. Select "Excel" as the data source from the list of connectors.
5. Navigate to the location of the Excel file you want to use and open it.
6. Select the objects required in the Excel workbook, launching the navigator dialog as shown in Figure 2.1 below.
7. In Navigator, "Select" the necessary spreadsheets by selecting the checkbox.
8. Select the "Load" option to import the chosen spreadsheets as separate tables in the Power BI Data Model.
9. Alternatively, select "Transform Data" to open the Power Query Editor if you need to apply business rules or modify the data before importing it.

| Figure 2.1 | Navigator to Select Spreadsheets |

Navigator

Display Options ▾

EuroMart Stores.xlsx [1]
Order Data

Order Data

Order ID	Order Date	Customer Name	Country	State
BN-2011-7407039	01-01-2011	Ruby Patel	Sweden	Stoci
AZ-2011-9050313	01-01-2011	Summer Hayward	United Kingdom	Engla
AZ-2011-6674300	04-01-2011	Devin Huddleston	France	Auve
BN-2011-2819714	04-01-2011	Mary Parker	United Kingdom	Engla
BN-2011-2819714	04-01-2011	Mary Parker	United Kingdom	Engla
AZ-2011-617423	05-01-2011	Daniel Burke	France	Auve
AZ-2011-617423	05-01-2011	Daniel Burke	France	Auve
AZ-2011-2918397	07-01-2011	Fredrick Beveridge	France	Prov
AZ-2011-2918397	07-01-2011	Fredrick Beveridge	France	Prov
AZ-2011-2918397	07-01-2011	Fredrick Beveridge	France	Prov
BN-2011-3248724	08-01-2011	Archer Mort	France	Lang
BN-2011-3248724	08-01-2011	Archer Mort	France	Lang
AZ-2011-6712797	11-01-2011	Evie Flockhart	Italy	Ligur
AZ-2011-4827146	11-01-2011	Faith Greenwood	Austria	Viens
AZ-2011-4827146	11-01-2011	Faith Greenwood	Austria	Viens
AZ-2011-6439906	11-01-2011	Summer Hayward	Spain	Murc
AZ-2011-6439906	11-01-2011	Summer Hayward	Spain	Murc
AZ-2011-7053593	11-01-2011	Gracie Powell	United Kingdom	Engla
AZ-2011-7053593	11-01-2011	Gracie Powell	United Kingdom	Engla
AZ-2011-5702370	12-01-2011	Hershel Snyder	Germany	Lowe
AZ-2011-5702370	12-01-2011	Hershel Snyder	Germany	Lowe
AZ-2011-5702370	12-01-2011	Hershel Snyder	Germany	Lowe

Load   Transform Data   Cancel

2.1.2 Sourcing data from SQL Server

A step-by-step guide for sourcing data from SQL Server in Power BI is as follows:

1. Open Power BI Desktop.

2. On the "Home" tab, select "Get data."

3. In the data source options, choose "SQL Server" from the list or search for it in the dialog box.

4. Select "SQL Server." A page named SQL Server Database opens up.

5. The server name has to be inserted. The database is optional.
6. Choose "Import" as the data connectivity mode.
7. Click "OK" on the screen as shown in Figure 2.2 below.

Figure 2.2 **Connecting to SQL Server**

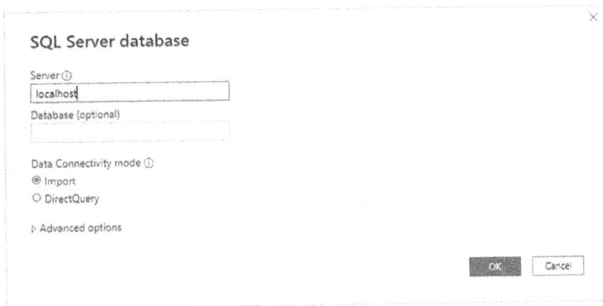

SQL Server database

Server ⓘ
localhost
Database (optional)

Data Connectivity mode ⓘ
⦿ Import
○ DirectQuery

▷ Advanced options

OK   Cancel

8. Another dialog box opens up, as shown in Figure 2.3 below, asking for credentials to be provided to the SQL server.

Figure 2.3 **Screen Two With Credentials**

SQL Server database

Windows

Database

Microsoft account

localhost

Use your Windows credentials to access this database.

⦿ Use my current credentials
○ Use alternate credentials
User name

Password

Back   Connect   Cancel

9. Select "Use my current credentials" and click Connect if your domain account has access, as this will use "Windows authentication." If your domain account

does not have access, choose "Database authentication" and enter the SQL Server username and password provided by your database administrator.

10. In the Navigator window:
- Browse and select a specific table from the database.
- Or, click Advanced Options to write a custom SQL query that returns the required table.

11. Click Load to import the selected data or Transform Data to modify it in Power Query before loading.

Figure 2.4	Warning for Accessing Data Source Using an Unencrypted Connection

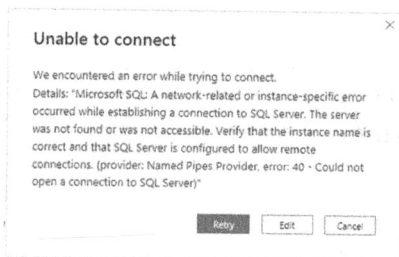

Sometimes, the user may see a warning note, as shown in Figure 2.4 above. It states that the server was inaccessible or that Power BI cannot access data sources using an unencrypted connection. When such a problem is encountered, select the tables or functions within the SQL Server database that must be imported into Power BI. The final step is to choose either Load or Transform Data.

2.1.3 Web as a data source

Data can be sourced from files stored on websites, especially internal corporate databases, or even embedded

HTML tables on web pages. This data source supplements the internal references publicly available on the internet for better information sourcing.

A step-by-step guide for sourcing data from the Web in Power BI is as follows:

1. Open "Power BI Desktop."
2. Click "Get Data" and select "Web" as the source.
3. Enter the URL where the data is located, and from the Navigator select the table you want.
4. Click "Connect" to access the web content, as shown in Figure 2.5 below.

Figure 2.5 | **Inserting the URL to Access Web Content**

Clicking on the Connect button enables the "Accessing the web content" dialog box. Next, "Web view" and "Table view" are displayed, and data can be loaded by choosing the required tables and then transformed to build visuals.

You have now learned to connect to various data sources with these operations. Once data sources are connected and loaded, the functions explained in the upcoming sections must be carried out.

2.2 Power Query Editor for Data Cleansing and Transformation

In this section, we will understand how to work on the imported data to ensure accurate results. This process is called the transformation of data and is made easy in Power BI through the Power Query Editor. This tool provides a simple user interface for cleansing data.

Some examples of data cleansing include deleting columns, filtering rows, splitting columns, replacing values, sorting, and custom calculations. After the required data cleansing, the data from various sources is combined.

This section will help us understand how to use Power Query Editor, transform data in Power BI, leverage R, and conduct AI insights calculations.

2.2.1 What is Power Query Editor

Power Query Editor is a user-friendly interface in Power BI for data cleansing, transformation, and other data management options. It is initiated by clicking on the "Transform Data" option in the Power BI ribbon.

The Power Query Editor View displays "New Source," which is similar to "Get Data" as seen in Section 2.1. "Queries" on the left side shows a list of all queries that are connected to various data sources, which can also be renamed, disabled, or organized into groups.

"Query Settings" on the right side enables renaming and editing the list of steps or transformations applied to the queries. This can also be relaunched from the View menu at the top of the Home page.

Figure 2.6 below shows some of the key interface areas in the Power Query Editor View.

Figure 2.6 Significant Interface Areas in the Power Query Editor View

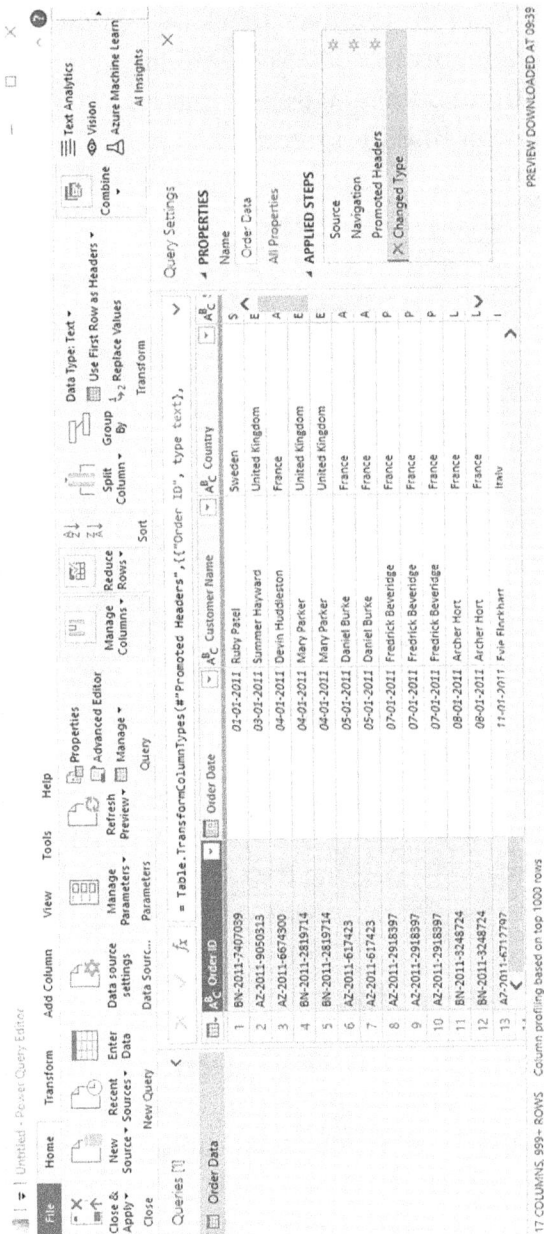

The Advanced Editor option on the top, next to the "Refresh Preview" button, facilitates M Queries written by the Power Query Editor. Every click in the Power Query Editor is automatically converted into the M formula language. All fundamental transformations can be facilitated using the Power BI Editor interface, as shown in Figure 2.7.

Figure 2.7 Advanced Editor View

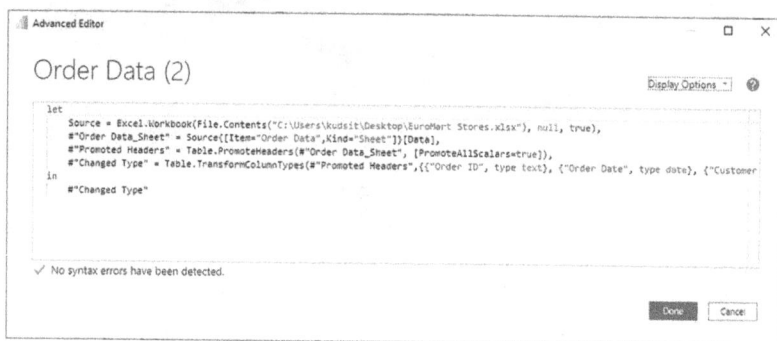

The "Applied Steps" section, located at the bottom right (shown in Fig. 2.6), allows you to manage transformations in Power Query. You can delete or modify incorrect steps, change their order if needed, and review previous steps to see how the data looked at an earlier stage. Once you finalize the transformations, clicking the "Close & Apply" button will load the processed data into the data model.

2.2.2 Transforming data

Data transformation is a critical step towards data preparation. Data from various sources can be transformed to improve quality and facilitate meaningful insights. The accuracy in data analysis and visualization results improves drastically if proper data transformation is facilitated.

It ensures that data is effectively cleaned, sorted, and formatted for analysis.

The following are the benefits of transforming data in Power BI:

1. It ensures that clean and structured data is loaded into the model.
2. It removes all sorts of inconsistencies, incomplete and redundant data elements, from the dataset.
3. It removes unnecessary columns and rows to improve the analytic performance of Power BI.
4. It combines data from multiple sources with consistency and standardization.
5. It facilitates complex data analysis and visualizations.
6. It minimizes errors in datasets, ensuring analytical accuracy.

In Power Query Editor, you can modify data using two main options: Transform and Add Column. While both help in refining data, they serve different purposes.

1. Transform Column

The "Transform" Column tab is used when you want to modify an existing column without creating a new one. Changes made here overwrite the original values. Some key transformations include:

- Changing data types, for example, converting text to numbers or dates
- Replacing values, for example, replacing nulls with a default value
- Splitting columns, for example, separating full names into first and last names

- Merging columns, for example, combining multiple columns into one
- Removing duplicates to clean the data

2. Add Column

The "Add" Column tab is used when you need to create a new column based on existing data while keeping the original column unchanged. Some common ways to add columns include:

- Conditional columns, for example, creating a column based on specific conditions
- Custom columns, for example, using formulas to generate new values
- Extracting text, for example, pulling out a portion of a string
- Creating an index or duplicate columns for reference

In the upcoming section, let's cover the following transformation processes in further detail:

1. Organizing data by using the first row as a header
2. Removing columns
3. Adding new columns

2.2.3 Organizing data by using the first row as a header

Organizing and naming columns in a dataset is the preliminary step in transforming data. Figure 2.8 below shows how data appears when loaded.

Usually, column headers are automatically imported from a data source, but Power BI often fails to capture the column headers. Select "Use First Row as Headers" from the Home ribbon's Transform tab.

Figure 2.8   Loading Data From a Source

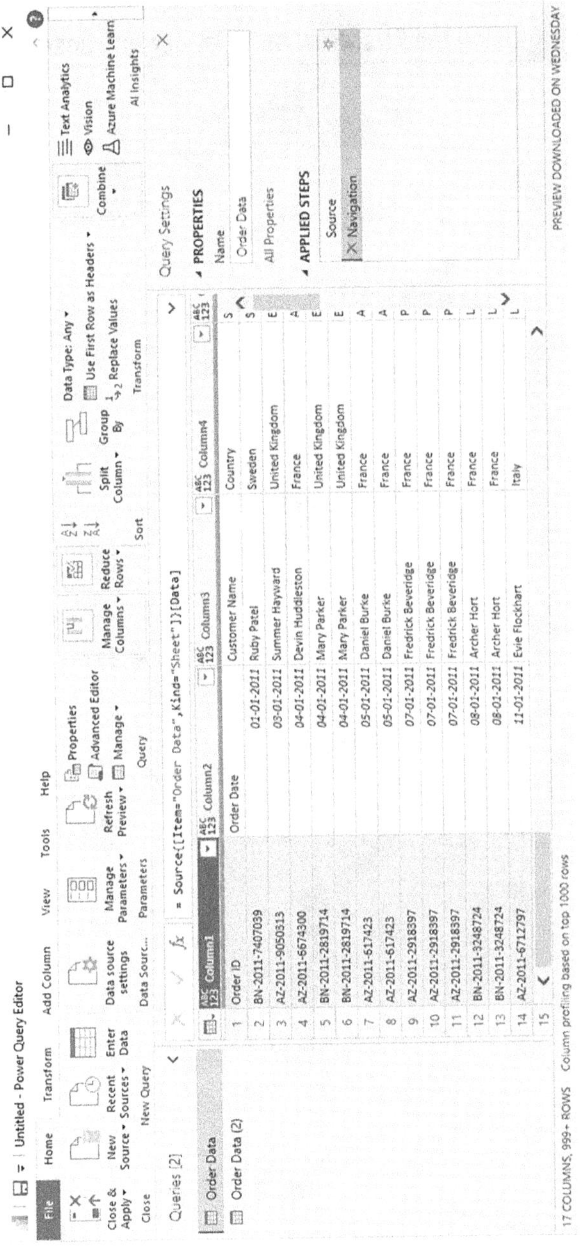

Then, the first row of the dataset will be used as the column header, shown in Figure 2.9 below:

Figure 2.9 Using the First Row as a Header to Transform Data

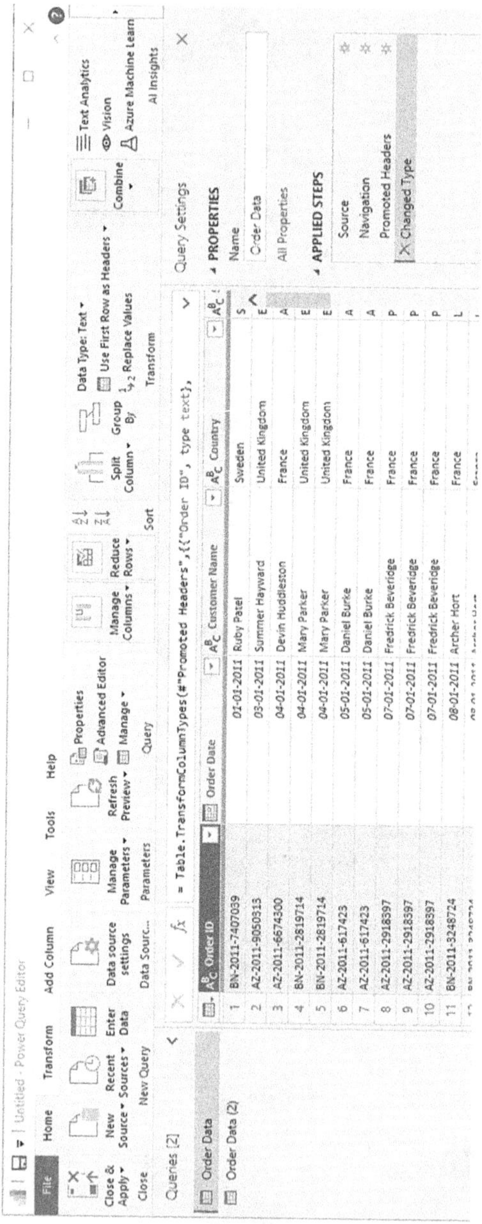

2.2.4 Removing columns

The data will now have several columns with headers. If some columns are not required, they can be removed in the Power Query Editor, or else the unused columns will take up unnecessary space in the data model.

Select all the necessary columns, then right-click and choose "Remove Other Columns" to keep only the selected ones. Alternatively, select the columns you want to remove, right-click, and choose "Remove Columns" to delete only the selected ones. After removing unnecessary columns, the Applied Steps window shows the query result of "Removed Other Columns" (Fig. 2.10).

Figure 2.10 Removing Other Columns in the Power Query Editor

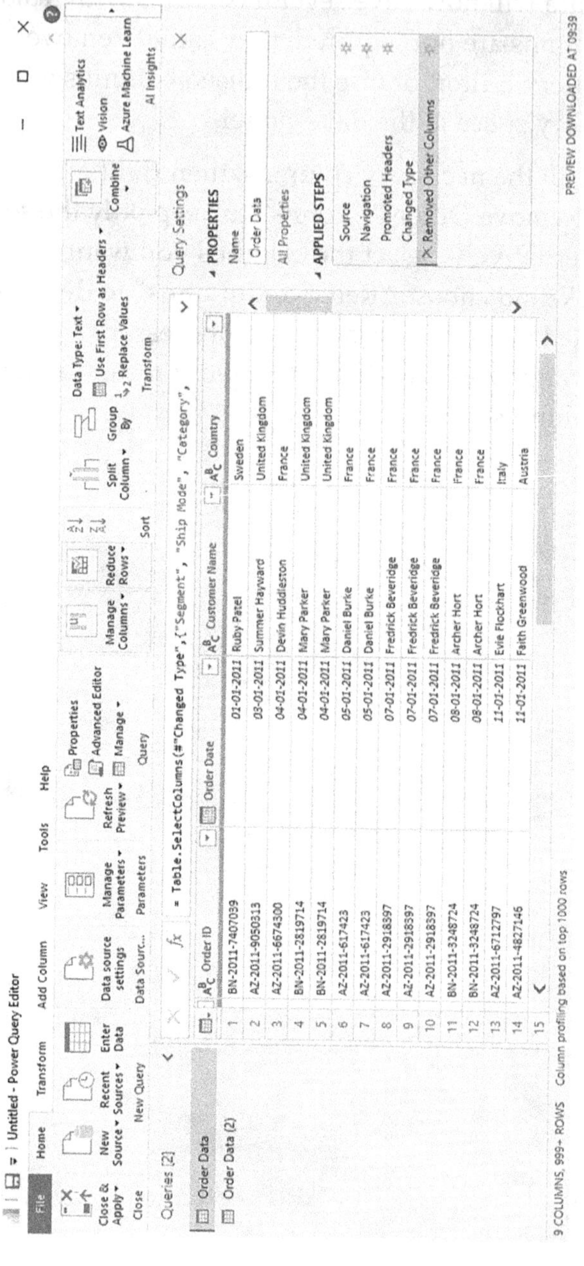

Columns not being used can also be removed from "Manage Columns" in the Home ribbon. This opens the "Choose Column" dialogue as shown in Figure 2.11 below. Here, we can select the columns we need to keep. If the selection goes wrong or needs some editing, it can be done by deleting or rearranging through Applied Steps.

Figure 2.11 **Choosing Required Columns From Manage Columns in the Home Ribbon**

2.2.5 Adding a new column

If a new column needs to be added, click "Column From Examples" in the Power Query Editor ribbon shown in Figure 2.12 below. Then select from "All Columns" to provide Power Query Editor with data that requires transformation.

Figure 2.12 Add Columns From Examples

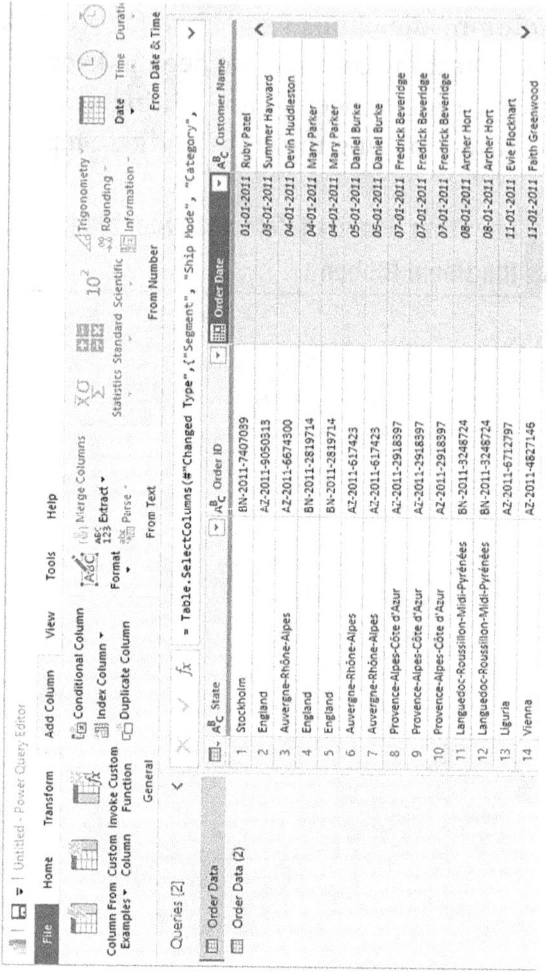

This will launch an "Add Column" window from examples where we must enter sample values for the newly created columns, as shown in Figure 2.13 below.

Figure 2.13 Add Column From Examples Interface

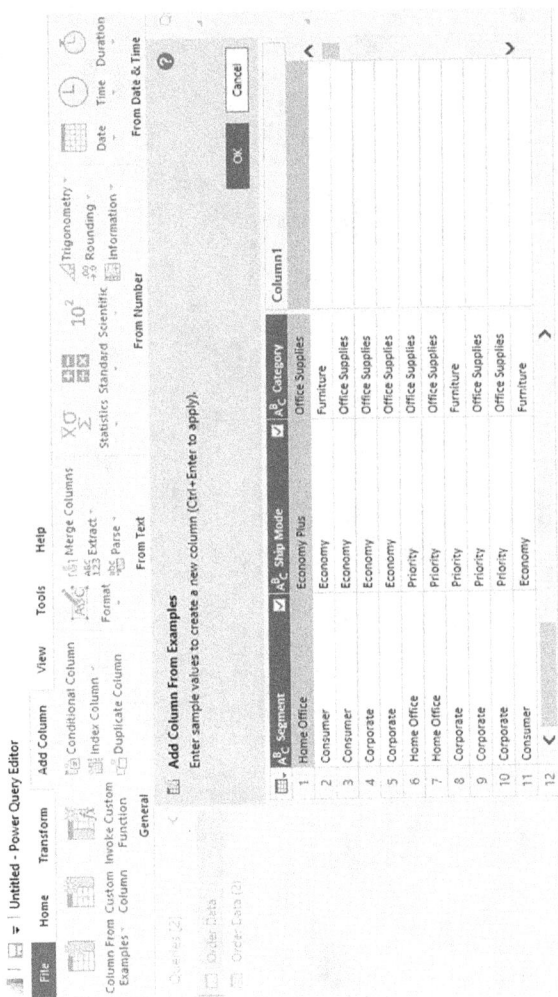

If you need to combine the State or Country, and/ or enter the name of the State or Country, press Enter after inputting the desired value to generate a newly merged column (Fig. 2.14). This operation should be applied to every row in the dataset to ensure uniformity.

Figure 2.14 New Column Added

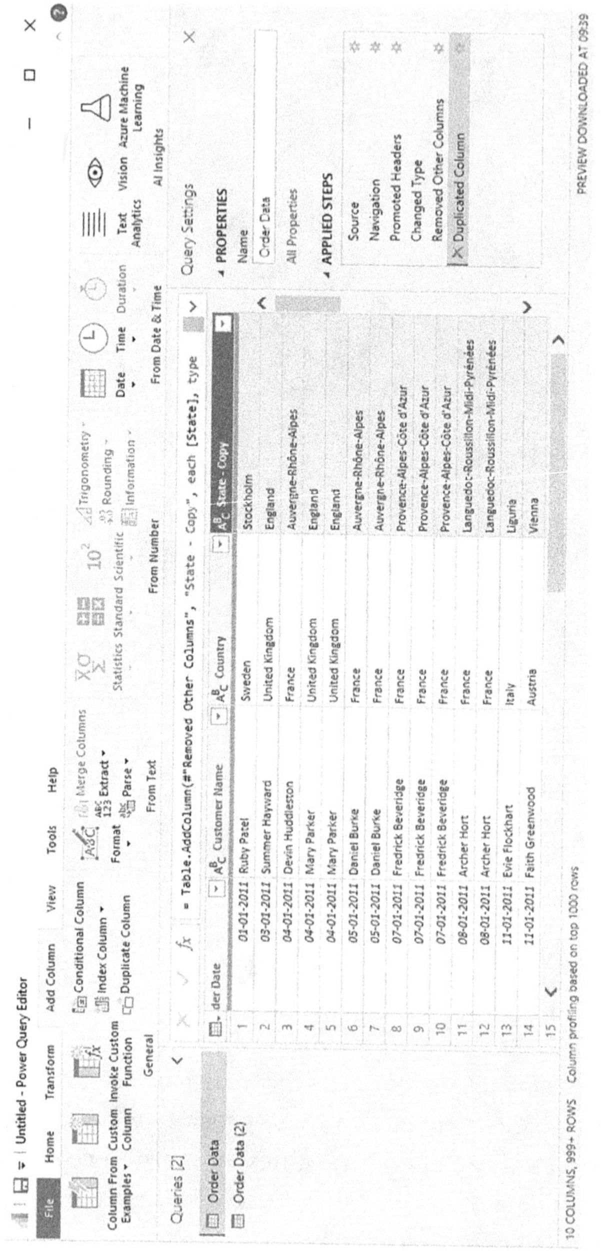

The column can also be renamed by clicking on the column header. Sometimes, "Add Columns From Examples" may prompt you to input multiple examples and correctly translate them to the query function. In such cases, additional examples need to be added.

If the column data type needs to be edited, right-click on the column that needs to be changed, then select "Change Type" to choose the new data type.

2.3 More Data Transformation Options

In addition to the three techniques discussed in the previous section, let's explore other transformation techniques that Power BI offers, such as Conditional Column, Fill Down and Fill Up, Unpivot Transform, Unpivot Other Columns, Unpivot Only Selected Columns, and Merge Query Transformation.

1. Conditional Column

You can use the "Conditional Column" feature from the "Add Column' ribbon in Power BI to create a new column based on specific conditions applied to an existing column. For example, you can create a new column named "Name of State" where, if the value in a selected column is *null*, the new column will display the corresponding *country name*. Refer to Figure 2.15 below for a visual reference.

Figure 2.15 Adding a Conditional Column

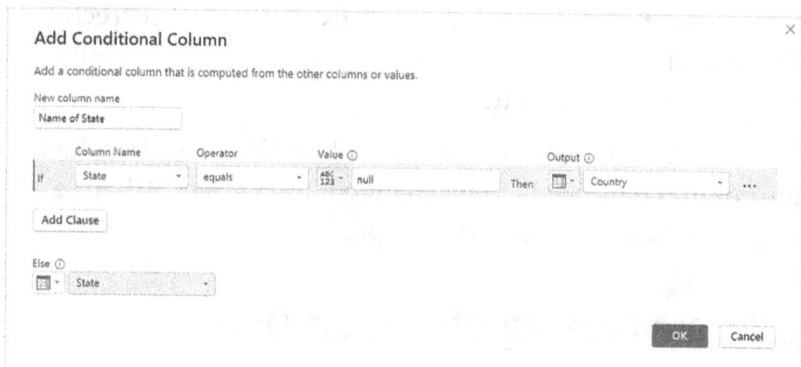

Add Conditional Column

Add a conditional column that is computed from the other columns or values.

New column name
Name of State

	Column Name	Operator	Value ⓘ	Output ⓘ
If	State	equals	null	Then Country

Add Clause

Else ⓘ
State

OK   Cancel

In the new column (Fig. 2.16), the results display the Name of the State. For example, as seen in Figure 2.16 below, if State is null, then the output will display the country; else it will display State as it is.

Figure 2.16 Result of Adding a Column

Month Number	Month Name	Year	State	Country	Name of State
1	January	2014	Carretera	Canada	Carretera
1	January	2014	Carretera	Germany	Carretera
6	June	2014	Carretera	France	Carretera
6	June	2014	Carretera	Germany	Carretera
6	June	2014	Carretera	Mexico	Carretera
12	December	2014	Carretera	Germany	Carretera
3	March	2014	null	Germany	Germany
6	June	2014	null	Canada	Canada
6	June	2014	null	France	France
6	June	2014	null	Germany	Germany
6	June	2014	null	Mexico	Mexico
7	July	2014	null	Canada	Canada
8	August	2014	null	Mexico	Mexico
9	September	2014	null	Germany	Germany
10	October	2013	null	Canada	Canada
12	December	2014	null	United States of America	United States of America
2	February	2014	Paseo	Canada	Paseo
2	February	2014	Paseo	Mexico	Paseo
6	June	2014	Paseo	Canada	Paseo
6	June	2014	Paseo	Germany	Paseo
7	July	2014	Paseo	Germany	Paseo
8	August	2014	Paseo	Mexico	Paseo
9	September	2013	Paseo	France	Paseo
9	September	2013	Paseo	Mexico	Paseo

2. Custom Columns

A "Custom Column" allows you to create a new column using custom formulas in Power Query Editor. Unlike conditional columns, which use predefined rules, custom columns offer more flexibility through mathematical operations, string manipulations, and logical expressions. For instance, you can combine the first and the last names into a full name or calculate a new metric using existing columns.

3. Fill Down and Fill Up

"Fill Down" and "Fill Up" are unique data transformation options applied to columns where a value shall replace all null values below or above a non-null value or until there is a non-null value again. The Fill Down option shall replace all of the null values below a non-null value, and the Fill Up option will do the opposite of Fill Down, where it would replace all the null values above a non-null value. It is also important to sort the data to ensure that the Fill Down and Fill Up transformations are successful.

4. Unpivot Transform

The "Unpivot Transform" function enables reorganizing the dataset to a more structured format and is best suited for Power BI applications for managers. This transformation makes data more accessible in real time and more acceptable for data analytics.

The dataset before unpivot operations is shown in Figure 2.17 below.

Figure 2.17 The Dataset Before Unpivot Operation

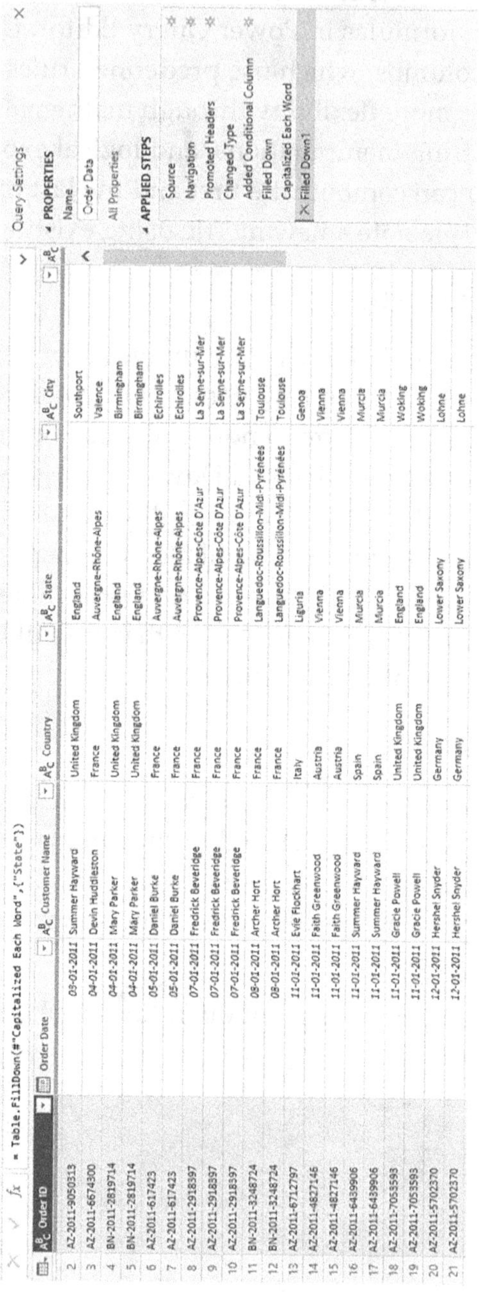

Formula: `= Table.FillDown(#"Capitalized Each Word",{"State"})`

Order ID	Order Date	Customer Name	Country	State	City
AZ-2011-9050313	09-01-2011	Summer Hayward	United Kingdom	England	Southport
AZ-2011-6674300	04-01-2011	Devin Huddleston	France	Auvergne-Rhône-Alpes	Valence
BN-2011-2819714	04-01-2011	Mary Parker	United Kingdom	England	Birmingham
BN-2011-2819714	04-01-2011	Mary Parker	United Kingdom	England	Birmingham
AZ-2011-617423	05-01-2011	Daniel Burke	France	Auvergne-Rhône-Alpes	Echirolles
AZ-2011-617423	05-01-2011	Daniel Burke	France	Auvergne-Rhône-Alpes	Echirolles
AZ-2011-2918597	07-01-2011	Fredrick Beveridge	France	Provence-Alpes-Côte D'Azur	La Seyne-sur-Mer
AZ-2011-2918597	07-01-2011	Fredrick Beveridge	France	Provence-Alpes-Côte D'Azur	La Seyne-sur-Mer
AZ-2011-2918597	07-01-2011	Fredrick Beveridge	France	Provence-Alpes-Côte D'Azur	La Seyne-sur-Mer
BN-2011-3248724	08-01-2011	Archer Hort	France	Languedoc-Roussillon-Mid-Pyrénées	Toulouse
BN-2011-3248724	08-01-2011	Archer Hort	France	Languedoc-Roussillon-Midi-Pyrénées	Toulouse
AZ-2011-6712797	11-01-2011	Evie Flockhart	Italy	Liguria	Genoa
AZ-2011-4827146	11-01-2011	Faith Greenwood	Austria	Vienna	Vienna
AZ-2011-4827146	11-01-2011	Faith Greenwood	Austria	Vienna	Vienna
AZ-2011-6439906	11-01-2011	Summer Hayward	Spain	Murcia	Murcia
AZ-2011-6439906	11-01-2011	Summer Hayward	Spain	Murcia	Murcia
AZ-2011-7053593	11-01-2011	Gracie Powell	United Kingdom	England	Woking
AZ-2011-7053593	11-01-2011	Gracie Powell	United Kingdom	England	Woking
AZ-2011-5702370	12-01-2011	Hershel Snyder	Germany	Lower Saxony	Lohne
AZ-2011-5702370	12-01-2011	Hershel Snyder	Germany	Lower Saxony	Lohne

Query Settings

▲ PROPERTIES

Name

Order Data

All Properties

▲ APPLIED STEPS

Source

Navigation

Promoted Headers

Changed Type

Added Conditional Column

Filled Down

Capitalized Each Word

× Filled Down

Figure 2.18 Results of Pivoted Data Transformation

	Order Date	Customer Name	Country	State	City	Region
1	01-01-2011	Ruby Patel	Sweden	Stockholm	Stockholm	North
2	03-01-2011	Summer Hayward	United Kingdom	England	Southport	North
3	04-01-2011	Devin Huddleston	France	Auvergne-Rhône-Alpes	Valence	Central
4	04-01-2011	Mary Parker	United Kingdom	England	Birmingham	North
5	04-01-2011	Mary Parker	United Kingdom	England	Birmingham	North
6	05-01-2011	Daniel Burke	France	Auvergne-Rhône-Alpes	Echirolles	Central
7	05-01-2011	Daniel Burke	France	Auvergne-Rhône-Alpes	Echirolles	Central
8	07-01-2011	Fredrick Beveridge	France	Provence-Alpes-Côte D'Azur	La Seyne-sur-Mer	Central
9	07-01-2011	Fredrick Beveridge	France	Provence-Alpes-Côte D'Azur	La Seyne-sur-Mer	Central
10	07-01-2011	Fredrick Beveridge	France	Provence-Alpes-Côte D'Azur	La Seyne-sur-Mer	Central
11	08-01-2011	Archer Hort	France	Languedoc-Roussillon-Midi-Pyrénées	Toulouse	Central
12	08-01-2011	Archer Hort	France	Languedoc-Roussillon-Midi-Pyrénées	Toulouse	Central
13	11-01-2011	Evie Flockhart	Italy	Liguria	Genoa	South
14	11-01-2011	Faith Greenwood	Austria	Vienna	Vienna	Central
15	11-01-2011	Faith Greenwood	Austria	Vienna	Vienna	Central
16	11-01-2011	Gracie Powell	United Kingdom	England	Woking	North
17	11-01-2011	Gracie Powell	United Kingdom	England	Woking	North
18	11-01-2011	Summer Hayward	Spain	Murcia	Murcia	South
19	11-01-2011	Summer Hayward	Spain	Murcia	Murcia	South
20	12-01-2011	Hershel Snyder	Germany	Lower Saxony	Lohne	Central
21	12-01-2011	Hershel Snyder	Germany	Lower Saxony	Lohne	Central

PROPERTIES

Name
Order Data

All Properties

APPLIED STEPS

Source
Navigation
Promoted Headers
Changed Type
Added Conditional Column
Filled Down
Capitalized Each Word
Filled Down1
X Pivoted Column

The "Unpivot Columns" option converts any selected column headers into row values and the data within those columns into a corresponding row (Fig. 2.18). Using this selection, any new columns added to the data source are automatically included in the Unpivot Transform. The results are shown in Figure 2.19 below:

Figure 2.19 Customer Details Based on State as a Result of Unpivoted Data

Customer Name	State
Ruby Patel	Stockholm
Summer Hayward	England
Devin Huddleston	Auvergne-Rhône-Alpes
Mary Parker	England
Mary Parker	England
Daniel Burke	Auvergne-Rhône-Alpes
Daniel Burke	Auvergne-Rhône-Alpes
Fredrick Beveridge	Provence-Alpes-Côte D'Azur
Fredrick Beveridge	Provence-Alpes-Côte D'Azur
Fredrick Beveridge	Provence-Alpes-Côte D'Azur
Archer Hort	Languedoc-Roussillon-Midi-Pyrénées
Archer Hort	Languedoc-Roussillon-Midi-Pyrénées
Evie Flockhart	Liguria
Faith Greenwood	Vienna
Faith Greenwood	Vienna
Summer Hayward	Murcia
Summer Hayward	Murcia
Gracie Powell	England
Gracie Powell	England
Hershel Snyder	Lower Saxony
Hershel Snyder	Lower Saxony
Hershel Snyder	Lower Saxony
Hershel Snyder	Lower Saxony

5. Unpivot Other Columns

This option converts all column headers not selected into row values and the data in those columns into a corresponding row. Using this selection, any new columns added to the data source are automatically included in the Unpivot transform as shown in Figure 2.20 below.

Figure 2.20 Country-Wise Results of Unpivoted Data

#	Attribute	Value	Attribute.1	Value.1
1	Country	Sweden	Order ID	BN-2011-7407039
2	Country	Sweden	Order Date	01-01-2011
3	Country	Sweden	Customer Name	Ruby Patel
4	Country	Sweden	State	Stockholm
5	Country	Sweden	City	Stockholm
6	Country	Sweden	Region	North
7	Country	Sweden	Segment	Home Office
8	Country	Sweden	Ship Mode	Economy Plus
9	Country	Sweden	Category	Office Supplies
10	Country	Sweden	Sub-Category	Paper
11	Country	Sweden	Product Name	Enermax Note Cards, Premium
12	Country	Sweden	Discount	0.5
13	Country	Sweden	Sales	-45
14	Country	Sweden	Profit	-26
15	Country	Sweden	Quantity	3
16	Country	Sweden	Feedback?	FALSE
17	Country	United Kingdom	Order ID	AZ-2011-9050313
18	Country	United Kingdom	Order Date	03-01-2011
19	Country	United Kingdom	Customer Name	Summer Hayward
20	Country	United Kingdom	State	England
21	Country	United Kingdom	City	Southport

PROPERTIES

Name

Order Data

All Properties

APPLIED STEPS

Source

Navigation

Promoted Headers

Changed Type

Added Conditional Column

Filled Down

Capitalized Each Word

Unpivoted Columns

× Unpivoted Other Columns

6. Unpivot Only Selected Columns

This option can convert any selected column header into row values and the data in those columns into a corresponding row. Using this selection, any new columns added to the data source will not be included in the Unpivot Transform.

This transform operation is shown in Figure 2.21, and the results of the unpivoted transformation are shown in Figure 2.22.

Figure 2.21 Customer, Country, and Product Name as Selected Columns for Unpivoted Data Transformation

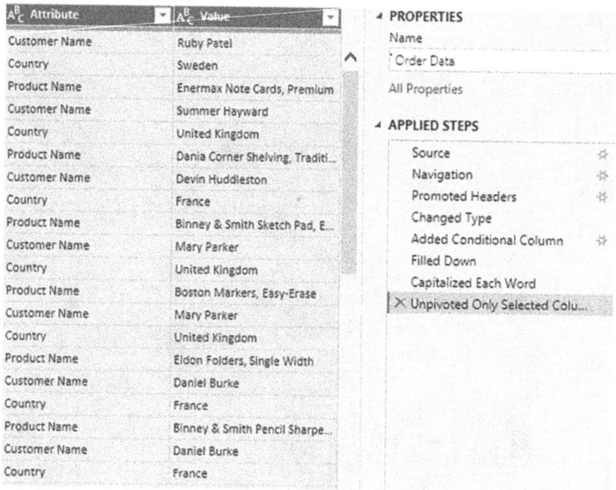

Figure 2.22 Results of Unpivoted Data Transformation

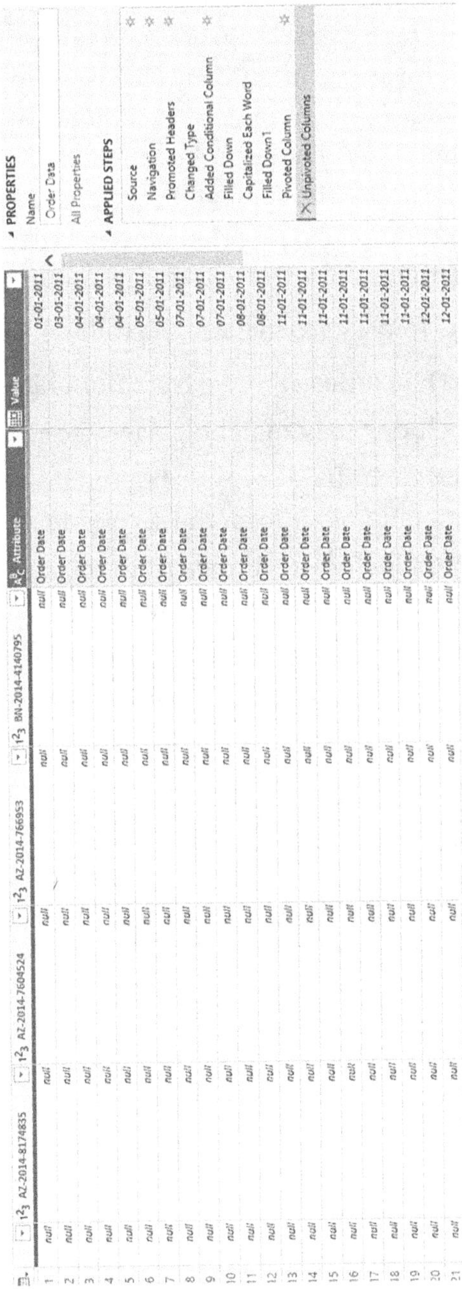

PROPERTIES

Name
Order Data
All Properties

APPLIED STEPS

Source
Navigation
Promoted Headers
Changed Type
Added Conditional Column
Filled Down
Capitalized Each Word
Filled Down1
Pivoted Column
X Unpivoted Columns

	AZ-2014-8174835	AZ-2014-7604524	AZ-2014-766953	BN-2014-4140795	Attribute	Value
1	null	null	null	null	Order Date	01-01-2011
2	null	null	null	null	Order Date	03-01-2011
3	null	null	null	null	Order Date	04-01-2011
4	null	null	null	null	Order Date	04-01-2011
5	null	null	null	null	Order Date	04-01-2011
6	null	null	null	null	Order Date	05-01-2011
7	null	null	null	null	Order Date	05-01-2011
8	null	null	null	null	Order Date	07-01-2011
9	null	null	null	null	Order Date	07-01-2011
10	null	null	null	null	Order Date	07-01-2011
11	null	null	null	null	Order Date	08-01-2011
12	null	null	null	null	Order Date	08-01-2011
13	null	null	null	null	Order Date	11-01-2011
14	null	null	null	null	Order Date	11-01-2011
15	null	null	null	null	Order Date	11-01-2011
16	null	null	null	null	Order Date	11-01-2011
17	null	null	null	null	Order Date	11-01-2011
18	null	null	null	null	Order Date	11-01-2011
19	null	null	null	null	Order Date	11-01-2011
20	null	null	null	null	Order Date	12-01-2011
21	null	null	null	null	Order Date	12-01-2011

7. Merge Query Transformation

Merge query transformation in Power BI helps join two tables with columns extracted from both tables. This enables the creation of meaningful outcomes to assist in managerial decision-making. A merge operation requires at least one common column (key) between the tables, and also, the columns need to have the same data type for exact merging. The required columns from both tables are selected and then joined by selecting a Join Type function.

The various Join Types include the following:

- **Full Outer:** Includes all rows from both tables.
- **Inner:** Includes only matching rows from both tables.
- **Left Order:** Includes all rows from the first table and only matching rows from the second table.
- **Right Order:** Includes all rows from the second table and only matching rows from the first.
- **Left Anti:** Returns only the rows from the first (left) table that do not have matching rows in the second (right) table.
- **Right Anti:** Returns only the rows from the second (right) table that do not have matching rows in the first (left) table.

To perform this function, open Power Query Editor, click on Home, select "Merge Queries", and select "Merge Queries as New" from the drop-down. Select two tables, and choose the common column to merge. As shown in Figure 2.23 below, population and area queries are selected.

Figure 2.23	Selecting Table and Matching Columns to Create a Merged Table

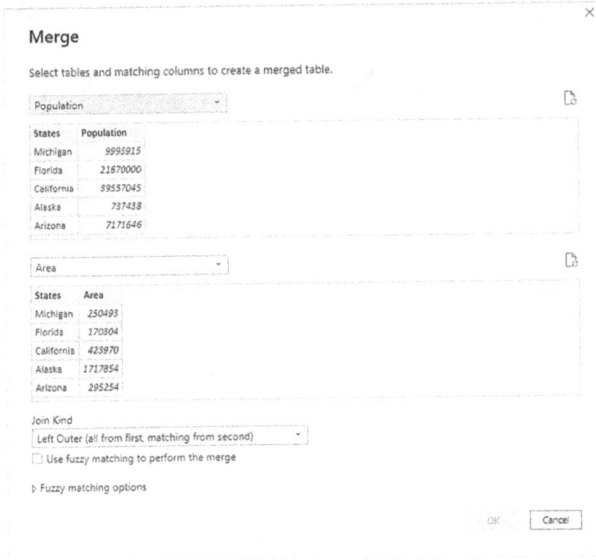

Merge

Select tables and matching columns to create a merged table.

Population

States	Population
Michigan	9995915
Florida	21670000
California	39557045
Alaska	737438
Arizona	7171646

Area

States	Area
Michigan	250493
Florida	170304
California	423970
Alaska	1717854
Arizona	295254

Join Kind

Left Outer (all from first, matching from second)

☐ Use fuzzy matching to perform the merge

▷ Fuzzy matching options

OK   Cancel

Tables and matching columns are selected to create a merged table by matching defined rows in the selected columns; refer to Figure 2.24.

Figure 2.24 Configuration to Merge Two Queries

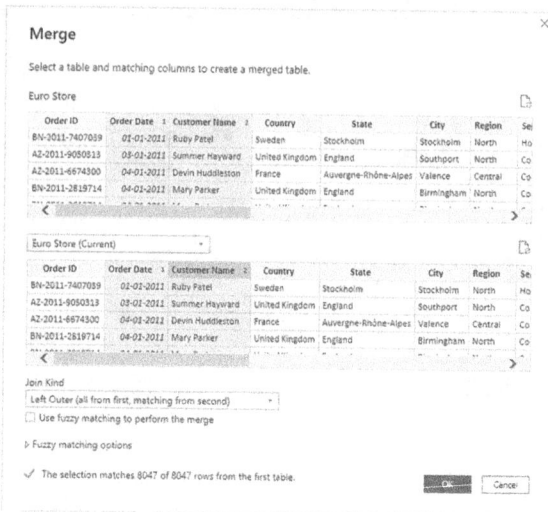

On clicking OK, a new query combines the results, and the new column can be renamed. The new column added will have a table value for each row. Now click "Expand" from the column header, as shown in Figure 2.25, and select the required columns.

Figure 2.25 Expand the Columns

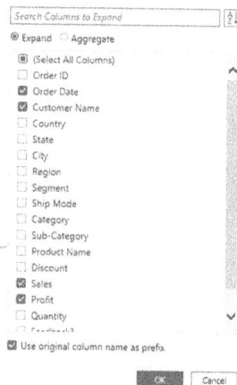

Rename the columns as required. Further, disabling the load option for the original queries can also be done in Power BI to generate the required data model.

While working with data that does not provide matching values, a more advanced feature called "Fuzzy Matching" can be applied to join two values based on their approximate similarity. In this way, the Merge Queries option, shown in Figure 2.26, helps join two queries together.

Figure 2.26 Configuring the Required Columns in the Merge

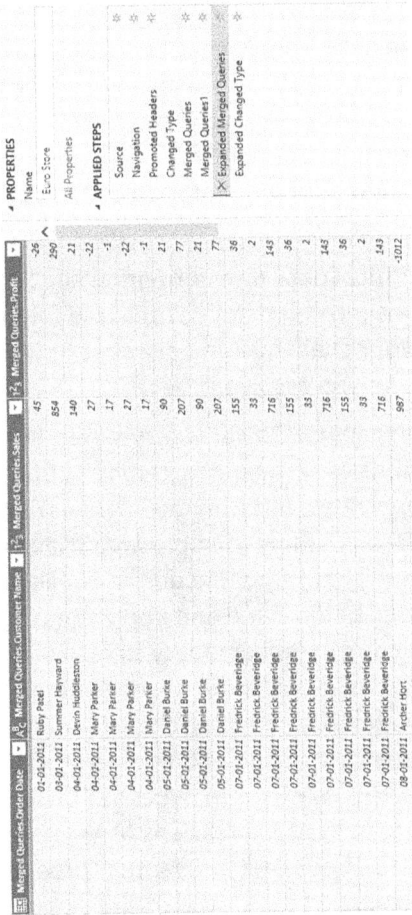

EXERCISE

We have listed some common data transformation challenges, followed by a solution to address them below.

Some of the common challenges include:

- Inconsistent formats across different data sources create issues.
- Cleaning and standardizing data before analysis is time-consuming.
- Reports take forever to load because of massive datasets.
- Combining data from Excel, SQL, and Application Programming Interfaces (APIs) always leads to mismatches.
- Duplicates keep creeping into reports.
- Filtering takes a long time for datasets that contain millions of records.

Consider a critical data transformation challenge that you have encountered before. Apply the following solution to your challenge and discover how Power Query can help you resolve it.

Solution: You can use Power Query's built-in transformations to standardize, remove duplicates, clean missing values, filter unnecessary data, and remove unused columns to improve efficiency. You can use Power Query's Merge function to check for data inconsistencies beforehand and apply the Unpivot Columns function in Power Query to restructure data for better analysis. Power Query's Remove Duplicates feature can create unique identifiers to avoid redundancy. You can also apply Natural Language Processing (NLP), use Text Analytics in Power BI, and leverage Data Analysis Expressions (DAX) functions. We will learn more about DAX in Chapter Three, Section 3.5.

2.3.1 Enabling and disabling load in Power Query

In Power BI, managing query load efficiently with Power Query is crucial for optimizing performance and maintaining a clean data model. The Enable Load option in Power Query determines whether a query's data is loaded into the Power BI data model. On the other hand, Disabling Load prevents unnecessary queries from consuming memory and storage.

1. When to Disable load?

Load should be disabled in the following scenarios:

- **Staging queries:** If a query is used only for transformations and is not needed in reports
- **Intermediate steps:** When queries are merged, and only the final result is required
- **Performance optimization:** When it is essential to reduce model size and improve refresh speed by keeping only important tables

2. How to Disable or Enable Load?

- In Power Query Editor, right-click the query and uncheck "Enable Load" to disable it.
- Queries with load disabled won't appear in the data model but can still be used for transformations.

2.3.2 Enabling Append Query

The function of appending queries is used to combine data from multiple tables vertically. The tables must have the same column structure, with the same column names and data types.

To perform Append Query, Open Power Query Editor, click on Home, and select Append Queries or Append Queries as New. Again, choose the tables to append. Click OK, and the data will be combined into a single table.

Here, rows from one table are added below the rows from another. Power BI aligns columns based on column name, and if columns do not match, it creates NULL values.

Merge Query and Append Query

A Merge Query is used when we need to combine related data from different tables. For example, to add product details to sales data, we use the merge function. This query combines tables horizontally, column-wise, and adds a new column from another table.

However, if we want to combine sales values from multiple years, we need to use the Append Query instead. The Append Query stacks similar datasets together by combining tables vertically and adding new rows from another table. It requires the tables to have an identical column structure.

Point to Remember

Merge Query works like a matchmaker for your data. It helps your data find the perfect partner and build a strong relationship. For example, a Merge Query helps to merge contact details (Name + Phone Number)

On the other hand, an Append Query stacks data vertically and helps you add new rows to the spreadsheet. For example, an Append Query is like adding more contacts to your phonebook.

2.4 R Script Transform and Leveraging R

Business rules can be applied to data by using the R language, a powerful scripting language in advanced analytics. R Transform is integrated into Power BI and can be leveraged to create a data model.

The first step is to install Microsoft R Open (an open-source platform by Microsoft Corporation) using the URL below, available on the internet: (https://www.microsoft.com/en-us/download/details.aspx?id=51205).

This will run the R script using the web link as shown in Figure 2.27.

Figure 2.27 Installing R in Power BI

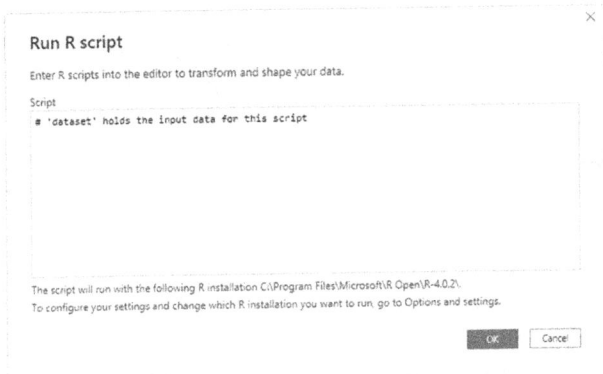

Download and run all the installations, accept all default settings, and integrate R with Power BI Desktop. From the "File" menu in Power BI, select "Options and Settings" to choose Options, as shown in Figure 2.28 below.

Figure 2.28 Integration and R Scripting

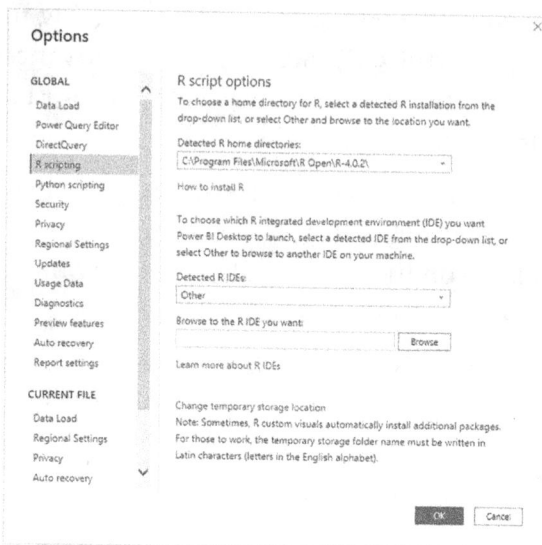

Before starting in Power BI, the MICE library must be installed to set up the R distribution. Launch Microsoft R Open. Then download R Studio. In the R console, input the following text, as shown in Figure 2.29, and press Enter:

install.packages("mice")

Figure 2.29 Input for R Console

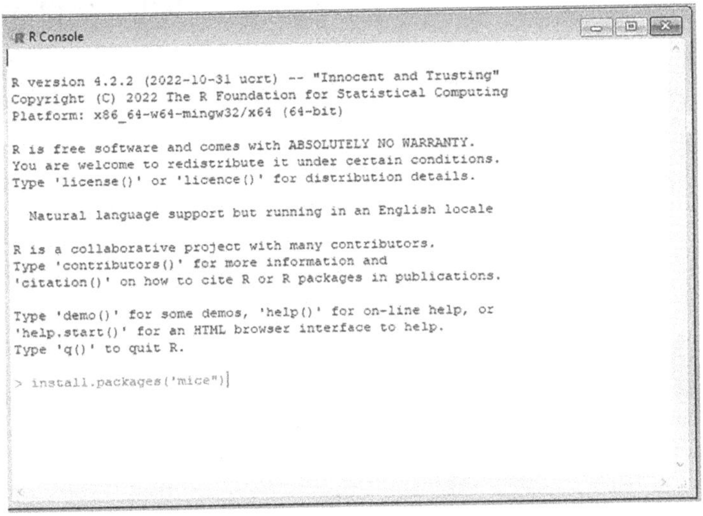

Next, an output will be generated, prompting you to close the R console window to launch Power BI Desktop (Fig. 2.30).

Figure 2.30 Output Window From R Console

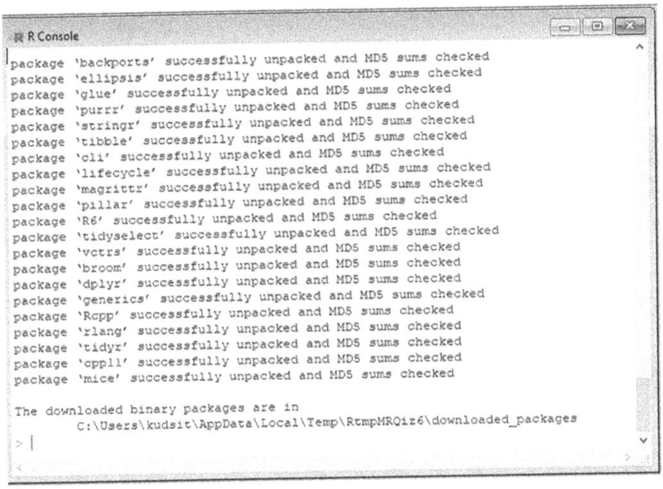

In the Power BI Desktop, connect the required data source, upload data, transform, and launch the Power Query Editor. Select the Run R Script (Fig. 2.31) to load the MICE library and detect missing values in the dataset with the script below, then click OK.

```
library(mice)
tempData<-mice(dataset, m=1,maxit=50,meth="pmm",seed=100)
completedData<-complete(tempData,1)
Output <- dataset
output$completedValues<-completedData$"SMi missing values"
```

Figure 2.31 **Running the R Script to Find Missing Values in the Dataset**

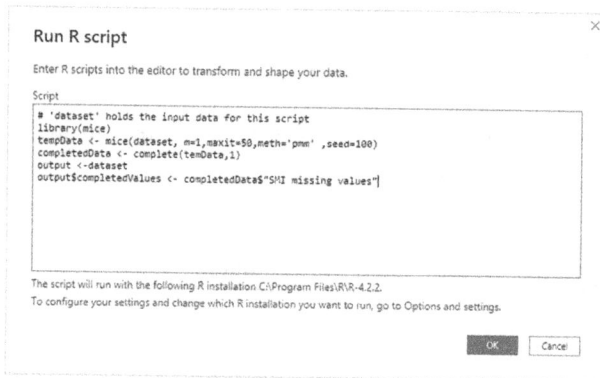

After running the R script to find missing values in the dataset, click on the hyperlink in the table to navigate to the corresponding data row. This allows you to verify the results of the newly applied transformation for identifying and detecting missing values. The new output will have the latest values seen based on the R script. Now, close and apply on the Home ribbon.

Thus, R Transform is an effective data source for creating visuals and reports in Power BI. Python is also used in Power BI to create new data connectors, transformations, and visuals as seen in Chapter One, Section 1.7.1. However, the usage of Python comes with certain challenges as discussed in the previous chapter.

2.5 AI-Powered BI for Sentiment Analytics

Customers post numerous reviews on various data sources and websites. Running AI algorithms can extract crucial data from these posts in the form of phrases, language, and images. Further, sentiment analysis can be applied to identify whether the response is positive or negative and enable subsequent categorization.

Power BI is equipped with AI insights, which can be enabled by setting up an AI workload and choosing the maximum amount of memory as a 20% limit. The Home ribbon in the Power Query Editor includes a Text Analytics option. After completing the required sign-in steps, select the Text Analytics algorithm with the Score Sentiment option. This will analyze the text in the Review Text column when you click OK. A new numeric column will be added with a value of 0 or 1 for every row in the dataset. A score closer to 1 indicates positive sentiments, and any score closer to 0 indicates negative sentiments.

In the initial part of this chapter, we understood the importance of preparing data to meet specific reporting needs. Then we progressed to learn about advanced data transformation methods, running R scripts for data modeling, and leveraging AI-driven sentiment analysis within Power BI. Let's revise our learnings from this chapter before moving to Chapter Three.

Chapter Summary

- Power BI can connect and sync with a variety of data sources. Key data sources are Microsoft Excel, SQL Server, and the Web. Power BI provides built-in connectors for integration with various databases and platforms.

- Data can be imported into Power BI by directly connecting to key sources such as Excel, SQL Server, and the Web, depending on where the data is stored.

- Power BI offers various data cleansing and transformation options through Power Query, enabling users to prepare structured, clean data for reporting. Transforming data at the import stage helps build efficient and accurate reports aligned with business objectives.

- Data can be optimized for import using Power Query and transformation tools in Power BI.

- The data source is selected based on the location of the data, and connectors are applied accordingly.

- Power Query Editor has a wide range of transformation functions available and is a powerful tool for applying business rules to transform incoming data. It includes diverse data transformation and cleansing features, ensuring that raw data is structured and clean for analysis and visualization.

- In Power Query, there are three main options to create new columns. The Custom Column option allows you to write formulas using the M language for advanced logic. The Conditional Column option lets you define new columns using if-then rules without needing to code. Lastly, the Column From Examples option enables you to create new columns by providing sample outputs, and Power Query automatically detects the transformation pattern.

- A Merge Query is used when we need to combine related data from different tables. Merge Query combines tables horizontally, column-wise, and adds a new column from another table. But if we want to combine sales values of multiple years, we need to use Append Query instead. Append Query stacks similar datasets together, combines tables vertically, adding new rows from another table, and requires an identical column structure.

- R Transform is an effective data source for creating visuals and reports in Power BI.

- Power BI is equipped with AI insights, which can be enabled by setting up an AI workload and choosing the maximum amount of memory as a 20% limit.

QUIZ

1. **Why is data transformation necessary?**
   a. Not necessary as the data is always perfect as it is.
   b. It helps to eliminate errors and customize data for specific purposes.
   c. It assists in increasing the volume of data.
   d. It helps to avoid advanced analytics.

2. **What is the primary purpose of Power Query Editor?**
   a. To create dashboards
   b. To transform and clean data
   c. To store data
   d. To delete data

3. **Identify which is not a source for importing data using the Power Query Editor.**
   a. Excel
   b. SQL Server
   c. Web
   d. PDF files

4. **Which data source can be directly accessed using Power Query Editor?**
   a. PDF files
   b. SQL Server
   c. PowerPoint slides
   d. Video files

5. **What is the benefit of sourcing data from SQL Server into Power BI?**

   a. Real-time data updates
   b. Limited data storage
   c. Manual data entry
   d. Restricted data access

6. **Identify the data transformation technique used in Power Query Editor to combine multiple columns.**

   a. Pivot
   b. Unpivot
   c. Merge
   d. Concatenate

7. **Identify the role of the "Fill Up" and "Fill Down" functions in Power Query Editor.**

   a. To fill in missing values
   b. To create new columns
   c. To remove rows from the data
   d. To export data to Excel

8. **Why is it required to run R scripts within Power BI?**

   a. To replace SQL queries
   b. To generate complex data models and conduct advanced analytics
   c. To build dashboards
   d. To create standard reports

9. **Why is it important to clean and transform data?**

   a. To reduce the size of the data
   b. To ensure data accuracy and relevance
   c. To hide data from other users
   d. To create more complex datasets

10. **Which feature in Power Query Editor is used to remove unwanted columns from a dataset?**

    a. Filter Rows

    b. Remove Columns

    c. Replace Values

    d. Pivot Column

Answers

1 – b	2 – b	3 – d	4 – b	5 – a
6 – b	7 – a	8 – b	9 – b	10 – b

Case Study 1

(Chapters 1 and 2)

How a Retail Chain Streamlined Market Trend Analysis for Smarter Decisions

Introduction:

The objective of this case study is to discuss foundational capabilities and the potential of Power BI for effective data visualization and transformation outcomes. This case enables you to get a clear understanding of data sources and cleansing techniques. Additionally, it discusses the creation of basic visualizations to present key insights, demonstrated through the case study of a retail chain.

A retail chain collects data on sales, customer demographics, and purchasing patterns. It has 45 stores spread across five states, and it deals in groceries, household items, and electronics. The management wants to identify market trends for this year and visualize them strategically.

Over the past year, sales have fluctuated significantly across regions and product categories. The Chief Executive Officer (CEO) believes that decisions are currently based on gut feeling rather than real data insights. To build a data-driven culture, the company hires a new business intelligence manager who introduces Power BI to support accurate storytelling and analytics.

The BI manager begins by training department heads on data analysis, visual storytelling, and data transformation for making informed decisions. They set up a Power BI dashboard using sales data from Excel files, customer feedback from online forms, and social media sentiment using R scripts. They also perform data cleansing and transformation functions on inconsistent product category names, dates, and missing values.

Challenges:

The BI manager identified several challenges, including:

- **Lack of structured data analysis:** Managers relied heavily on Excel reports that were often delayed and prone to manual errors.
- **Disparate data sources:** Sales data, customer feedback, and inventory reports were scattered across different formats (Excel, CSV, SQL database, and online forms).
- **Poor data quality:** Missing values, inconsistent category names, duplicate entries, and mismatched date formats created barriers to meaningful analysis.
- **Limited awareness about data visualization tools:** Department heads were unfamiliar with Power BI and its benefits in deriving insights.
- **Inability to gauge customer sentiment:** Although customer reviews and feedback were collected, there was no structured way to analyze them for strategic insights.

Solutions implemented:

The retail company leveraged Power BI in four stages for enhanced data analysis:

1. **Power BI implementation and training**

   - Installed Power BI Desktop across departments and trained managers on building basic dashboards.

- Explained the building blocks of Power BI—datasets, reports, dashboards, and dataflows—and how they could be used in daily decision-making.

2. Data integration and transformation

- Imported data from various sources (Excel, SQL databases, online survey forms).
- Used Power Query Editor to:
  - **a.** Remove duplicate rows.
  - **b.** Clean column headers.
  - **c.** Fix inconsistent product category names.
  - **d.** Convert text dates into standard date formats.
  - **e.** Merge datasets to create a unified view of sales and customer feedback.

3. Leveraging R and AI for advanced analytics

- Used R scripts in Power BI to conduct sentiment analysis on open-ended customer feedback from Google Forms and social media.
- Created AI-powered visuals to classify customer responses as positive, neutral, or negative.

4. Storytelling with data

- Designed interactive dashboards showing:
  - **a.** Region-wise sales trends
  - **b.** Product category performance
  - **c.** Customer sentiment heatmaps
- Used slicers and filters to allow store managers to drill down into state- or store-level data.

This case reinforces that in the era of Industry 4.0, BI tools are not just IT solutions but strategic enablers for competitiveness and sustainable growth. Companies that invest in data literacy, tools like Power BI, and continuous upskilling are more likely to thrive in today's volatile and tech-driven business environment.

Case assignment:

1. Import sales data from Excel and SQL databases.
2. Clean and transform data using Power Query Editor (e.g., remove duplicates, handle missing values).
3. Visualize metrics such as monthly sales trends, top-selling products, and customer segmentation.
4. Discuss the importance of visualizing this data for decision-making.

Sample datasets for reference: You can input these datasets in Excel/CSV formats for direct upload to Power BI.

Date	Product	Name	Category	Sales	Units sold	Customer age	Gender	Region
1/1/2024	P001	Smart Watch	Electronics	200	1	35	M	North
1/1/2024	P002	Jeans	Apparel	100	2	28	F	East
2/1/2024	P003	Smart Phone	Electronics	800	1	40	M	South
2/1/2024	P004	Blender	Home Appliances	150	1	32	Undisclosed	West

Case discussion questions:

You may answer these descriptive and application-based questions based on your understanding of the case.

1. Why is it important for this retail company to shift from instinct-based decisions to data-driven storytelling?

2. Discuss how Power BI can help managers make better business decisions. Refer to any three features.

3. Name and explain any two major building blocks of Power BI that the BI manager would have used in the dashboard.

4. What steps must be followed in using Power Query Editor to clean and transform this data?

5. Give examples of three data sources to build a comprehensive dashboard for this company.

6. Explain how R scripts and AI integration can help analyze customer sentiment from social media comments.

7. What challenges might arise during the data transformation process, and how can Power BI help address them?

8. Why is data cleansing a critical step?

This page is intentionally left blank

CHAPTER 3

Data Modelling With Power BI

Key Learning Objectives

- Learn how to create data models by examining relationships between various data sources.
- Understand how to manage complex relationships within datasets, enhancing the performance of data models.
- Demonstrate how usability enhancements in data models support business needs.
- Identify methods for data optimization for effective data processing and analysis.

Usually, it takes months to work with a data model in a rigid corporate environment, and many enterprise models fail, pointing to reasons such as high costs, infrastructural issues, or workforce management inefficiencies. However, Power BI helps to remove barriers that may account for the failure of enterprise projects and provides an agile approach to building data models.

This chapter outlines relationships between different data sources to create and develop an intelligent data model. It focuses on building connections among datasets, working with complex relationships, and adding usability enhancements that stress the performance of the data model. These improvements contribute to the success of BI projects and support managers in making informed decisions.

Before we explore these aspects, let's understand what a data model is and its role in creating relationships and enabling data transformation in Power BI. Data modeling refers to the process of creating a structured representation of data. It defines how data is organized and stored in a system. It mainly involves designing schemas, relationships, and hierarchies for efficient data retrieval and analysis.

Data modeling is crucial for managers as it offers a clear framework to understand complex data, ensuring data integrity and scalability across organizations. It supports them in deriving actionable insights for effective decision-making.

Power BI plays a pivotal role in data modeling, providing user-friendly tools for designing and managing data models. It equips managers to create relationships between datasets confidently and optimize models for performance. Power BI can handle large, diverse datasets, advanced analytics, and visualization requirements. Thus, it bridges the gap between raw data and strategic insights and aids as an effective tool for data-driven management.

Imagine a wholesale company wants to analyze its sales. They have a Sales Table with information like units sold, dates of sales, and customer details. They also have a Customer Table with customer names and regions, and a Product Table with product names and categories. In Power BI, data modelling functions connect these tables using common fields like Customer ID and Product ID.

Once connected, you can easily build reports like "Total Sales by Region" or "Top-Selling Products by Category." You don't need to deploy complex formulas every time—the model handles it for you. This saves time and helps you focus on developing strategic insights, not technical details.

3.1 Building Relationships

The first and most important step in data modeling is to define and build relationships for seamless integration with various datasets. Based on cardinality, there are three types of relationships in Power BI:

1. **One-to-One**

    In a One-to-One relationship, each row in Table A has exactly one corresponding row in Table B. For example, each employee will have one salary record. Employee names will be in Table A, and their corresponding salaries will be in Table B.

2. **One-to-Many**

    In a One-to-Many relationship, one value in a column in Table A corresponds to multiple related rows in another column in Table B. Suppose Table A consists of customer details, then Table B corresponds to the orders made by each customer. In this relationship, a customer can make multiple orders, which would be reflected in Table B.

3. Many-to-Many

In a Many-to-Many relationship, multiple rows in one table will relate to many rows in the next table. For example, Table A shows student details and Table B shows course details. Here, each student can be in many courses, and each course has many students, thus creating many-to-many relationships between tables.

In Power BI, Filter Direction shows how data filters from one table to another table through relationships. A Single Direction filter flows in one direction, that is, from one side. For example, selecting a region in a "Region" table filters the "Sales" table, not vice versa. In Bidirectional Filters, the filter flows both ways between the tables; they are useful in complex models, which have many-to-many relationships.

Relationships are built by connecting data sources so that filtered visuals and reports can be created quickly in Power BI from multiple datasets. Some characteristics of the relationships include auto-detected relationships, active and inactive relationships between two tables, relationships built in a single column, and relationships automatically filtering one side of a relationship to the many sides.

Power BI automatically detects and creates these diverse relationships between tables through auto-detection. This requires accuracy as each pair of tables may have one active relationship and many inactive relationships. Most relations are built based on a single column; auto-detection works by identifying common columns across tables. These single columns serve as a unique identifier to ensure clarity in data linking.

3.2 Importing Data Tables into a Data Model

To support the analysis of data, a data table must be imported. From the Get data option, select the Excel file, choose Order Data, and click the Load option, as seen in Figure 3.1.

Figure 3.1 Importing Data by Loading

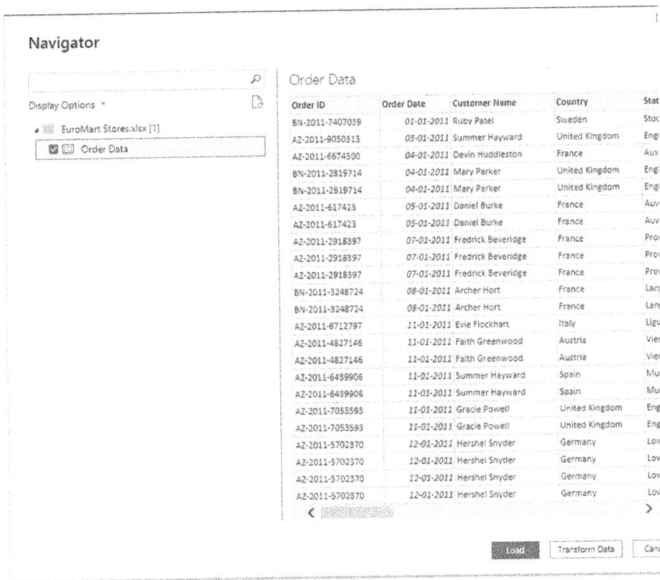

After loading, verify that all auto-detected relationships have been created, as shown in Figure 3.2, the Relationship View of the data.

Figure 3.2 Relationship View of Data

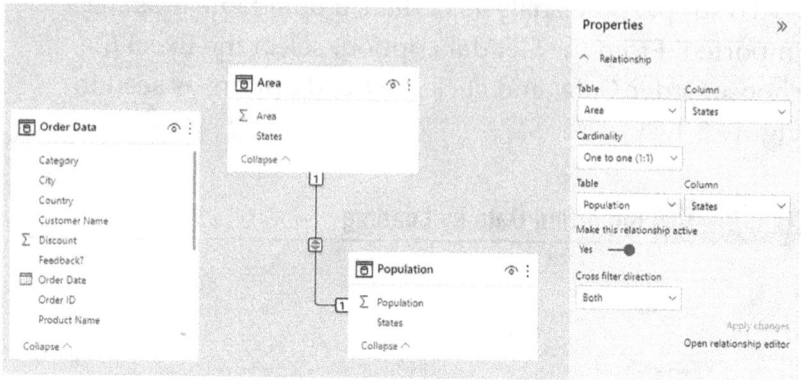

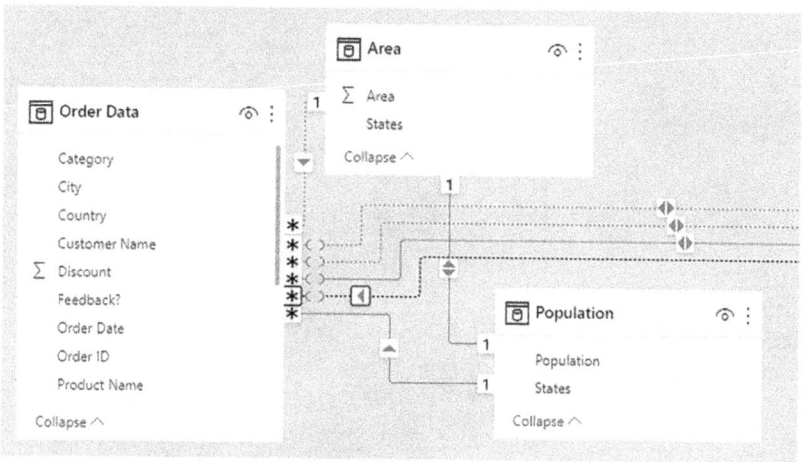

3.2.1 Managing relationships

Power BI provides a centralized interface for managing relationships across data tables. Figure 3.3 shows the Model View to Manage relationships, which will appear on the Home ribbon.

Figure 3.3 | **Manage Relationships in Model View**

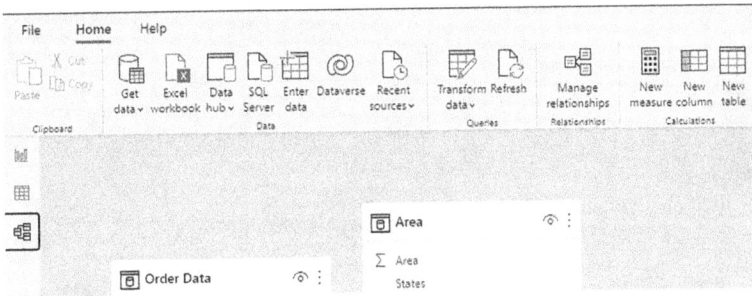

Under the Home tab of Model View in the ribbon, there is a "Relationships" group of commands. There is a "Manage relationships" button in this group. Clicking on this, a view appears, as shown in Figure 3.3 above, which helps us manage the relationships. Similarly, we can manage relations in the Report View by clicking the Modeling tab in the ribbon (Fig. 3.4).

Figure 3.4 | **Manage Relationships in Report View**

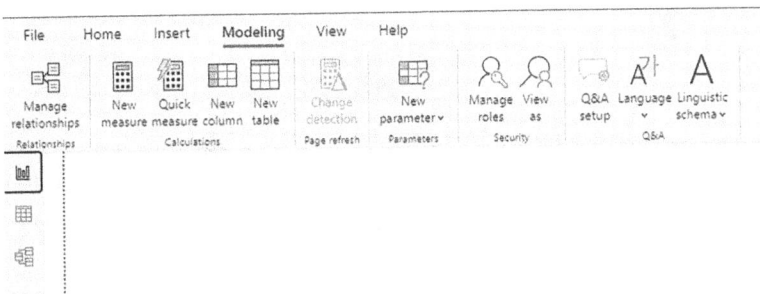

If you are in the Data View, relationships can be managed by clicking the Table tools ribbon, as shown in Figure 3.5 below.

Figure 3.5 Manage Relationships in Data View

The Manage Relationships View in the Model, Report, and Data Views opens the Manage Relationships Editor, allowing you to create new relationships and edit or delete existing ones.

3.2.2 Manage Relationship Editor

Figure 3.6 shows the Manage Relationship Editor, which presents the current relationships in the model.

| Figure 3.6 | Manage Relationships Dialog Box |

Manage relationships

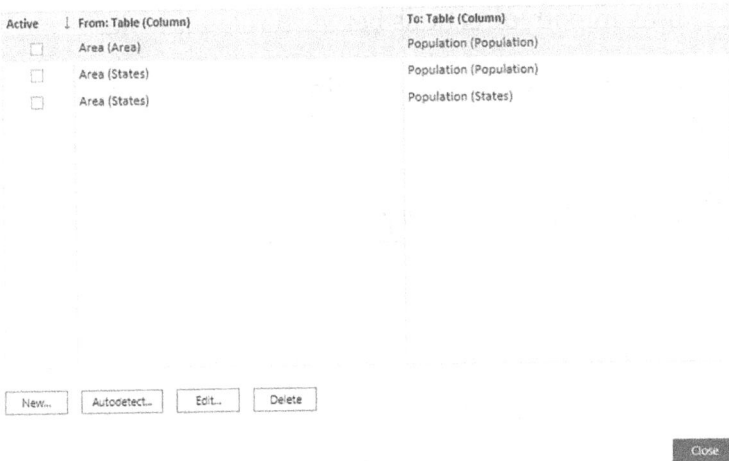

Active	↓ From: Table (Column)	To: Table (Column)
☐	Area (Area)	Population (Population)
☐	Area (States)	Population (Population)
☐	Area (States)	Population (States)

| New... | Autodetect... | Edit... | Delete |

Close

There are four buttons in the lower portion of this page, namely, New, Autodetect, Edit, and Delete. The "New" button helps to create new relationships. The "Edit" tab is used for editing an existing relationship, and the "Delete" tab is for deleting an existing relationship. The "Autodetect" button shows the available relationships and helps to identify relationships between tables and columns.

1. Edit data relationship

To edit a relationship, click on the Relationship checkbox and the "Edit" button. This opens up the Edit Relationships dialogue box. The checkbox identifies whether the relationship is active or inactive.

In Power BI, relationships between tables are typically identified as "Many-to-One." This means that multiple rows in one table (the "many" side) relate to a single row in another table (the "one" side). The "cross-filter direction" can be set to either "single (default)" or "both." By default, Power BI allows filtering from "one" side to the "many" side. However, enabling "bidirectional filtering" (both sides) allows filters to flow in both directions between related tables.

Figure 3.7 shows tools for editing the relationship between two datasets in the Edit Relationship dialog box.

Figure 3.7 Editing Relationship

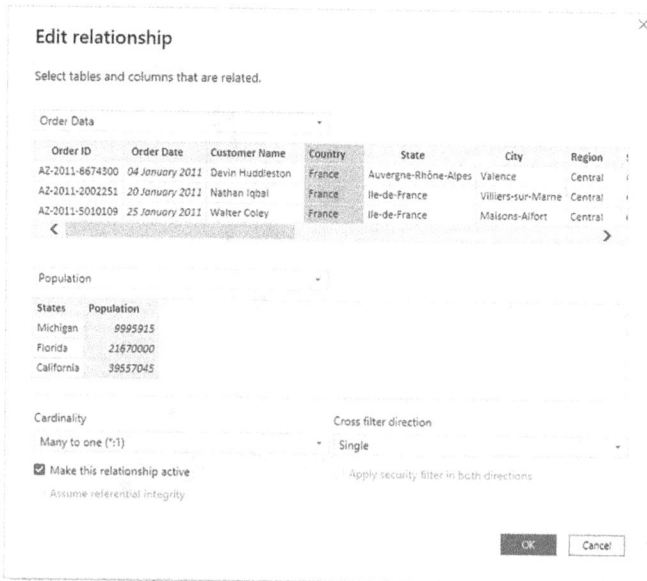

2. Create and delete a new data relationship

In Power BI, we can create and also delete a new data relationship. Within the Manage Relationships dialog box, click the "Create" button. Select the tables for which a new relationship needs to be created.

Figure 3.8 Creating a New Relationship

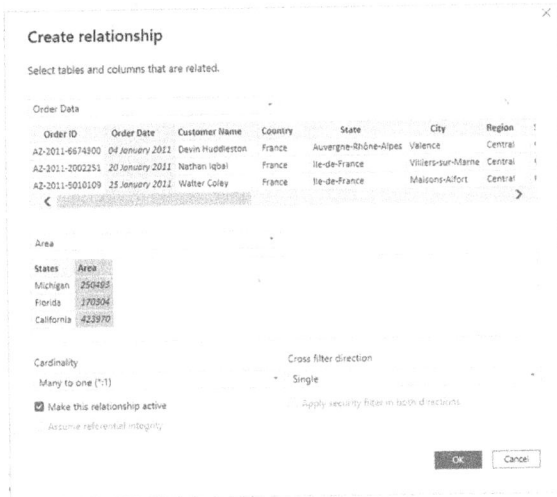

Figure 3.8 above shows the steps in creating a new relationship for tables. The Order Data from the Stores database and Area (Country, State, City, Region, etc) from which the order is generated is selected from the drop-down list.

There can be only one active relationship between tables in Power BI; all filtering will happen through this active relationship. To create new relationships, open Manage Relationships from the Home ribbon. In our example, we are creating a new relationship between the Order Data and the Area by selecting from the list of columns.

Within Manage Relationships, click to open the Create Relationship Editor. Power BI automatically updates cardinality, whether the relationship is active or not, and also updates the cross-filter direction. Now, click OK to close the editor. Again, if relationships are to be deleted, choose the delete option in Manage Relationships, as shown in Figure 3.9.

Figure 3.9 Deleting Relationships

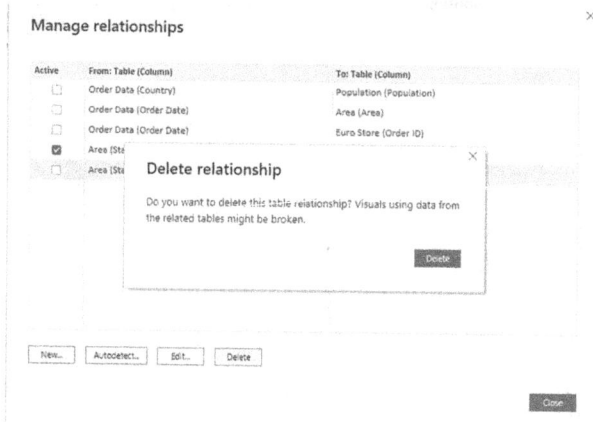

Disabling the Auto-Create Relationship feature in Power BI is considered a best practice, as relying on it is generally not recommended. When this feature is enabled, Power BI automatically attempts to create relationships between tables based on column names and data types as soon as they are imported. This might seem convenient, but it can lead to incorrect relationships.

To maintain better control over the data model and ensure relationships are explicitly defined and accurate, it's best to disable the Auto-Create Relationship setting manually.

POINT TO REMEMBER

Before creating a new relationship, ensure that the columns you link have matching data types. Mismatched data types, for example, text vs. number, will prevent Power BI from establishing a valid relationship.

To disable automatically created data tables from the file, navigate to Options and Settings and then to the Options window, as shown in Figure 3.10. Under Global, choose Data Load and uncheck the Auto Date/ Time for new files in the bottom part.

Figure 3.10 **Disabling Automatically Created Data Tables**

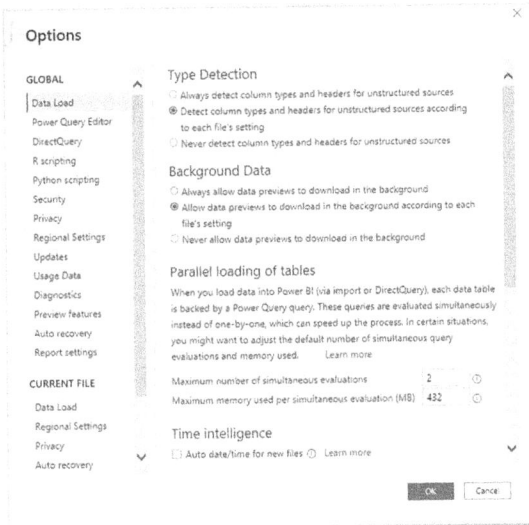

3.3 Usability Enhancements in Power BI

Usability enhancements can be leveraged to improve the overall user experience when interacting with the data model. Significant enhancements are listed here:

1. Hiding tables and columns
2. Renaming tables and columns
3. Default summarization
4. Displaying one column but sorting by another
5. Data categorization
6. Creating hierarchies

Let's understand these user enhancements in detail in the following section:

1. Hiding tables and columns

Some tables will be available in a data model, but shall not be used in the report. Similarly, some columns may be required to create relationships between tables, but they will not be part of the report. Since they are not part of the report, those tables and columns must be hidden from the Report View to reduce complexity.

To do this, right-click on the object that must be hidden and then select Hide in Report View, as shown in Figure 3.11.

Figure 3.11 In the Data View Option, Selecting the Column to be Hidden in the Report View

In the Report View, choose the option Hide. In the Model View, right-click on the column that needs to be hidden and then select Hide in Report View, as shown in Figure 3.12. Similarly, go to each table and hide the columns that need to be hidden.

Figure 3.12 Selecting Hide in Report View

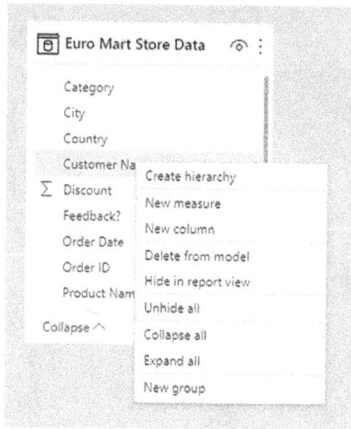

The hidden columns will still be visible in the Data and Relationship View. Hidden columns can be identified if they have slightly lighter text than the columns that are not hidden. They also have a visibility icon on the left of the column name, as shown in Figure 3.13.

Figure 3.13 Hidden Columns Indicated With Icon

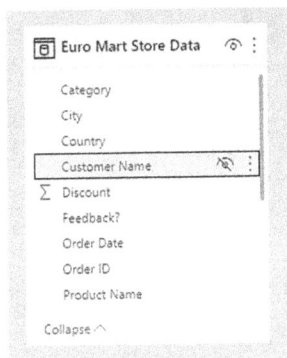

2. Renaming tables and columns

To enable easy use of data models and avoid duplication, tables and columns must be renamed depending on the end user's needs and understanding. A column with a list of Customer Names can be renamed as Customer, or the sales team can rename it as Client. Tables and columns can be renamed in all three views: Report, Data, or Model View.

a. Renaming in Report View

Right-click and rename the table in Report View per the user's understanding, as done in Figure 3.14.

Figure 3.14 Renaming Table

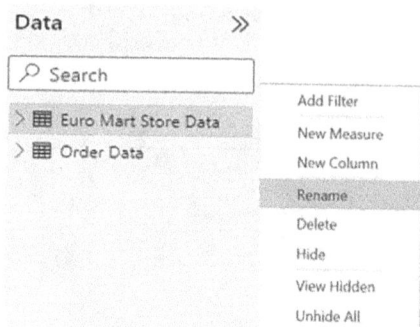

b. Renaming in Data View

In the Data View, right-click the column that needs to be renamed. Figure 3.15 shows selecting the column to be renamed.

Figure 3.15 Renaming the Customer Name Column in the Data View

Order ID	Order Date	Customer Name	Country
AZ-2011-6674300	04 January 2011	Devin Huddleston	France
AZ-2011-2002251	20 January 2011	Nathan Iqbal	France
AZ-2011-5010109	25 January 2011	Walter Coley	France
AZ-2011-2397035	07 February 2011	Millie Newman	France
AZ-2011-4069925	01 March 2011	Oscar Clayton	France
AZ-2011-3714764	11 March 2011	Ashton Charles	France
AZ-2011-332801	19 April 2011	Koby Tompson	France
BN-2011-5672017	27 April 2011	Louie Knight	France
AZ-2011-2112563	10 May 2011	Francesca Bowen	France
AZ-2011-7005483	13 May 2011	Robert James	France
BN-2011-4249147	03 June 2011	Ada Dalton	France
AZ-2011-3901505	27 June 2011	Kayla Tearle	France
AZ-2011-6011646	09 July 2011	Nancy Fike	France
AZ-2011-3858939	29 September 2011	Julian Mack	France
AZ-2011-2730322	04 October 2011	Mark Washington	France

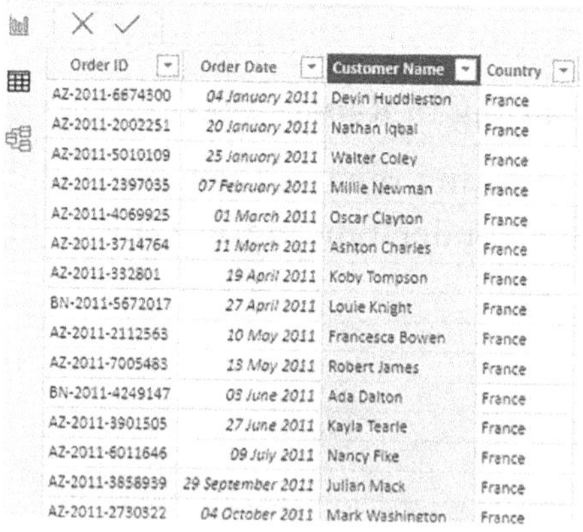

The column Customer Name is renamed Customer, as shown in Figure 3.16.

Figure 3.16 **Renaming Customer Name to Customer**

Order ID	Order Date	Customer	Country
AZ-2014-9634517	23 April 2014	Aaron Bootman	Italy
AZ-2011-9409671	04 April 2011	Aaron Bootman	United Kingdom
AZ-2011-3937280	30 August 2011	Aaron Bootman	Italy
AZ-2014-9634517	23 April 2014	Aaron Bootman	Italy
BN-2014-2854953	11 March 2014	Aaron Bootman	Germany
AZ-2011-9409671	04 April 2011	Aaron Bootman	United Kingdom
AZ-2012-9056595	12 March 2012	Aaron Bootman	Germany
BN-2014-1772108	07 February 2014	Aaron Bootman	United Kingdom
AZ-2012-608163	20 March 2012	Aaron Bootman	United Kingdom
AZ-2011-3937280	30 August 2011	Aaron Bootman	Italy
AZ-2013-4015759	13 August 2013	Aaron Bootman	France
AZ-2011-2169445	21 March 2011	Aaron Bootman	Italy
AZ-2011-2169445	21 March 2011	Aaron Bootman	Italy
AZ-2012-9056595	12 March 2012	Aaron Bootman	Germany
AZ-2012-9056595	12 March 2012	Aaron Bootman	Germany
BN-2014-2854953	11 March 2014	Aaron Bootman	Germany
AZ-2012-9056595	12 March 2012	Aaron Bootman	Germany
BN-2012-6348676	21 August 2012	Aaron Bootman	Netherlands

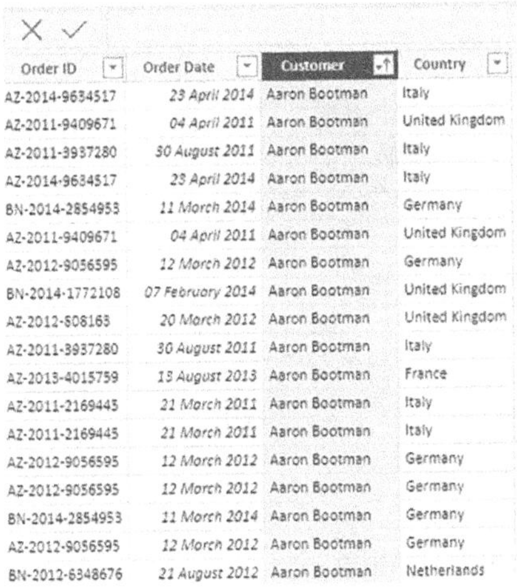

c. Renaming in Model View

In the Model View, right-click on Euro Store data, then select Rename for any column of choice. Rename the Feedback column as Responses, as shown in Figures 3.17 and 3.18.

Figure 3.17 **Renaming Column in Model View**

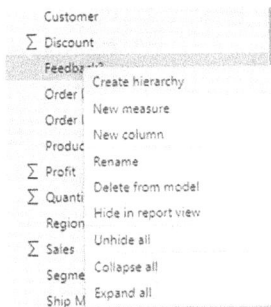

Figure 3.18 Column Gets New Names as Responses

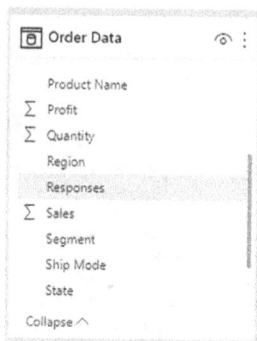

3. Default Summarization

Power BI assigns a default summarization, a sum operation denoted by a Sigma symbol, to those numeric columns that do not have a relationship. As shown in Figure 3.19, the columns Discount, Profit, Quantity, and Sales have been assigned default summarization by Power BI in the Report View.

Figure 3.19 Default Summarization Assigned to Columns

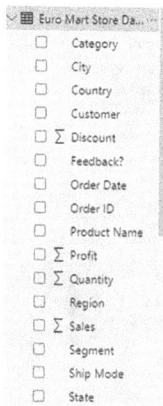

However, there are some issues related to default summarization. The columns identified by Power BI are descriptive attributes that help explain the data. This may confuse report developers if those columns are automatically aggregated when added to a report. Thus, columns should not be aggregated, and default summarization must be avoided.

To avoid default summarization, select Report View. Expand the data table, choose the Profit column, in which the default summarization is to be avoided. The Column Tools ribbon then appears across the top. Click the dropdown for Summarization and select Don't Summarize, as shown in Figure 3.20. Repeat the process for other columns that need to be disaggregated, removing default summarization.

Figure 3.20 Removing the Default Summarization for the Profit Column

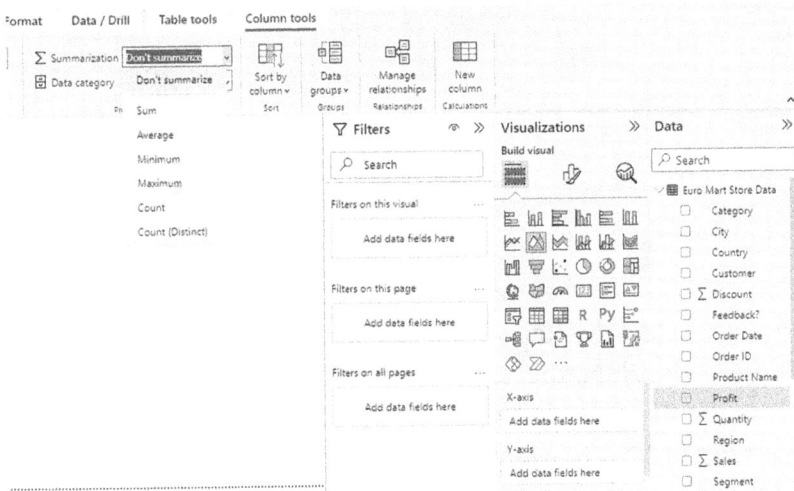

4. Displaying one column but sorting by another

This usability enhancement can be applied when we must display column names and then sort in a particular format by another column. For example, the month's title can be sorted alphabetically. Or instead, the months can also be sorted chronologically, while the report displays the month names and sorts them by their corresponding month numbers, as shown in Figure 3.21 below. You can select the column that you want to sort, and then use the "Sort by Column" option to specify another column based on which the selected column should be sorted.

Figure 3.21 Changing the Sort Order of a Column

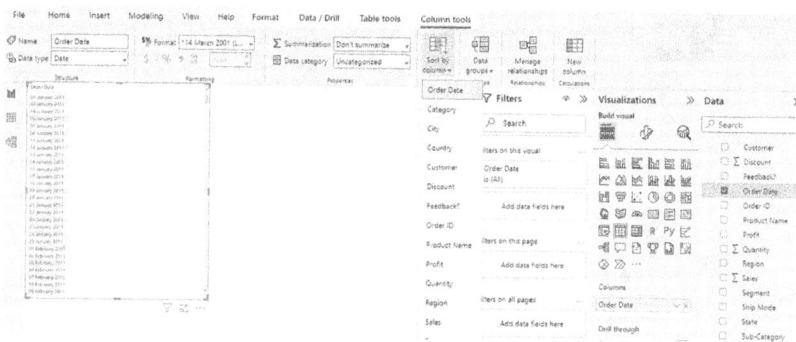

First, select the Report View, expand the Date table, select English Month Name, and then select the Column Tools. From the drop-down for Sort by Column, select Month Number of Year to categorize columns and improve the user experience in the report.

5. Data categorization

Based on data types, column names, and relationships in the data model, Power BI makes assumptions about columns, and these assumptions are used in the Report View to build visualizations and enhance user experience. Power BI selects different types of visuals for each column and decides on column placements within the fields. When Power BI identifies a column with numeric values on the many sides of a relationship, a default aggregation is assigned.

Power BI assumes that we want to aggregate the data, so it automatically places the numeric columns in the values area of a report. There are 13 diverse data categorization options shown in Figure 3.22. These classifications allow for improving user experience by reducing and possibly eliminating inaccurate results.

Figure 3.22 Data Categorization Options

The most commonly used data categorization in Power BI is for classifying geographical data. When geographical data is added to a map, Bing Maps makes certain assumptions about methods to map data, which can show incorrect results. This can be overcome through data categorization and using the data category option available as a usability enhancement option in Power BI.

Figure 3.23 Modifying Data Category in the Report View

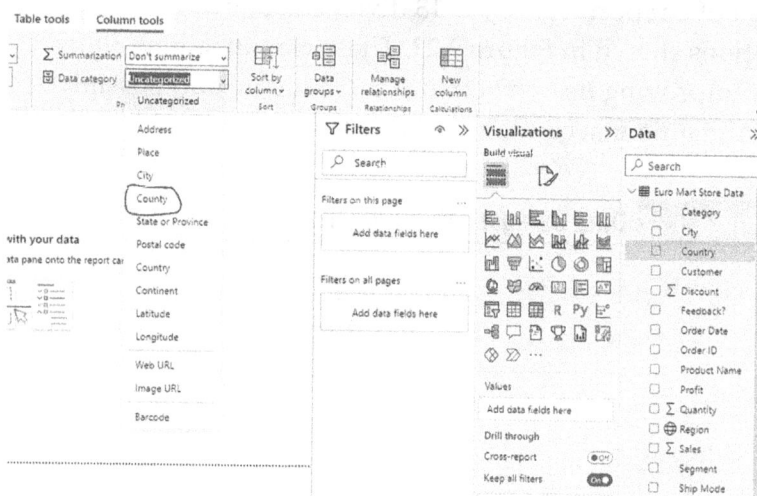

Classifying geographical columns in the data model helps Bing Maps correctly map data with accurate results. Proper classification and categorization can solve the issue of mapping geographical locations.

6. Creating hierarchies

Hierarchies enable storing information about relationships within data. When a hierarchy is added to the data model, as shown in Figure 3.24, Power BI will store the relationship for the user.

Figure 3.24 Creating Hierarchy

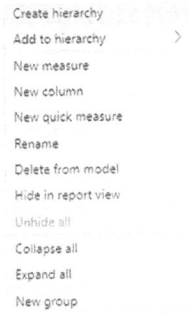

Create hierarchy
Add to hierarchy   >
New measure
New column
New quick measure
Rename
Delete from model
Hide in report view
Unhide all
Collapse all
Expand all
New group

Predefining and creating hierarchies help to organize attributes and show relationships in data. Additionally, it can add analytical value to the visualization by drilling down and rolling up data. Examples of a common hierarchy include: Country/ State/ City.

Figure 3.25 Adding Attributes to the Hierarchy

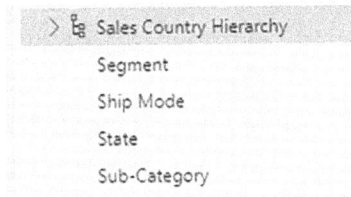

> Sales Country Hierarchy

Segment

Ship Mode

State

Sub-Category

At this stage, a new hierarchy has been created with a single column and can be renamed as Sales Country Hierarchy, as shown in Figure 3.25 above. In some cases, the order of attributes such as the sales country, state, segment, subcategory, or shipping mode may be incorrect. To rearrange the order, right-click on Sales Country and click Move Up.

Power BI also automatically creates a date hierarchy (year, quarter, month, day) for any date field added to the data model. This feature is helpful for time-based reporting and analysis. However, if the default hierarchy is not required for reporting purposes and only the base date field is used in visuals, it is recommended to remove or disable the auto-generated date hierarchy. This helps reduce the data model's size and optimize performance.

ACTIVITY

How do usability enhancements improve the efficiency and interpretability of a Power BI data model for end users? Discuss with an example where these enhancements significantly impact decision-making.

Data modeling serves as the backbone of organizational decision-making. With all these detailed enhancements we've learnt so far, modifications can be made to improve the effectiveness of the data model. This enhances user experience and makes the model intelligent, easy to understand, and navigate.

So far, we have explored how data modeling helps organize data efficiently, laying the foundation for building robust models. With these fundamentals in place, we can now turn our focus to evaluating data model performance—a crucial next step, covered in the following section.

3.4 Performance of a Data Model

A data model's performance is critical to identifying how design decisions affect performance today and in the future. This performance is measured through query execution and processing efficiency.

- **Query performance:** shows how quickly visualizations and reports provide results. Processing performance measures how long it would take to perform a data refresh on the underlying dataset.

  If the model size is small with simpler relationships, then query execution will be faster. Also, efficiently written DAX expressions enhance query speed. If the datasets are large, then users could use pre-aggregated tables to enhance the performance of the model.

- **Processing performance:** is critical when working with regularly updated or real-time data sources. In such cases, apply incremental refresh to minimize full reloads of data and discard unused ones to reduce model size and improve refresh speed.

- **Importing data:** is the standard methodology used to connect data in Power BI; this enables all queries to be answered from an in-memory cache. The imported dataset must undergo a data refresh operation to provide rich insights and enhance the model's performance.

- **Data refreshing:** includes importing only the required columns and removing all other columns from the data model, similar to rows.

- **Query folding:** the process of pushing work back to the underlying data source, can also significantly improve the processing performance of a data model.

Some of the best practices for improving the performance of a data model are as follows:

- Keeping the model lean by including only what's necessary and removing unnecessary columns and tables.

- Normalizing the model with a clear fact and dimension table structure to improve performance and clarity.

- Checking for auto date/time that can add hidden tables that bloat the model.

- Variables in DAX help improve readability and performance by reducing redundant calculations.

- **The Direct Query function:** is most commonly applied in query performance when the dataset is too large to import to Power BI. Instead of storing data in Power BI, queries are sent in real time to the underlying source whenever a user interacts with a report. However, since each user interaction generates a query against the source system, performance can become a concern, particularly if the queries are complex. To address this, creating aggregations is the best practice.

- **Creating aggregations:** is a robust methodology for enhancing query performance as it significantly reduces the number of rows queried. As a result, it improves performance and is often used with Direct Query. An aggregated table can be designed by understanding the data and considering the end user's requirements. This table can replace the original table, which stores more rows of data. This allows for maintaining both performance and data fidelity while reducing the load on the data source.

The performance of a data model is also influenced by the type of data model used. Power BI supports various data models based on how data is accessed and stored. Let us briefly learn about the major types of data models.

3.4.1 Types of data models

Data modeling should effectively present data, extract the data's analytical value, and support insight-driven evaluations. Power BI uses three data models to carry out these functions: flat models, star schemas, and snowflake schemas.

1. Flat data model

A flat data model is a simple table with all the descriptive attributes and measurable items; it doesn't have any supporting tables. This model is not flexible and intelligent, and as a result, cannot support complex analyses.

2. Star schema

The second type of data model, the star schema, is preferred in Power BI as it supports two types of tables— fact tables and dimension tables. The model is called a star because the dimension table surrounds the fact table and appears like a star.

3. Snowflake schema

As the name suggests, a snowflake schema resembles a snowflake rather than a star, supporting more advanced analytical requirements. In a snowflake schema, a product dimension can be divided into product category, subcategory, and specific category.

Figure 3.26(A) is the flat model, which stores all the data in just one table. Figure 3.26(B) represents the star schema, which connects a central fact table to dimension tables, and Figure 3.26(C) represents the snowflake schema that further normalizes dimension tables for data integrity.

Figure 3.26 (A) Flat Data Model

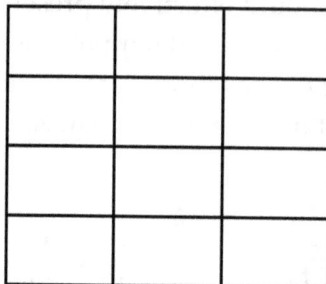

Figure 3.26 (B) Star Schema

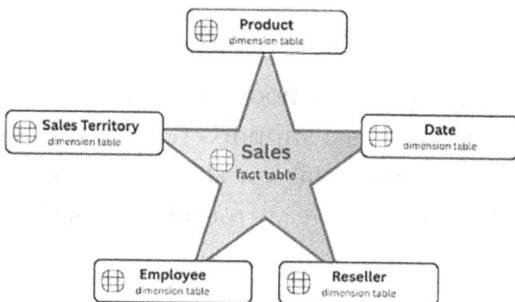

Figure 3.26 (C) Snowflake Schema

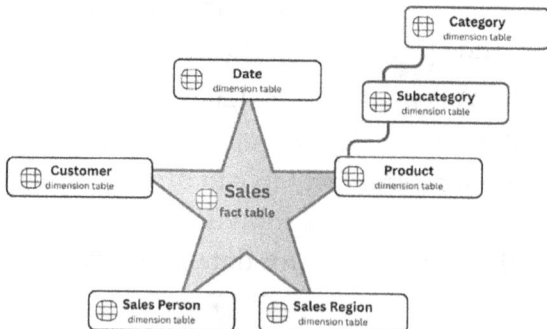

In this section, we explored how to evaluate the performance of data models and understood the relevance of optimizing data processing for seamless analysis. Having discussed various data models that serve distinct roles in structuring data for analysis, we now have a solid understanding of data modeling and performance optimization. In the upcoming section, we shall discuss Data Analysis Expressions, a powerful formula language in Power BI.

3.5 Data Analysis Expressions (DAX)

Data Analysis Expressions (DAX) is a formula language similar to Excel functions. It is used in Power BI, Excel Power Pivot, and SQL Server Analysis Services (SSAS) to perform data calculations and create custom measures. It involves filtering, aggregating, and manipulating data to derive information and insights.

DAX uses a formula language to calculate performance measures such as total sales over a period, profit margins from costs and revenue streams, gross profit margin, and forecast and trend analysis. It enables cross-table calculations through various operations of data aggregations, filtering, and conditional formatting. It is flexible enough to handle various scenarios and perform complex calculations that generate valuable findings.

DAX capabilities are beneficial across industries. For example, if a toy manufacturing company requires checking its sales performance across different regions, it can use DAX to compute various measures. This includes region-wise total sales, cumulative sales to track sales progression, month-to-date or year-to-date metrics, comparative analysis, and even trend analysis.

DAX is also applicable to an e-commerce platform to classify and sort online customers based on their buying behavior and patterns. It can calculate customer retention rates by identifying the number of repeat purchases, and also help identify high-value customers by studying spending patterns above a threshold limit. DAX applications are also seen in the healthcare industry, where professionals measure the waiting time of patients across different departments and compare it with departmental resource allocation.

DAX is a critical functionality in Power BI as it enables users to create advanced calculations and transform data for actionable intelligence. By enabling advanced calculations and formulas, DAX supports complex problem-solving. It permits creating groups and enables filtering datasets for custom grouping based on specific requirements. So when DAX is integrated in Power BI, it can convert static datasets to interactive data models, enabling substantive analysis across multiple domains.

FUN FACT

Did you know that DAX in Power BI was inspired by Excel formulas? Microsoft designed DAX to be intuitive and familiar to Excel users, especially for those who work with functions like SUM, IF, and VLOOKUP.

Let's understand the basics of using DAX in Power BI through the following section.

3.5.1 Creating calculated columns using DAX

Power BI Desktop has a built-in functionality called IntelliSense to assist in writing code and auto-completion.

This helps explore new functionalities in the DAX language. All we need to do is type in the formula bar.

Click on Data View and New Column in the Table Tools ribbon, as shown below in Figure 3.27.

Figure 3.27 **Creating a New Calculated Column**

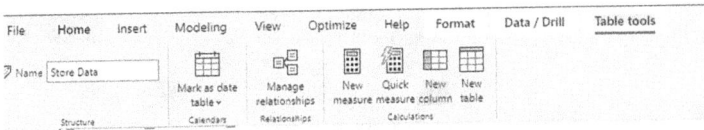

On clicking New Column, in the formula bar, we can see Column "=" as shown in Figure 3.28.

Figure 3.28 **Formula Bar**

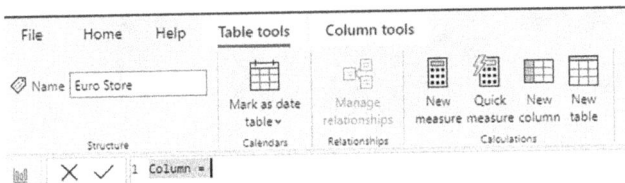

Name the new column by replacing the default text with the complete desired name. Move the cursor after the equals sign and enter a single quote character. A list of autocomplete options, created through IntelliSense, appears preceding the formula bar.

The first option displayed in the list would be the name of the table we selected. The table's name is automatically added to the formula bar by pressing Tab, as shown in Figure 3.29.

Figure 3.29 Adding a New Column

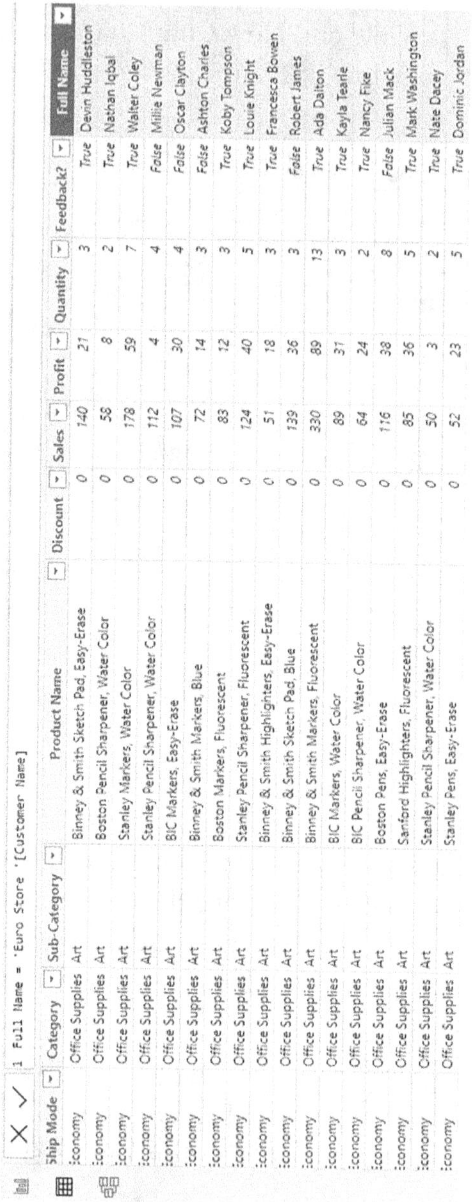

`1  Full Name = 'Euro Store'[Customer Name]`

Ship Mode	Category	Sub-Category	Product Name	Discount	Sales	Profit	Quantity	Feedback?	Full Name
Economy	Office Supplies	Art	Binney & Smith Sketch Pad, Easy-Erase	0	140	21	3	True	Devin Huddleston
Economy	Office Supplies	Art	Boston Pencil Sharpener, Water Color	0	58	8	2	True	Nathan Iqbal
Economy	Office Supplies	Art	Stanley Markers, Water Color	0	178	59	7	True	Walter Coley
Economy	Office Supplies	Art	Stanley Pencil Sharpener, Water Color	0	112	4	4	False	Millie Newman
Economy	Office Supplies	Art	BIC Markers, Easy-Erase	0	107	30	4	False	Oscar Clayton
Economy	Office Supplies	Art	Binney & Smith Markers, Blue	0	72	14	3	False	Ashton Charles
Economy	Office Supplies	Art	Boston Markers, Fluorescent	0	83	12	3	True	Koby Tompsson
Economy	Office Supplies	Art	Stanley Pencil Sharpener, Fluorescent	0	124	40	5	True	Louie Knight
Economy	Office Supplies	Art	Binney & Smith Highlighters, Easy-Erase	0	51	18	3	True	Francesca Bowen
Economy	Office Supplies	Art	Binney & Smith Sketch Pad, Blue	0	139	36	3	False	Robert James
Economy	Office Supplies	Art	Binney & Smith Markers, Fluorescent	0	330	89	13	True	Ada Dalton
Economy	Office Supplies	Art	BIC Markers, Water Color	0	89	37	3	True	Kayla Tearle
Economy	Office Supplies	Art	BIC Pencil Sharpener, Water Color	0	64	24	2	True	Nancy Fike
Economy	Office Supplies	Art	Boston Pens, Easy-Erase	0	116	38	8	False	Julian Mack
Economy	Office Supplies	Art	Sanford Highlighters, Fluorescent	0	85	36	5	True	Mark Washington
Economy	Office Supplies	Art	Stanley Pencil Sharpener, Water Color	0	50	3	2	True	Nate Dacey
Economy	Office Supplies	Art	Stanley Pens, Easy-Erase	0	52	23	5	True	Dominic Jordan

In the square bracket, choose the first option from the drop-down list [Customer Name]; pressing tab will autocomplete it. The formula bar is shown in Figure 3.30.

Figure 3.30 Formula Bar

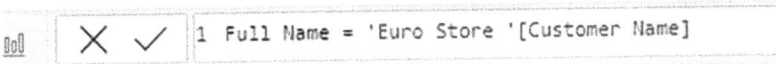

```
1 Full Name = 'Euro Store '[Customer Name]
```

Again, to add the country name of each customer, add a space followed by the country name using the ampersand sign (&) to combine both strings. The ampersand takes both the parameters, converts them to strings, and merges them. Quotes must be used on both sides of the string; the completed DAX formula is shown in Figure 3.31, and the result of the completed expression in the table is shown in Figure 3.32 below.

Figure 3.31 DAX Expression in the Formula Bar

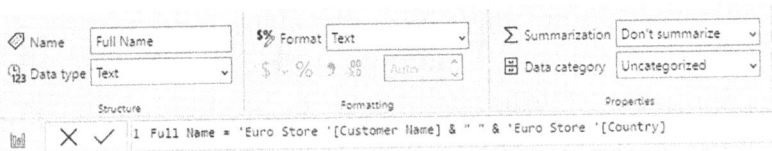

Name	Full Name	$% Format	Text	∑ Summarization	Don't summarize
Data type	Text	$ ~ % 9 .00 .0	Auto	Data category	Uncategorized
Structure		Formatting		Properties	

```
1 Full Name = 'Euro Store '[Customer Name] & " " & 'Euro Store '[Country]
```

Figure 3.32 Results of the Expression, Customer Name, and Country

Full Name ▼
Devin Huddleston France
Nathan Iqbal France
Walter Coley France
Millie Newman France
Oscar Clayton France
Ashton Charles France
Koby Tompson France
Louie Knight France
Francesca Bowen France
Robert James France
Ada Dalton France
Kayla Tearle France
Nancy Fike France
Julian Mack France
Mark Washington France
Nate Dacey France
Dominic Jordan France
Lilly Le Grand France

Example:

Assume you are going to manage a dataset for an internationally branded retail company. The dataset will include customer information, including names, the country they belong to, and other necessary details. Now, to make the dataset more user-friendly and content-rich for analysis, you decide to create a column that combines each customer's name with their respective country.

For this, we can use the ampersand symbol in a DAX formula, which will help to combine two text strings into one. Also, we can include a space between the customer's name and the country's name for better readability.

FullCustomerInfo = [Customer Name] & " (" & [Country] & ")"

This is the DAX formula to create a new calculated column combining the customer name and country name to which the customer belongs.

Let's break down the formula to this:

[Customer Name]" ("[Country]")"&

Customer Name refers to the name of the customer, followed by adding a space and an opening parenthesis for formatting. Again, Country Name, for each customer, followed by a closing parenthesis to complete the formatting, and finally, concatenating these elements into a single string. The results in the new column will look like this

John Joice (USA)

Priya Kumar (India)

This simple use of DAX is an example of how calculated columns can enrich a dataset for better reporting and analysis.

3.6 String Functions to Create Calculated Columns

String functions are tools in Power BI designed to format and analyze text data. Users can rely on these functions to extract specific parts of a string, combine multiple strings, or replace characters. These operations enhance the usability and presentation of textual information.

String functions are useful for cleaning and preparing data. They can also be used for creating calculated columns and can add meaningful context to reports. Let us see how we can create a calculated column using string functions.

We have seen how to create a calculated column in Section 3.5.1. We can now make a computed column to store a month-year value with a two-digit month and four-digit year separated by a dash. The calculation is "MM-YYYY."

Select the Date table, click on New Column from the Table Tools ribbon, enter the code below in the formula bar, and press Enter to get the new calculated column, as shown in Figure 3.33.

Month Year = 'Date (Order)' [Month Number of Year]

Figure 3.33 **Result of Using the String Function in DAX to Create Columns**

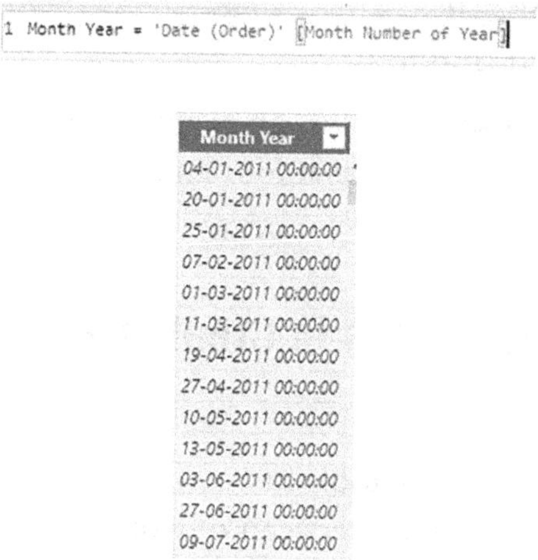

```
1  Month Year = 'Date (Order)' [Month Number of Year]
```

Month Year
04-01-2011 00:00:00
20-01-2011 00:00:00
25-01-2011 00:00:00
07-02-2011 00:00:00
01-03-2011 00:00:00
11-03-2011 00:00:00
19-04-2011 00:00:00
27-04-2011 00:00:00
10-05-2011 00:00:00
13-05-2011 00:00:00
03-06-2011 00:00:00
27-06-2011 00:00:00
09-07-2011 00:00:00

While validating the code, the results display only a single-digit month with no leading zero. The code must be re-edited to display double-digit months, as shown along with the results in Figure 3.34.

Figure 3.34 Displaying Date-Month-Year

```
1 Month Year = "0" & 'Order Data'[Month Number of Year]
```

Month Year
004-01-2011
020-01-2011
025-01-2011
007-02-2011
001-03-2011
011-03-2011
019-04-2011
027-04-2011
010-05-2011
013-05-2011
003-06-2011
027-06-2011
009-07-2011
029-09-2011
004-10-2011
011-11-2011
027-11-2011
029-11-2011
002-12-2011
027-12-2011
014-01-2012

To further optimize and only display the two-digit month, we need to use the "RIGHT function." This function helps to show only a specified number of characters from the right side of a string. Results are shown in Figure 3.35.

Figure 3.35 Results Displaying Two-Digit Month Only

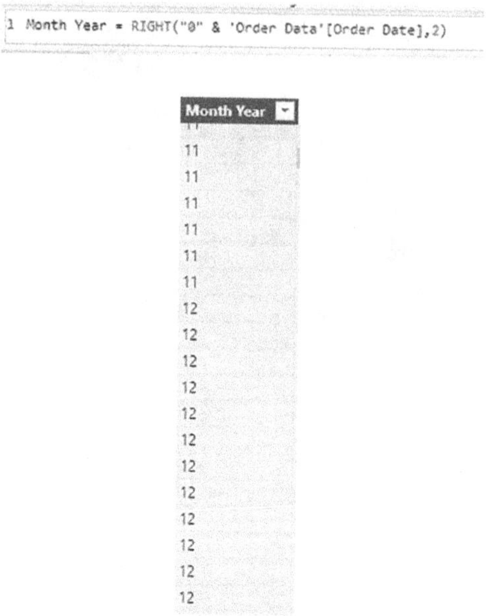

```
1  Month Year = RIGHT("0" & 'Order Data'[Order Date],2)
```

Month Year
11
11
11
11
11
11
12
12
12
12
12
12
12
12
12
12
12

Further, the "FORMAT function" allows one to work on a date column and customize it in several ways, but the resulting data type will be in text format. To create a new calculated column, click New Column from the Table Tools ribbon in the Data View. The formula bar and the results of the new calculated column would look like Figure 3.36.

Figure 3.36 Applying the Format Function to Create a New Calculated Column

```
Month Year Format = FORMAT('Order Data'[Order Date], "MM-YYYY")
```

Month Year Format
01-2011
01-2011
01-2011
02-2011
03-2011
03-2011
04-2011
04-2011
05-2011
05-2011
06-2011
06-2011
07-2011
09-2011
10-2011
11-2011
11-2011
11-2011
12-2011
12-2011

3.7 Calculated Measures

Calculated measures are powerful analytical tools; they differ from calculated columns as calculated measures are dynamic and can change as the filter content changes. These measures can be assigned to any table and extended to folders within the table. They automatically interact with all the relationships in the data model.

Calculated measures support additional metrics for visualizations and reports to obtain deeper insights into the transformed data. For example, if we want to calculate sales only for a specific product category of office supplies:

Sales = CALCULATE ([Total Sales], FILTER (Products, Products[Category] = "Office Supplies"))

Let's carry out a calculated measure for total sales and profit. Select the table and click New Measure from the Table Tools ribbon, as shown in Figure 3.37 below.

Figure 3.37 Creating a New Measure

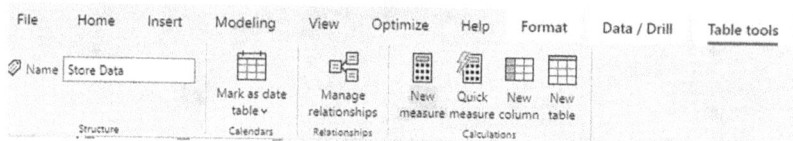

Once the measure has been created, click the Measure Tools ribbon as shown in Figure 3.38 and change the formatting to English (United States). The Total Sales are the sum of the sales amounts within the current filter context.

Figure 3.38 Changing the Formatting

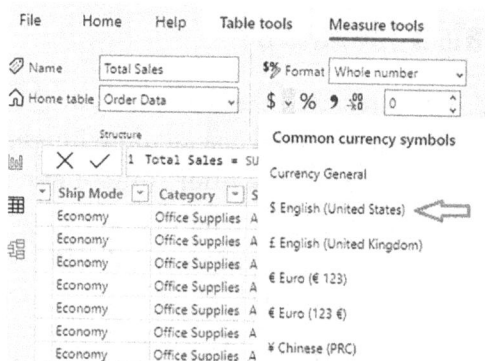

Next, let's carry out a calculated measure for Total Profit. Select the table and click the New Measure, similar to how the calculated measure for Sales was created. The DAX formula would be:

Profit = SUM ('Total Sales' [Sales Amount]) - SUM ('Total Sales' [Total Cost])

Unlike calculated columns, calculated measures need not be assigned to a specific table here. As a result, measures can be transferred to random tables and moved from one table to another by changing the Home table.

Let's take an example. A sales manager wants to prepare a month-wise sales report, considering variables such as region-wise and product-wise total sales, and profit. Let's use calculated measures to calculate total sales and profit using DAX in Power BI.

The equation in DAX to calculate total sales and profit is as follows:

Total Sales = SUM(Sales[SalesAmount])

Profit = SUM(Sales[SalesAmount]) - SUM(Sales[Cost])

Now, using filters, we can find the region-wise and product-wise total sales. The DAX equation will recalculate the sales and profits upon selecting the required region or the product category. Further visual representations, like bar charts or line charts, can be chosen to represent sales and profits across regions and product categories. Various insights can be gathered as to whether Region A is better than other regions based on sales value contributing to profits, or profit margins of Category X products are better than Y and Z types, and so on.

In this chapter, we gained an in-depth understanding of DAX, String Functions, and Calculated Measures. These three concepts enrich data models to perform complex analyses and present reliable insights. In Chapter Four, our focus will be on visualizing data. We shall explore a range of built-in visuals and learn how to apply them effectively to convey information. We will also study how to create and integrate custom visuals, leveraging cross-filtering and cross-highlighting features, and how to use various filtering options for visual storytelling.

Chapter Summary

- Data modeling in Power BI should ensure that the data is understandable, scalable, and flexible, and it should be able to edit relationships and create new ones.

- Power BI allows users to create data models by establishing complex relationships between data sources.

- Usability enhancements include summarization, categorization, hiding, renaming, and deleting columns.

- A data model's performance is critical to identifying how design decisions affect performance today and in the future. This performance is measured through query execution and processing efficiency.

- DAX is a formula language in Power BI for advanced calculations and real-time, engaging decision-making.

- DAX brings intelligence to data models and enables the creation of custom calculations, dynamic aggregations, and row-level calculations.

- String functions are essential for cleaning, manipulating, and transforming text data within datasets.

- String functions allow formatting of names, extracting substrings, and making datasets clearer and report-friendly.

- Calculated columns and measures are important tools in Power BI for performing custom calculations.

- Calculated columns are added to the data model and are used to calculate values row by row. They are often used when you need new data fields.

- Measures, on the other hand, are used to create summary values like totals, averages, or percentages and are calculated only when used in a visual. Using calculated measures, one can define measures that respond to filters and slicers to craft meaningful KPIs and summary statistics that enhance decision-making.

- Understanding the difference between calculated columns and measures helps build more efficient and powerful reports.

QUIZ

1. **What is the key benefit of using Power BI compared to traditional methods?**
   a. Removes barriers to high costs
   b. Increases the cost of data projects
   c. Limits data processing capabilities
   d. Requires extensive coding knowledge

2. **What is the importance of managing complex relationships within datasets?**
   a. To increase the number of data sources
   b. To reduce the usability of the data model
   c. To enhance the performance and reliability of data models
   d. To simplify the data model

3. **How do you enhance the usability of a data model?**
   a. By adding irrelevant data sources
   b. By reducing data visualization capabilities
   c. By limiting data processing options
   d. By simplifying user interfaces and improving data accessibility

4. **How does Power BI contribute to the success of BI projects?**
   a. By eliminating the need for data models
   b. By increasing the complexity of data processing
   c. By providing an agile approach to data modeling
   d. By restricting the use of relational data sources

5. **Which feature in Power BI allows the creation of relationships between different datasets?**

    a. Data Transform
    b. Visualizations Pane
    c. Dashboard Creation
    d. Data Modeling

6. **What is the role of usability enhancements in data modeling?**

    a. To confuse the user experience
    b. To eliminate relationships between datasets
    c. To support business needs and improve data model efficiency
    d. To complicate the presentation of data models

7. **Which relationship allows multiple records in one table to be related to multiple records in another table?**

    a. One-to-One
    b. One-to-Many
    c. Many-to-Many
    d. Many-to-One

8. **Which feature in Power BI helps identify and resolve relationship issues in data models?**

    a. Relationship View
    b. Dashboard Creation
    c. Visualizations Pane
    d. Query Editor

9. Which of the following DAX formulas correctly defines a calculated measure for Profit in Power BI using a Sales table that includes SalesAmount and Cost columns?

   a. Profit = Sales[SalesAmount] - Sales[Cost]

   b. Profit = SUM(Sales[SalesAmount])
      - SUM(Sales[Cost])

   c. Profit = CALCULATE(SUM(Sales[SalesAmount]
      - Sales[Cost]))

   d. Profit = SUMX(Sales, Sales[SalesAmount]
      - Sales[Cost])

10. Which feature allows creating new columns or tables based on existing data?

    a. Data Visualization

    b. Data Transform

    c. Data Analysis Expressions (DAX)

    d. Dashboard Creation

Answers

1 – a	2 – c	3 – d	4 – c	5 – d
6 – c	7 – c	8 – a	9 – b	10 – c

This page is intentionally left blank

CHAPTER 4

Exploring Visuals and Charts

Key Learning Objectives

- Understand various built-in visuals in Power BI and their applications.
- Learn to create and add custom visuals in Power BI using cross-filtering and cross-highlighting.
- Get familiar with various applications of filtering options for data visualization.

Power BI is a powerful tool that creates impactful visualizations and dashboards to bring data to life. Visuals that can be generated through Power BI are vast, and this chapter aims to focus on basic configurations for each of the built-in visuals and how to acquire custom visuals.

It will enable you to understand the rapid update cycle in Power BI that assists in adding visuals over time. These functions can be found under Preview Features in Power BI Desktop Options. The chapter will also cover other visualization tools that Power BI offers, such as Visualizations in Report View, Cross-filtering and Cross-highlighting, Slicer Visual, Tabular Data and Table Visualization, and Categorical Data Visualization.

Further, this chapter covers commonly used Power BI visualizations for analyzing trend data, including Line Charts, Area Charts, Combo Charts, Funnel Charts, Ribbon Charts, and Waterfall Charts.

Let's begin with Preview Features in Power BI.

4.1 Preview Features

We have seen how data is imported and modeled according to specific requirements in Power BI. We will now understand how visuals are enabled in Power BI. Preview Features are a set of tools and functionalities that equip users to access upcoming features and explore advanced visualization options.

The Preview Features tool in Power BI enables testing features like data enhancements, connectivity, or integration tools, and provides access to new visual styles before they are deployed. Some examples of tools that are tested are: advanced visuals, new chart types, AI-powered visuals, and new types of slicer options.

The Preview Features function is essential for visualizations as it helps to explore advanced visuals, such as interactive charting tools, which may be missing from the visual experience otherwise. By previewing features through this tool, users can leverage the latest visualization strategies in Power BI.

Figure 4.1 shows how to access the Preview features.

Step 1: Click File.

Step 2: Go to Options and Settings.

From Options, select Preview Features and then select the box next to the Shape Map visual and the Azure Map visual.

Figure 4.1 **Power BI Preview Features**

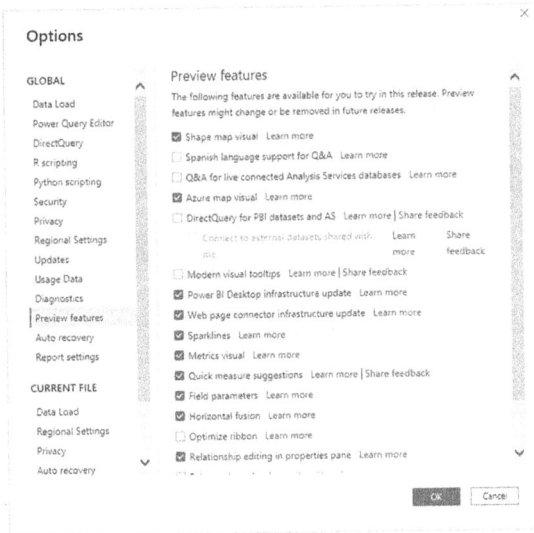

Once enabled, it requires restarting the Power BI Desktop, after which a notification pops up, as shown in Figure 4.2 below. When features are moved from the preview, they automatically fall off the preview list and are available upon loading the Power BI Desktop.

Figure 4.2   Restarting the Power BI Desktop Notification

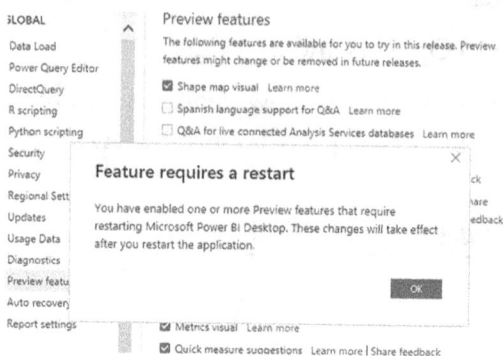

4.2 Visualizations in Report View

Report View in Power BI is useful in creating data visualizations and is the default view (shown in Fig. 4.3) when Power BI is launched. This view displays the Report Canvas (Fig. 4.3), page navigation, and panes for customizing visualizations within the report. Report Canvas is the primary design area containing all report visuals.

Practical Tip

To enable Preview Features, go to File > Options and Settings > Options > Preview Features and toggle on the features you want to try.

Figure 4.3   Report View

> ### POINT TO REMEMBER
>
> Report View is the primary workspace in Power BI
> for designing and customizing data visualizations, the
> central hub for creating impactful reports.

As shown in Figure 4.4, more visuals can be imported to
the Visualizations pane, which offers a menu of options to
access custom visuals from an app source or local files.

Figure 4.4 Options for More Visuals

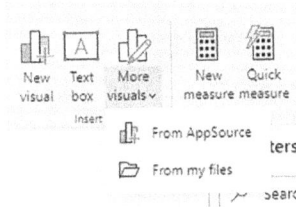

As shown below in Figure 4.5, applying "Filters on this
page" applies visuals on the selected page, and the "Filters
on all pages" option applies to every visual on every page.
The "Filters on this visual" option becomes available only
when a particular visual is selected, and the filter applies
exclusively to that visual.

Figure 4.5 — Applying Filters

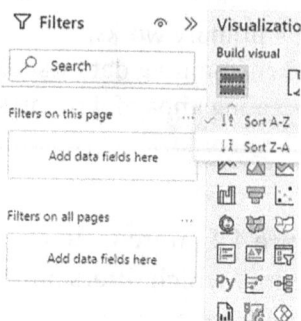

The Visualizations pane shown in Figure 4.6 consists of the following four sections:

1. Visuals section
2. Field section
3. Format section
4. Analytics section

Figure 4.6 — Visualizations Pane

The Visuals section shown in Figure 4.6 above displays all visualizations with enabled preview and imported custom visuals. The Field section displays different areas in the visualization. On the other hand, the Format section, as shown in Figure 4.7, controls the look, feel, and formatting options, which include font size, color, and label settings.

Figure 4.7 **Format Page**

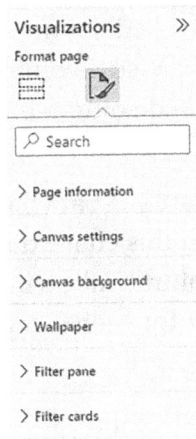

The fourth section, the Analytics section, allows static and data-driven lines like minimum, maximum, threshold, mean, and median lines varying based on visual selection.

The Field pane displays all fields to be added to visuals and filters, and the Navigation pane is used to select the report page that needs to be displayed on the canvas. Pages can be added by clicking the plus button, as shown in Figure 4.8, at the end of the page list.

Figure 4.8	Adding New Pages From the Field Pane

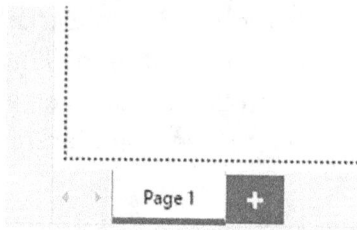

Further, to create a stacked column chart in the Report Canvas, click on the New Visuals button in Power BI. This action adds a blank stacked column chart to the canvas, ready to be configured.

A stacked column chart is a bar chart used to compare data across categories. In this chart, data series are stacked vertically within each column, allowing multiple data series to be visualized together for each category in a segmented form.

A stacked column chart requires two key elements to populate the visual: values for the X-axis and the Y-axis. The X-axis typically represents "categorical data" such as City, Name, Category, or Product, while the Y-axis displays "numerical data" like Profit, Units Sold, or Sales Amount.

For example, by selecting two fields—*Country* for the X-axis and *Profit* for the Y-axis, as shown in Figure 4.9, the visual displays the Sum of Profit by Country on the Report Canvas.

Figure 4.9 Creating Visuals

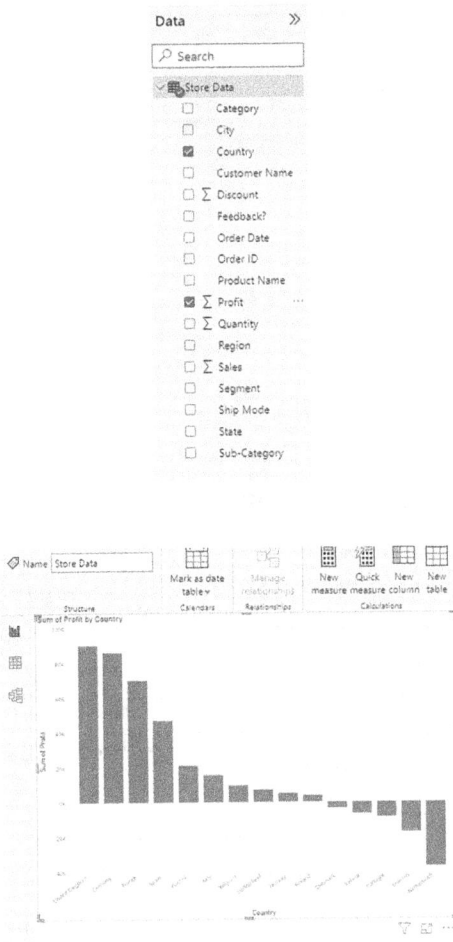

New visuals can also be created from the Field pane. For example, by selecting 'Segment' and 'Profit' from the Field pane, Power BI generates visuals that display segment-wise total profits, as shown in Figure 4.10. A new visual is created based on the data field selected, generally a column chart for numeric fields and a table for non-numeric fields. Further, the desired visualization can also be generated if required.

Figure 4.10 Creating Visuals by Selecting Variable Boxes From the Field List

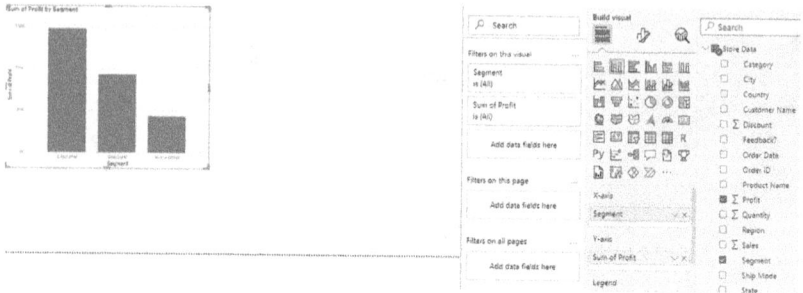

Customized visualizations can be created from the Visualizations pane, enabling you to select the visualization needed and then select the fields from the list. This leads to the desired visuals appearing in the Report Canvas.

Take the example of a retail store that wants to analyze yearly sales performance across different product categories. Using visualization features in Power BI, we can create a sales trend line chart using the year as the field on the X axis and total sales on the Y axis. This line chart will depict sales trends over the years.

If we have five regions as fields for geographical data and total sales as a field for the value, then we can use a Map visual to display the sales across different regions. From the map, we can identify the best-performing and the least-performing regions with respect to sales volume. Figure 4.11 shows profits for categories and segments.

Figure 4.11 Creating Customized Visuals Showing Profit by Categories and Segments

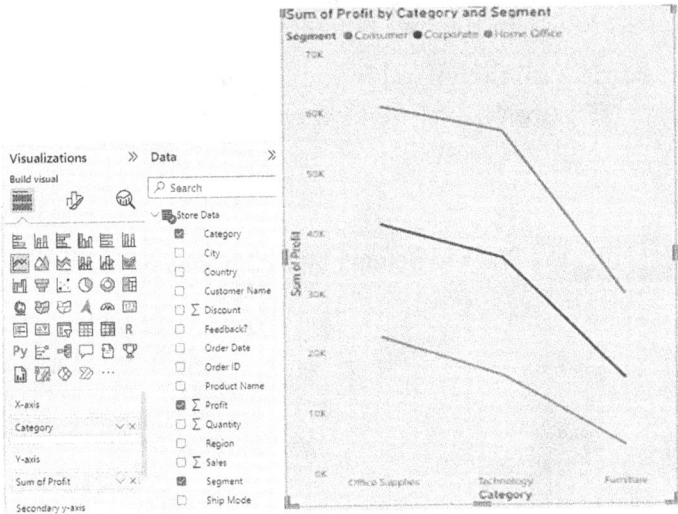

4.3 Cross-Filtering and Cross-Highlighting

One of the most significant features of Power BI for managers is the ability to allow them to interact with the visualization and filter visuals on the page so that particular questions about the data can be answered. This process is called cross-filtering: empowering managers to decide how to filter visuals based on specific business requirements. Managers and data analysts can add more visible and explicit forms of visuals with the help of Slicer Visuals from the Visualizations pane, which we will explore in Section 4.4

Cross-highlighting is the default interaction between two visuals, which offers flexibility in deciding which visuals should be incorporated in a report. Let's create two visuals to understand the cross-filtering and cross-highlighting features of Power BI. For instance, let's consider the data models of Total Sales and Ship Mode and follow the process below:

1. Select a stacked column chart from the Visualizations pane and anchor it on the Report Canvas.

2. From the Field pane, check the Total Sales and Ship Mode in the axis bucket.

3. Resize the visual in the Report Canvas, as shown in Figure 4.12, to make it easier to read. Now, there is only one visual on the Report Canvas.

Figure 4.12 **Stacked Column Chart Showing Sales and Ship Mode**

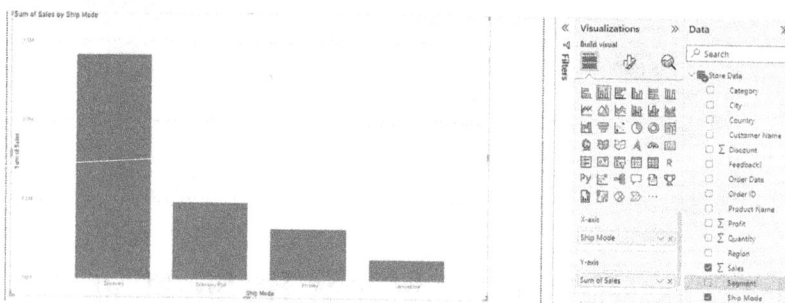

4. Next, let's add one more visual to the canvas by clicking on the empty space.

5. Now, from the Visualizations pane, select the Pie Chart, which will be added to the Report Canvas, and if needed, the visual can be moved to a preferred location in the canvas.

6. In the Field pane, check the Country, and it should go to the Legend bucket.

7. In the values bucket, the Sum of Profit should be added.

8. Check Figure 4.13 to verify; two visuals can be seen in the Report Canvas.

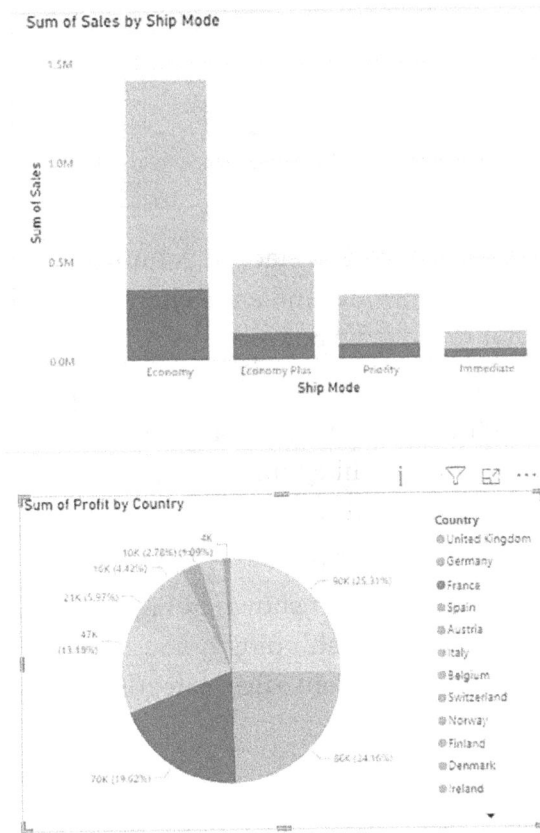

Figure 4.13 Stacked Column Chart and Pie Chart

The two visuals include a stacked column with Total Sales, based on Ship Mode, and a pie chart that shows the country's Total Profit from Sales.

Further, we can analyze sales data of a company that transports products using various shipping modes. This dataset includes metrics like total sales, profit margins, and the geographical distribution of sales. The visuals on the Report Canvas provide insights into these metrics.

The stacked column chart shown in Figure 4.14 represents total sales across different shipping modes. The pie chart displays the total profits from sales, categorized by country.

| Figure 4.14 | Cross-Highlighting the Economy Mode of Shipment |

Sum of Sales by Ship Mode

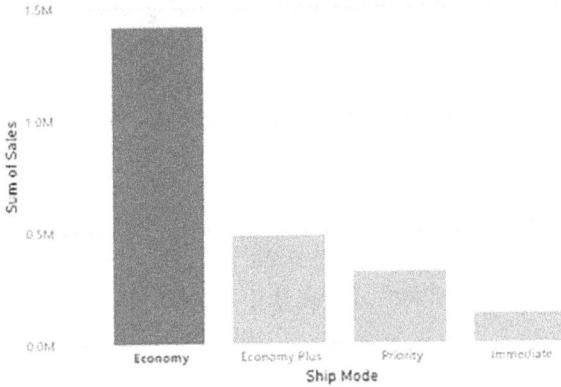

Sum of Profit by Country

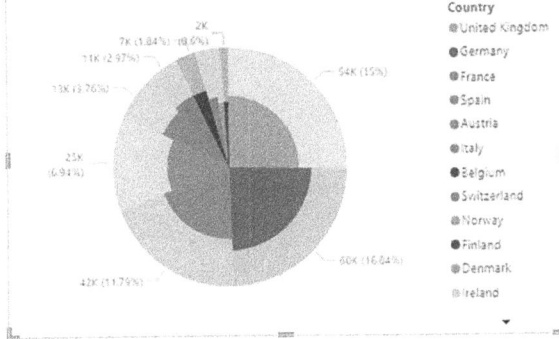

To see how cross-highlighting works, click the left mouse button on the Economy bar of Ship Mode on the X axis. We immediately see that the pie chart, shown in Figure 4.14 above, has been changed to a smaller highlighted area. The pie chart now shows profits only from countries where economy shipping was used.

For the United Kingdom, the Sum of Profit was 25%; for the highlighted Economy shipment mode, it is 15%, similar to other countries. A similar type of highlighting can be done by selecting a pie chart slice, which will then highlight a corresponding subset of the stacked column, as shown in Figure 4.15.

Figure 4.15 Cross Highlighting a Slice of the Pie Chart

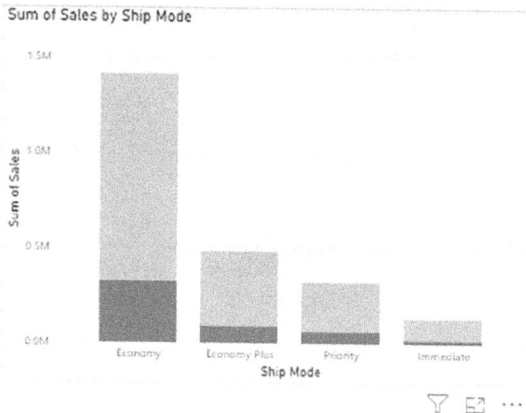

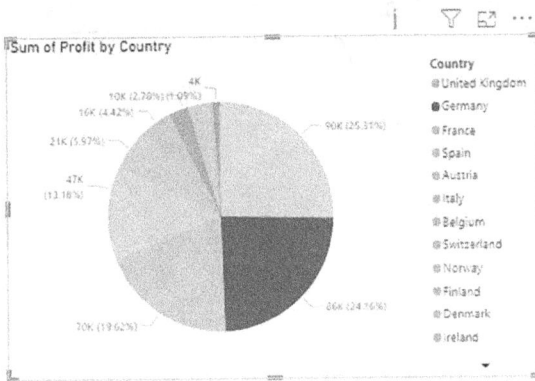

Using the cross-highlighting feature, we can quickly assess how shipping modes affect profits across different countries. This Power BI feature helps managers and analysts to report data across all visualizations. Almost everything inside a visual can be selected, and when selected, it would affect the other visuals within the same report page.

In some situations, a unique visual may not require to be filtered by anyone but still must be controlled. To do this, after selecting the visual, click on the Format ribbon and choose the Edit Interactions option, as shown in Figure 4.16.

Figure 4.16 Edit Interactions Option

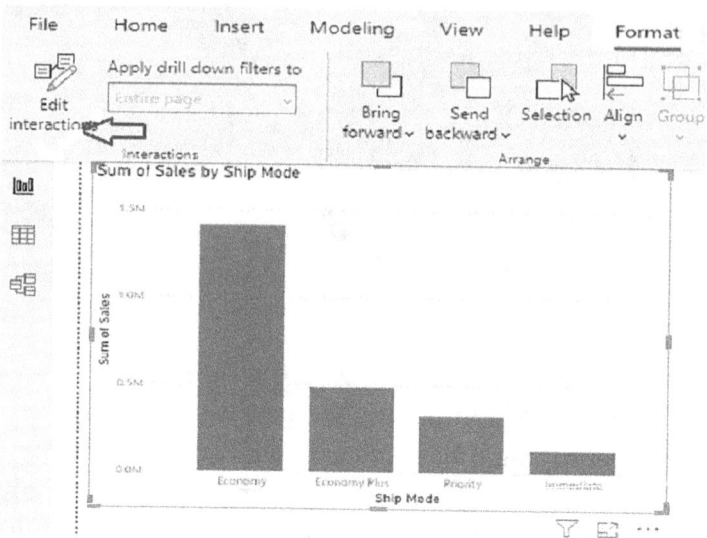

On selecting it, new icons appear next to the other visuals, as shown in Figure 4.17.

Figure 4.17 New Icons With Edit Interactions

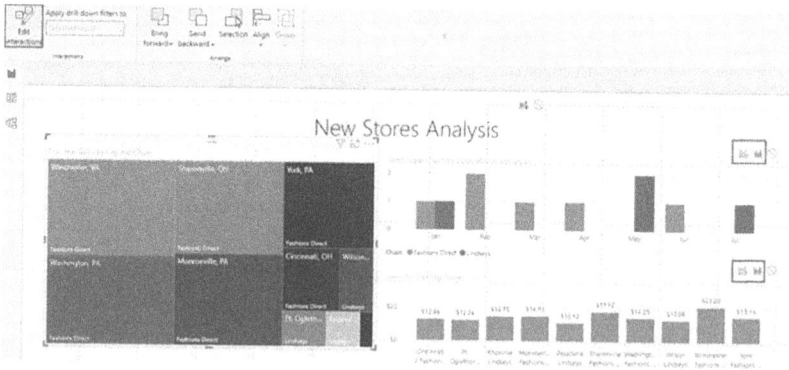

Open Store Count by Open Month and Chain

Jan | Feb | Mar | Apr | May | Jun | Jul

Chain ● Fashions Direct ● Lindseys

| $12.36 | $12.26 | $14.75 | $14.93 | $10.92 | $12.92 | $16.25 | $13.08 | $21.22 | $15.16 |

Cincinnati 2 Fashion... | Ft. Ogdether... | Knoxville Lindseys | Monroev... Fashions... | Pasadena Lindseys | Sharonville Fashions... | Washingt... Fashions... | Wilson Lindseys | Winchester Fashions... | York Fashions...

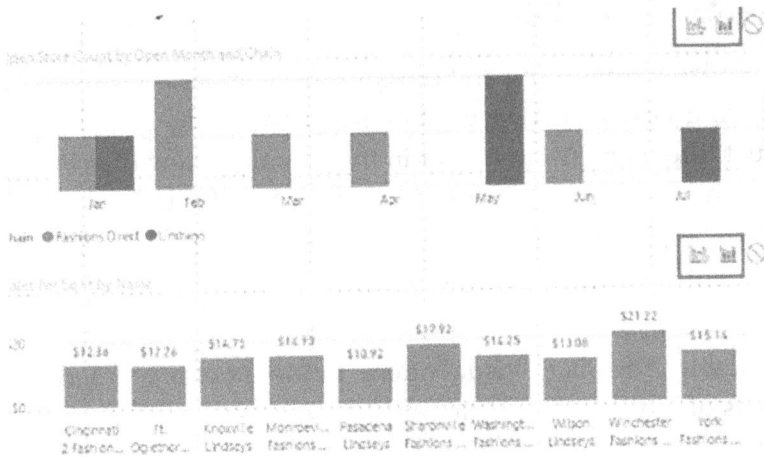

The first icon, showing a bar chart with a funnel, indicates whether the visual will be cross-filtered.

The second icon, showing a bar chart without a funnel, enables cross-highlighting. Here, only part of the data in the target visual is highlighted based on the selected value.

The third icon shows a circle with a diagonal line, which means no interaction. The selected visual will not affect the target visual through filtering or highlighting.

When a chart is selected, we can decide if any other visuals would be affected by cross-highlighting or cross-filtering from the chart. This option must be applied to every individual visual, as every visual would provide options for no interaction and filtering, and only a subset of visuals, including pie charts and bar diagrams, allows highlighting.

The default interaction behavior is highlighting; if highlighting is unavailable for the visual, the default behavior would be filtering. If you have selected the last option, which is "Circle," then no changes will occur in that visual.

4.4 Slicer Visual

Cross-highlighting and cross-filtering are options for filtering visuals. However, if managers and data analysts must filter something absent in the visuals, a new filtering option known as Slicer Visual needs to be adopted.

The Slicer Visual tool allows a single field to be displayed, narrowing the portion of the dataset. Depending on the data type of that field, various presentation options are made available. The Slicer Visual offers multiple options based on types of data, such as String or Text Values, Numeric, and Date.

4.4.1 Setting up the Slicer for string/ text

Here's how you can set up the Slicer tool in Power BI for string/ text:

1. To begin with, make sure that no visuals are selected in the Report Canvas by clicking in the blank area.

2. From the Visualizations pane, select the Slicer and move it to a convenient space in the canvas.

3. Anchor points can be used to resize the visual to fit the correct size.

4. From the Field pane, check the box "Sales Quantity" from the Store data and add it to the Field bucket. The Slicer shows a list view and a detailed canvas view as shown in Figure 4.18.

Figure 4.18 Slicer List View and Slicer Showing Sales Quantity in the Report Canvas

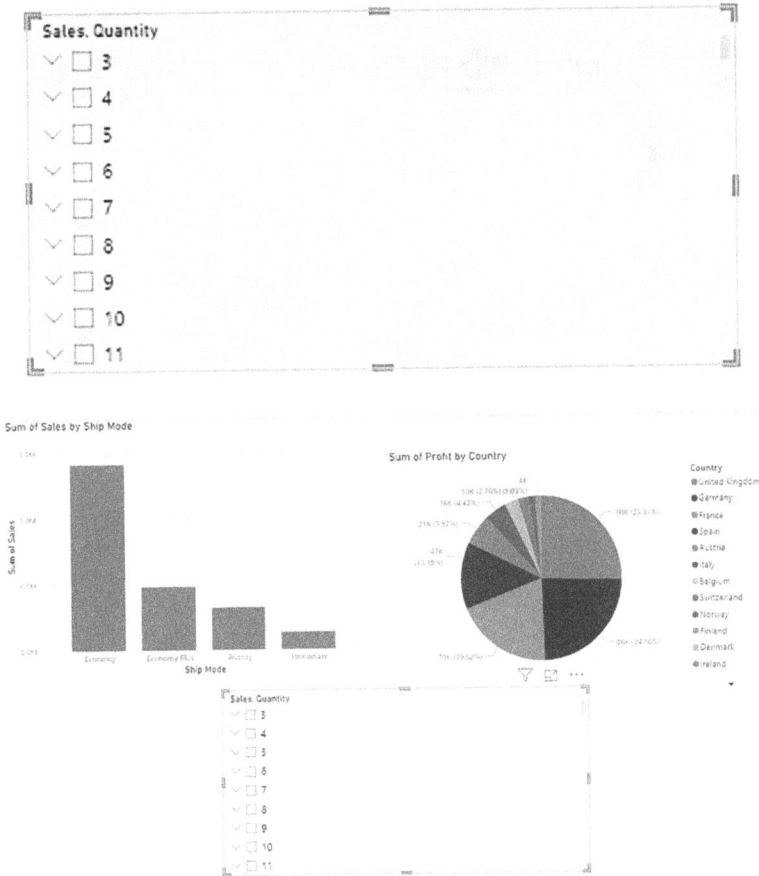

5. The List view enables users to see the list of all options, so the filter can be applied using the specific required field.

6. Checking a particular field of sales quantity results in filtered visuals for the exact quantity selection.

The Sum of Sales by Ship Mode based on the selected Quantity and the Sum of Profits country-wise based on the amount chosen are filtered as shown in Figure 4.19.

Figure 4.19 Slicer for Filtering Visuals Concerning Sales Quantity

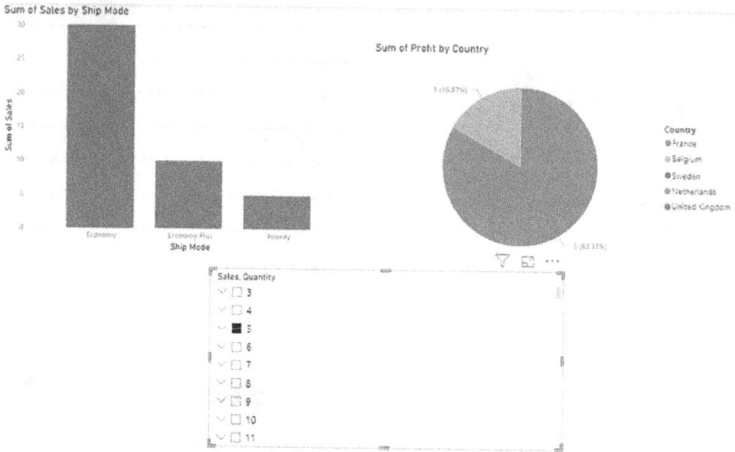

In case we opt for a sales quantity of 8 units, the stacked column and the pie chart will be filtered, as shown in Figure 4.20. The Slicer not only accepts a single field but can also accept multiple fields, which can be added to the Slicer Field bucket. The slicer would display a stepped list with a drop-down set of values.

Figure 4.20 Slicer Filtering Visuals for Varied Quantity

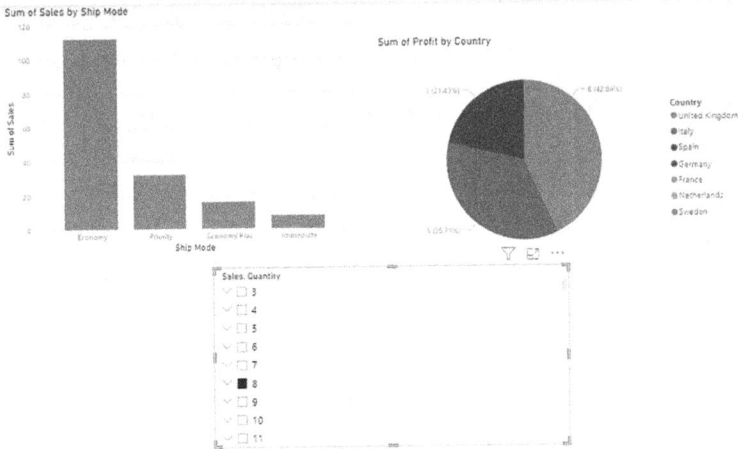

The hierarchies can be defined in the data model, or they can even be dragged from the table into the Slicer. Refer to Figure 4.21 to see the stepped list.

Figure 4.21 Stepped List

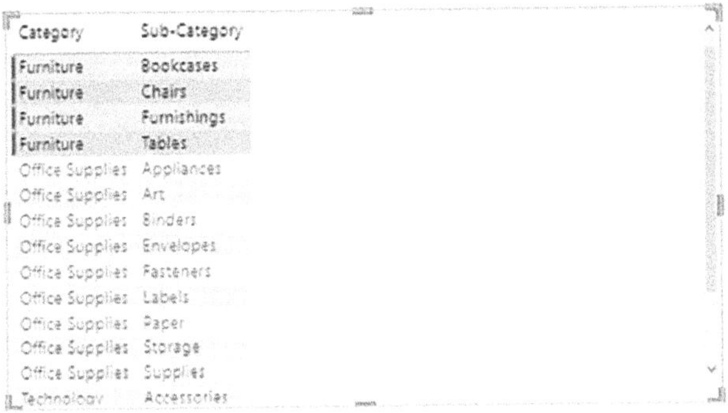

Slicers can also be used for numeric values like sales value (covered in Section 4.4.2) as well as for text or categorical data such as city, state, or even product category. Let's see how Slicer works for categorical data, such as for a state.

Suppose your dataset contains sales data from multiple states; you can insert a Slicer for a particular State column. All visuals (charts, tables, maps) on the page will automatically update to show data only for that selected state. This helps focus the analysis on a particular geographical area/ state without navigating away.

Another feature of Slicers is its ability to add Search, which improves the experience of managers and analysts when they work with large lists. To access the Search functionality in a Slicer, click the three dots (ellipsis) at the top-right corner of the Slicer. From there, you can find the Search option shown in Figure 4.22.

Figure 4.22 Enabling Search

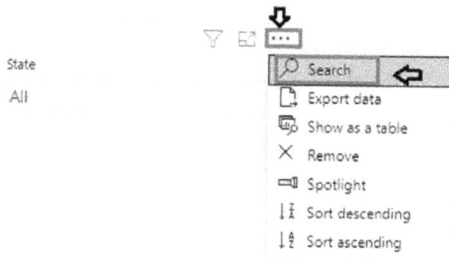

4.4.2 Setting up the Slicer for numeric data

If numeric data needs to be selected, similar to string options, we need to go to the Visualizations pane. Then, we need to select the Slicer, ensuring no visuals are selected in the Report Canvas. Filtering can be done on any numeric or date column of the data model.

Create a Slicer Visual and select numeric data for the field, as shown in Figure 4.23. Immediately, a new presentation for the filter can be seen on the canvas. There would be a numeric field that can give a range of values to filter the visuals on the page.

Figure 4.23 Selecting Numeric Data in the Slicer

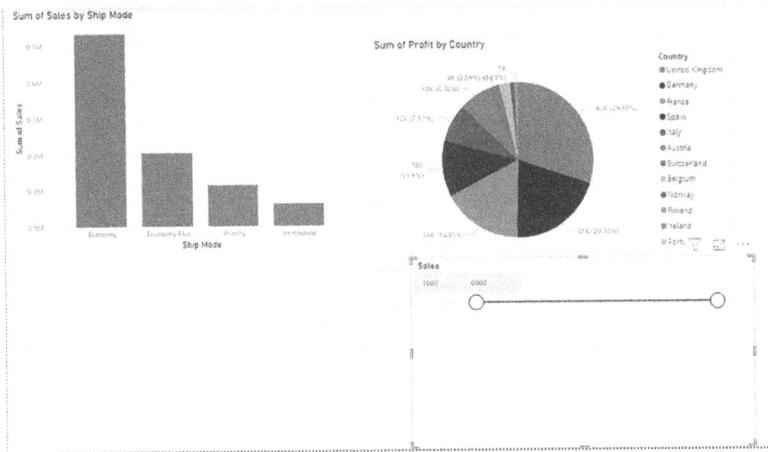

The Slicer can also be used in the List format by clicking the down arrow on the upper right corner of the Slicer. The drop-down menu contains a list of values selected from a specific field. A range of values between two points can be chosen to filter the data. Similarly, values less than or greater than a specific value can be adjusted using the sliding scale to filter the visuals.

When the price, size, or rating values change, managers can use the drop-down list to select data points between values greater than or less than a particular value for filtering visuals. Filtering date in the Slicer Visual is shown in Figure 4.24.

Figure 4.24 Date Field on Slicer

Businesses and analysts can use various ways to filter visuals, including Cross-filtering and Slicer Visuals, to filter data for meaningful results. The Report page, after generating the required visualizations, needs to be renamed from Page 1 by right-clicking Page 1 at the bottom part, as shown in Figure 4.25.

Figure 4.25 Option to Rename the Page

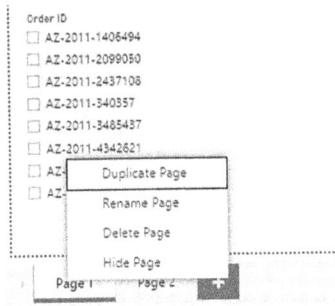

The Report page filtering visuals based on Order ID for a specified period, depicting the country-wise Sum of Profits, is shown in Figure 4.26.

Figure 4.26 Order ID, Period, and Country-Wise Sum of Profits

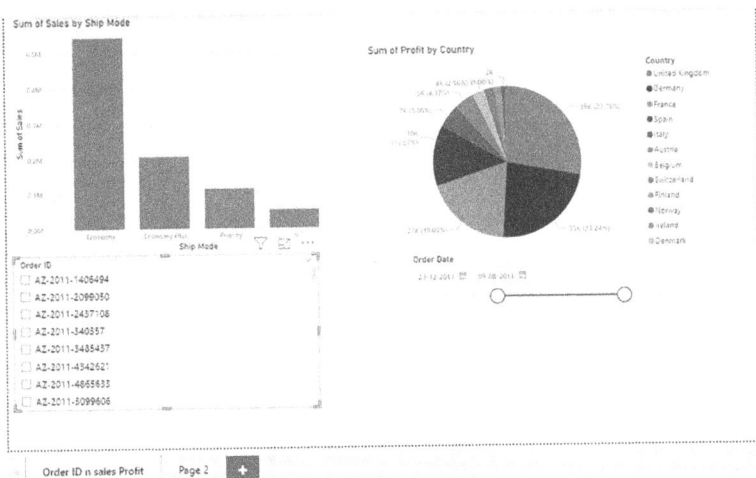

For a multi-page report in Power BI, users may want to apply a single filter across multiple pages. So, instead of adding the same Slicer to every page and manually selecting the same filter repeatedly, we can use Sync Slicers to control Slicers across multiple report pages. For example, if a user selects the United Kingdom on page 1, then page 2, page 3, page 4, and so on, will automatically filter for the United Kingdom.

4.5 Tabular Data and Table Visualization

Although data can be visualized in many ways using various filtering options, if we want to see and compare detail-level data, a table or matrix visual option can be used.

4.5.1 Table View

A Table View can be set up by selecting Table from the Visualizations pane, resizing to the required space in the canvas, and then from the Fields pane, checking the boxes: Country, the sum of sales, the sum of profit, the sum of quantity, and discount.

Figure 4.27 shows the table with the checked fields.

Figure 4.27 Table Visualization Based on Specific Fields

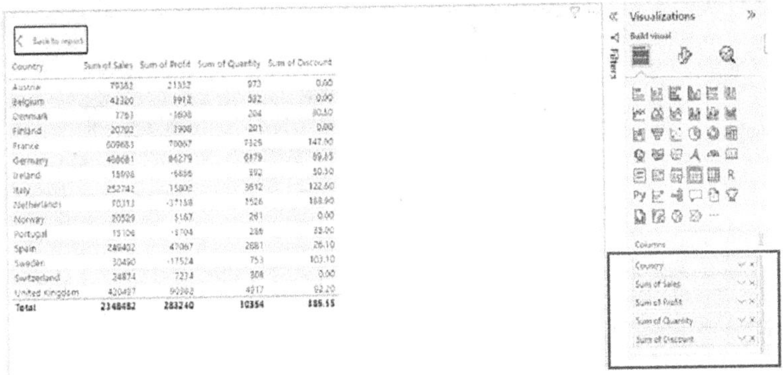

The table appearance can be further adjusted to enhance it by selecting the format of the visual from the Visualizations pane, as shown in Figure 4.28.

Figure 4.28 Format the Visual Option

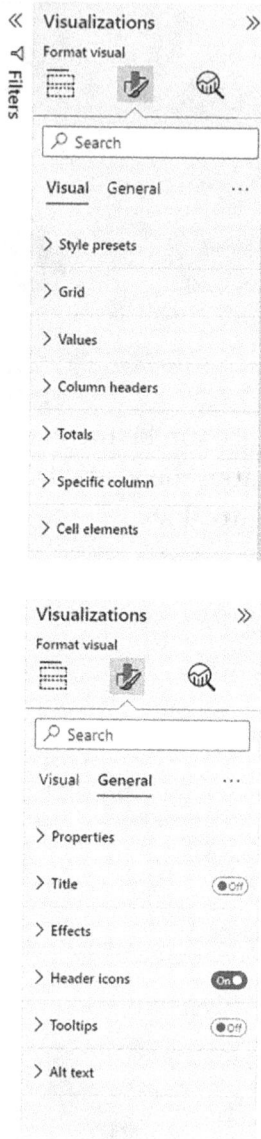

Power BI allows users to quickly switch between different aggregation functions for numerical columns within visualizations. This can be done by using the down-arrow icon next to the field name, either in the Field pane or directly on the visual field well.

For this purpose, select a visual in the Visualizations pane. Then, go to the Values field. Click the down-arrow next to a numerical field (Sales or Quantity). Then choose the desired aggregation, Sum (default) or Average, or Minimum/ Maximum, etc., depending on context.

The size of the data text can be adjusted by adjusting the Text Size to a larger font for easy visibility. The column headers section can also be expanded. Applying Conditional Formatting will change the appearance of data in visuals based on the values of the data itself. It is a powerful tool for drawing attention to key metrics, outliers, or performance thresholds.

Customized text and background colors can also be provided to enhance the look and feel of the table from the Conditional Formatting option. The table, after applying various formatting options, would look like Figure 4.29.

Figure 4.29 Table With Background Conditional Formatting

Country	Sum of Sales	Sum of Profit	Sum of Quantity	Sum of Discount
Denmark	7763	-3608	204	30.50
Portugal	15106	-8704	286	35.00
Ireland	15998	-6886	392	50.30
Norway	20529	5167	261	0.00
Finland	20702	3908	201	0.00
Switzerland	24874	7234	308	0.00
Sweden	30490	-17524	753	103.10
Belgium	42320	9912	532	0.00
Netherlands	70313	-37188	1526	188.90
Austria	79382	21332	973	0.00
Spain	249402	47067	2881	26.10
Italy	252742	15802	3612	122.60
United Kingdom	420497	90382	4917	92.20
Germany	488681	86279	6179	89.85
Total	2348482	283240	30354	885.55

Let's take an example, where we have a table visual showing the following columns of Sales Amount, Profit, Quantity, and Discount with respect to country-wise distribution. We want to highlight sales performance, green for high sales, yellow for medium sales, and red for low sales.

To do this, click on the table visual in the Visualizations pane. Again, move to the Values section and click the down-arrow next to Sales Amount. Select Conditional Formatting and choose Background color or Font color. Now, choose Format by setting custom rules and click OK. The Sales Amount column in the table visual will change color based on the value ranges, making it easy to spot performance trends visually.

4.5.2 Matrix View

The Matrix View in Power BI enables managers to select a category for rows and columns to view detailed data at cross-sections of those two categories. This view aggregates data and equips analysts to drill down into the data in a more granular format.

To operate the Matrix View, choose Matrix from the Visualizations pane and from the Field pane, drag Region and Country as Row, Order data as Columns, Sum of Profits, and Sum of Sales as values. The matrix created is shown in Figure 4.30. The insights from matrix visuals are better than those of table visuals.

Figure 4.30 Matrix Visual With Fields

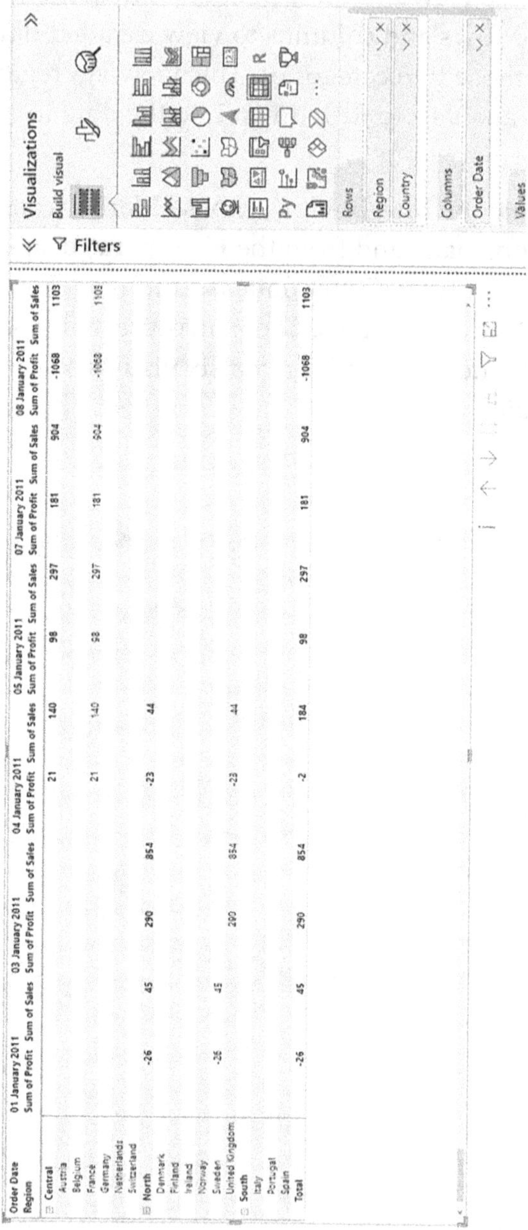

Here, various types of formatting options can be used to enhance the appearance of the Matrix View to draw out critical information. Since hierarchies are present, options to drill up and drill down, which expand the data field, are available in the bottom portion of the Report Canvas. Figure 4.31 shows the Table and Matrix View next to each other, making it possible to identify the difference in detail.

Figure 4.31 | **Table and Matrix Visual View**

Country	Sum of Profit	Sum of Quantity
Austria	21332	973
Belgium	9912	532
Denmark	-3608	204
Finland	3908	201
France	70067	7329
Germany	86279	6179
Ireland	-6886	392
Italy	15802	3612
Netherlands	-37188	1526
Norway	5167	261
Portugal	-8704	286
Spain	47067	2881
Sweden	-17524	753
Switzerland	7234	308
United Kingdom	90382	4917
Total	283240	30354

Segment Country	Consumer Sum of Profit	Sum of Sales	Corporate Sum of Profit	Sum of Sales	Home Off Sum of Pr
Austria	12028	43461	5925	20587	3
Aaron Cunningham	52	687			
05 August 2011	52	687			
Adam Bentley	182	571			
Aidan Hayward			8	54	
Aidan Rowe	66	499			
Alex Greenwood	34	83			
Alexander Bond			28	113	
Alfonso Gomez			33	147	
Ali Mander-Jones					
Amanda Hutcherson			5	27	
Amber Adams			11	69	
Amy Nixon	273	719			
Andy Henderson					
Angelina Beeton	652	2347			
Angus De Groot			7	146	
Total	147447	1236282	92634	738137	43

4.6 Categorical Data Visualization

For categorical data, bar charts, column charts, pie charts, treemaps, and scatter charts are used to represent values proportionally, making it easier to distinguish differences across categories. These visuals also come with features of filtering, highlighting, and the use of drill-downs.

1. Bar and column charts

Bar and column charts are almost similar except in their orientation. Bar charts use horizontal rectangular bars, where the length is proportional to the amount of data. Column charts display vertical bars in both stacked and clustered formats.

For setting bar charts, from the Visualizations pane, select the stacked bar chart and resize it as required on the Report Canvas. Drag the country data field to the Y axis and the sum of profit to the X axis to determine profits across the country.

Extend the visual to break down each country's profit by category and drag the category to the Legend bucket. Figure 4.32 illustrates a bar chart showing country-wise profit in various categories.

Figure 4.32 Bar Chart Showing Country Profits in Various Categories

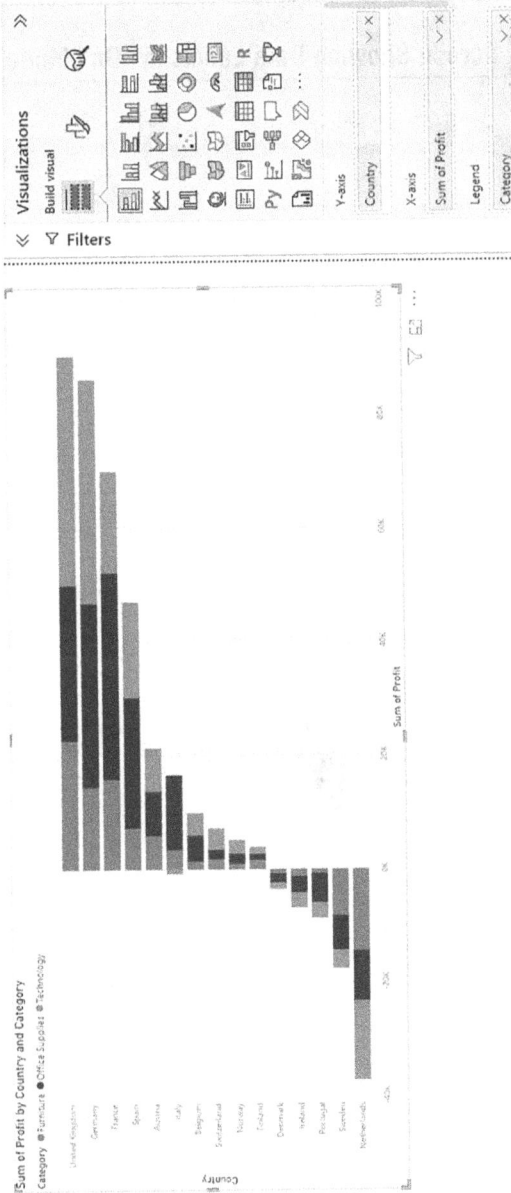

Further, in the Format section, turn on the Data Labels so that the bar chart has data labels enabled, as shown in Figure 4.33.

Figure 4.33 Screen Showing Data Labels in "On" Mode

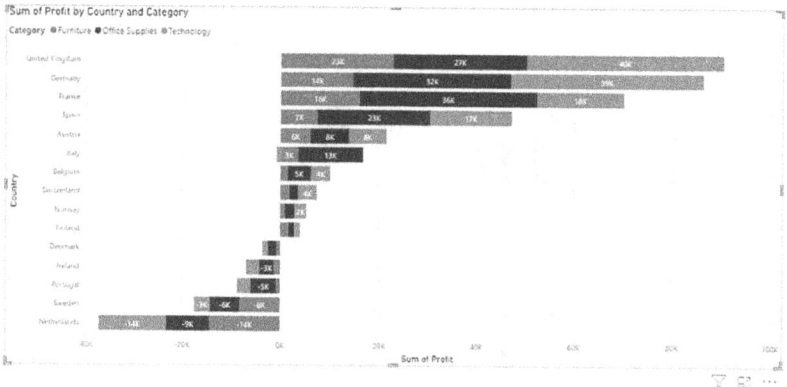

Figures 4.34–4.36 show some of the standard charts.

Figure 4.34 Clustered Bar Chart

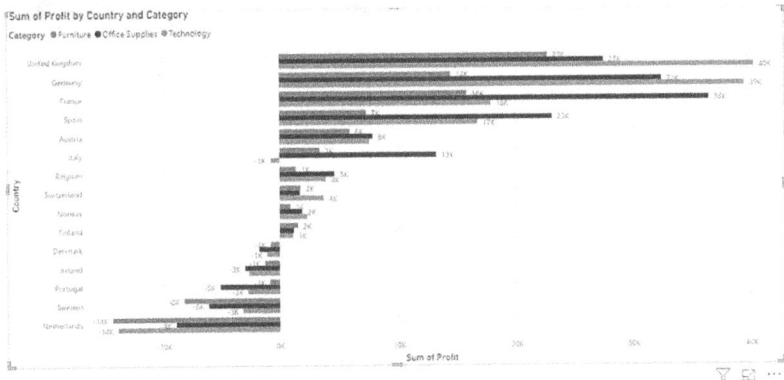

Figure 4.35 Clustered Column Chart

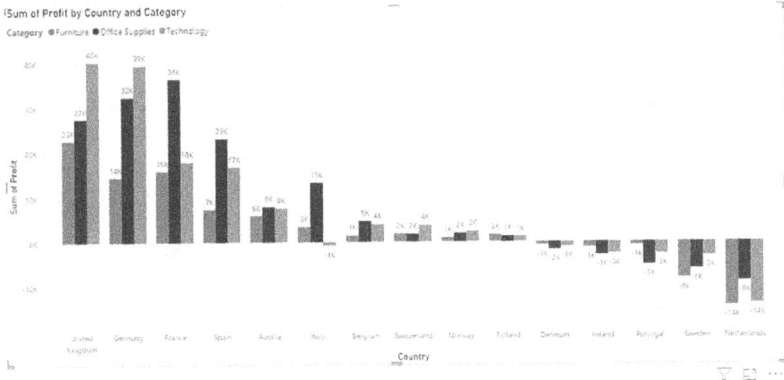

Figure 4.36 100% Stacked Bar Chart

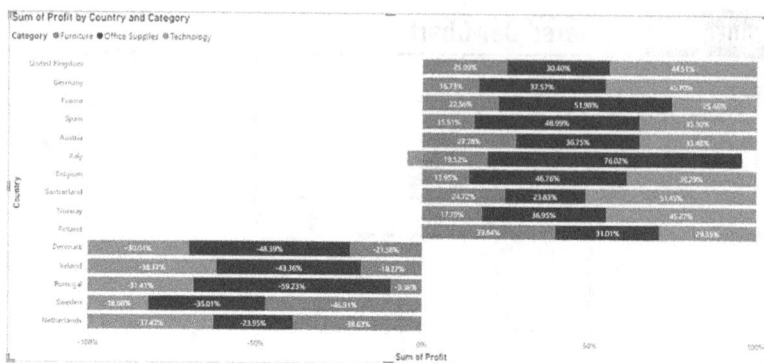

2. Pie charts

Pie charts enable visualizing a particular section compared to the whole section and enable cross-highlighting. Donut charts also provide a similar functionality, but they have a hollow center, which allows for labeling. Pie charts can be accessed from the Visualizations pane.

Consider that we have a dataset with sales data and various columns with data relating to country, profit, and other related fields, as quoted in previous examples. Select the Country as the Legend and the Sum of Profits as Values to generate the pie chart.

This chart allows users to compare profit contributions from different countries visually. Also, this selection can be followed to generate donut charts using the same steps. Figure 4.37 displays the pie chart and the donut chart.

Figure 4.37 Pie Chart and Donut Chart

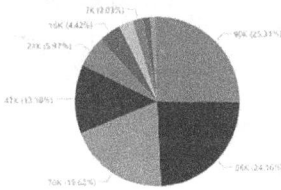

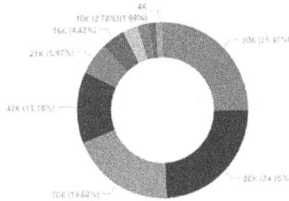

This pie chart displays segments representing the country-wise total profits, and the size of each segment corresponds to its profit contribution relative to the whole dataset. Thus, it shows a clear distribution of profits across different countries, helping to identify high and low-performing countries.

A donut chart provides a similar breakdown with a central blank space, which offers an aesthetic design and space for additional annotations, if any. The donut chart, displayed alongside the pie chart, reinforces insights by offering an alternative design option with varied visualization preferences.

Data labels in these visualizations can be customized by selecting a label style option. The font size can also be changed, as filtering data may affect the chart's readability.

3. Treemap

A Treemap represents hierarchies in the data by nesting data in rectangles commonly referred to as branches. These branches are described in various colors. Categories can be added to the Details bucket to create small rectangles within the branches, referred to as leaves. Treemaps are usually used when bar and column charts get cluttered with many categories.

Figure 4.38 shows the Country as the branch, the Category of items as the leaves, and the Value as the Sum of Profits. So, the sum of profits based on each category in each country is shown on the Treemap.

Figure 4.38 Treemap

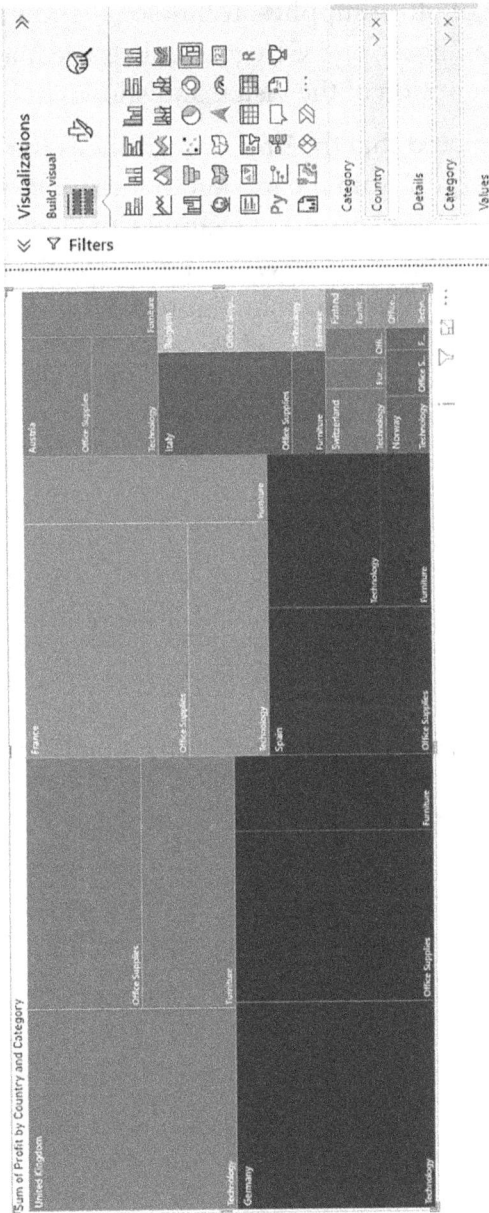

The size of each rectangle corresponds to its value, which is the total profit or the sum of the profits. The leaf is a category of office supplies, technology, and furniture. Legend, Data Labels, and Category Labels are made available in the Format option of the visual and shown in Figure 4.39.

It is to be noted that the Treemap arranges the rectangles by size, the largest from the top left to the smallest in the bottom right of the canvas. For example, the United Kingdom is the most profitable country, and Finland is the least profitable country, as shown in Figure 4.39.

Figure 4.39 Treemap Visual With Details Displayed

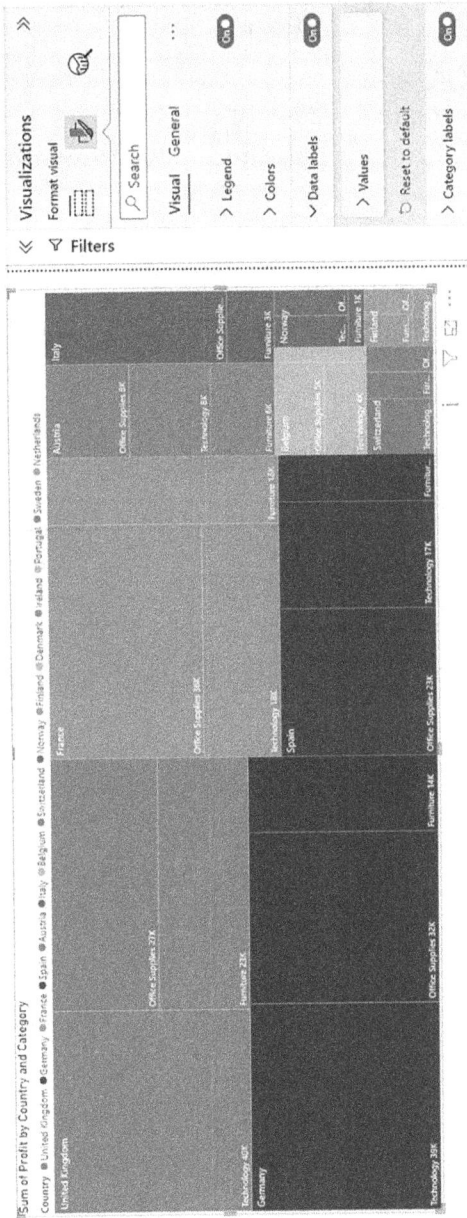

4. Scatter chart

A scatter chart, called a bubble chart, shows the relationship between two or three numerical values. It helps in identifying correlations, clusters, trends, and outliers in your data. To create a scatter plot, select the scatter chart from the Visualizations pane and move to an area in the canvas.

From the Field pane, drag the Sum of Sales to the X axis, Profit to the Y axis, Quantity to the Size Bucket, and Country to the Legend bucket. The visual would look as shown in Figure 4.40.

Figure 4.40 Scatter Plot Showing Sales, Profit, and Quantity by Country

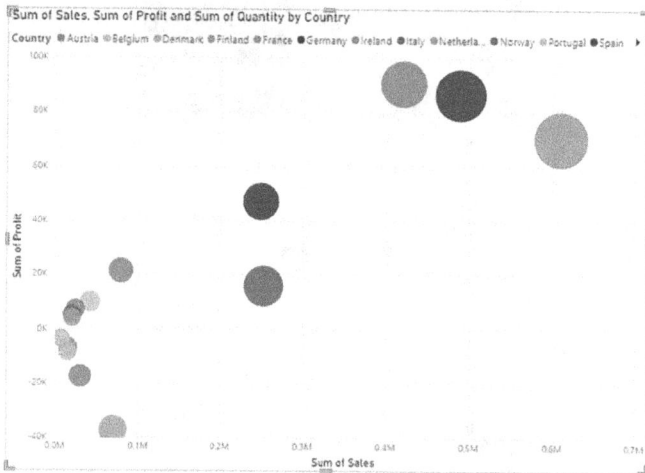

Each bubble represents a country. The horizontal (X) position shows how much that country contributed to total sales. The vertical (Y) position shows how much profit was made in that country. We can analyze whether higher sales

correlate with higher profit, or if some countries are selling more but earning less.

The size of each bubble is determined by the quantity sold. Larger bubbles represent countries with higher sales volume, regardless of revenue or profit. This helps distinguish between high-volume, low-profit vs low-volume, and high-profit markets.

Figure 4.41 Play Axis in Scatter Chart

One unique feature of the scatter chart is to bring data to life through the Play Axis, where a small animation can be brought into the visual, as shown in Figure 4.41 above. When we add the Month to the Play Axis bucket, a play button will appear along with the 12 months, and when we press the play button, bubbles will move to display values at specific times.

Scatter plots are commonly used in many functional areas, including marketing, sales, finance, and operations. They serve as a critical visualization tool in these fields by helping identify trends, correlations among variables, factors, and clusters, and facilitating informed decision-making.

For example, scatter plots are used in marketing and sales domains to visualize customer purchase frequency against transaction value, to identify high-valued and low-valued customers. They are also used in the Human Resource domain to visualize years of experience against salary to identify compensation trends.

4.7 Trend Data Visualizations

Over time, data trends reflect significant changes in value. Power BI helps visualize these trends and total values across time frames. Commonly used visualizations for trend data include Line and Area Charts, Combo Charts, Funnel Charts, Ribbon Charts, and Waterfall Charts.

1. Line chart and area chart

A line chart is the most basic and standard tool for representing and analyzing data. From the Visualizations pane, select the line chart and move it to the required space on the canvas. From the Field pane, drag the Order Date and Category to the X axis and the Sum of Sales and Profit to the Y axis to display the line chart. Figure 4.42 shows the sum of sales and profit by order date and category.

Figure 4.42 Line Chart

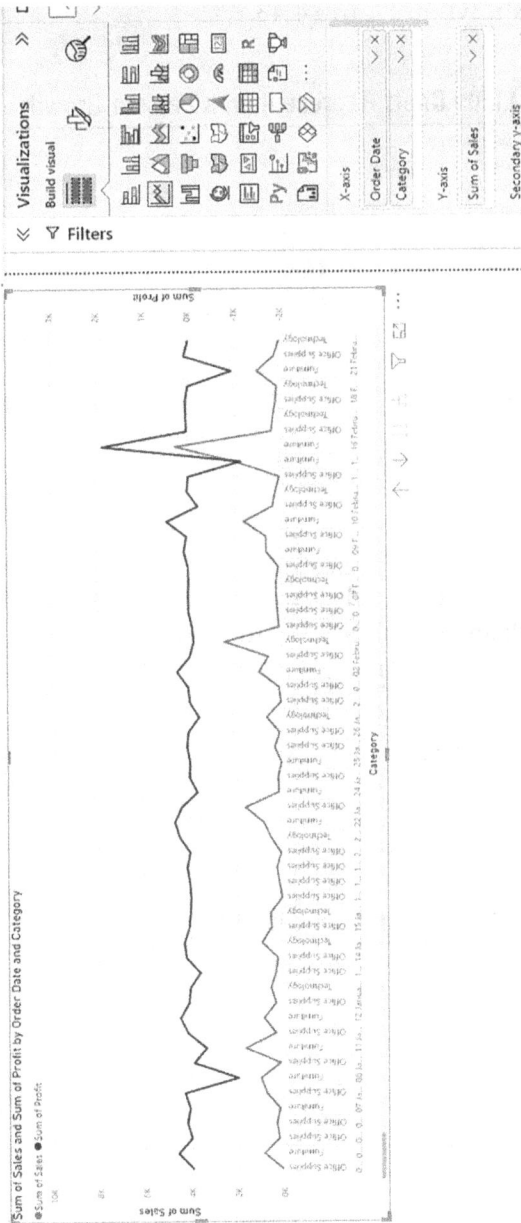

Here, we see that there is a significant growth in the sales and profits for the furniture category on the order date of 16 February, shown in Figure 4.43.

Figure 4.43 Line Chart Representing a Peak in Growth

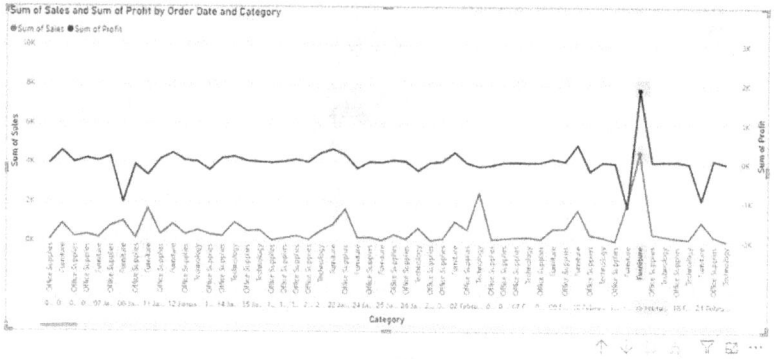

Line chart is one of the oldest types of charts, first used by Scottish engineer William Playfair in 1786 to represent economic data trends (Spence, I., & Wainer, H., 2017).

Drill up can also be used to format the visual and view trends across years, as shown in Figure 4.44. (Spence, I., & Wainer, H., 2017).

Figure 4.44 Drill Up Format in Line Chart

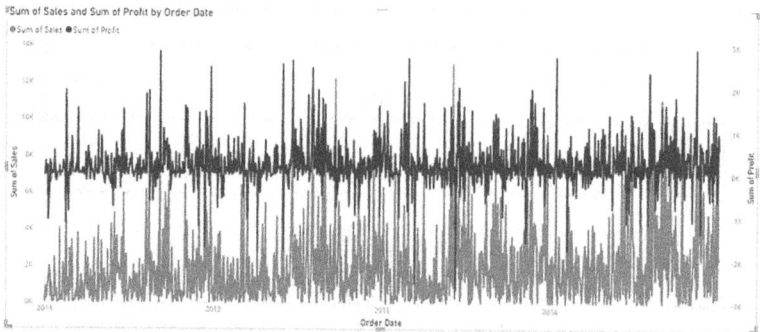

Area charts are also based on line charts, showing areas in colors between axes and lines representing volume, as shown in Figure 4.45.

Figure 4.45 Area Chart

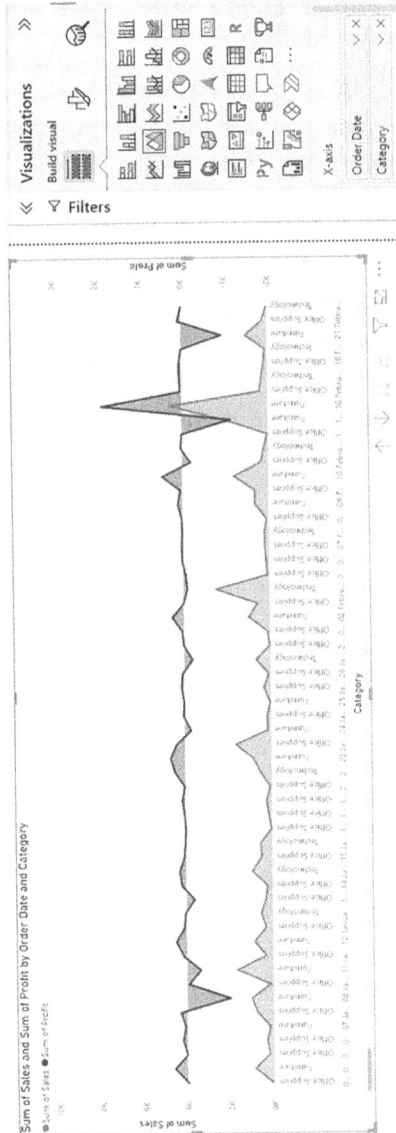

2. Combo charts

Combo charts combine line charts and column charts in stacked or clustered columns, which helps to compare data at a glance. Here, two equal or distinct fields can be taken in each axis, either numeric or percentage.

Select the line and stacked column chart from the Visualizations pane and resize it to the required area in the Report Canvas. Drag the Country field to the shared axis bucket and Order Quantity to the columns values bucket, and then drag Profit to the line values bucket.

Now, there are two Y axes: one is order quantity, and the other is profit. Expand the hierarchy by one level to get data points between the two variables. This is seen in Figure 4.46, which represents columns showing order quantity and the line as profit. It's clear from the figure that when the quantity sold is higher, the profit is also higher.

Figure 4.46 Combo Charts

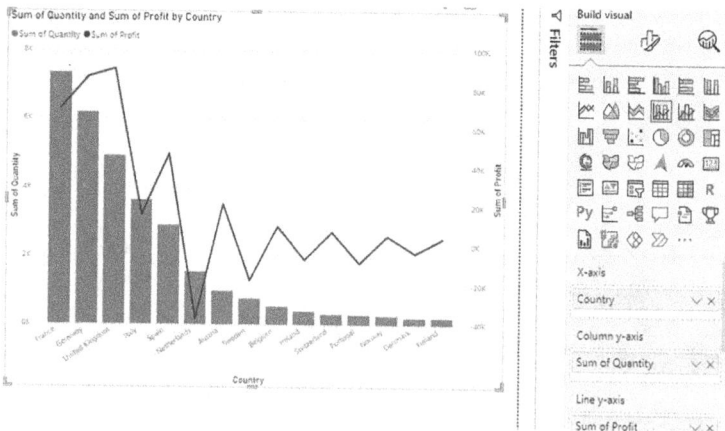

> ### HIGHLIGHT
>
> A combo chart lets you mix bar and line charts, making it one of the best ways to compare trends and totals in one visualization. They help in combining two different types of data (e.g., revenue as bars, profit margin as a line).

3. Funnel charts

Funnel charts have a unique appeal and show the percentage difference between values, with the highest value at the top and the lowest at the bottom. Each stage in the funnel shows the percentage difference between itself and the previous stage and compares it to the highest stage. Hence, funnel charts are an excellent fit for visualizing linear processes in three or four stages.

This chart is chosen from the Visualizations pane and sized to the area in the Report Canvas. Drag the Country list or Date to the Category axis and Sales to the Values bucket. Sales by Country ranking from highest to lowest is shown in Figure 4.47, enabling us to identify the countries that make the highest sales value. France had 100% and Denmark contributed only 1.27% of the total sales, making it the lowest among all countries.

Figure 4.47 Funnel Chart

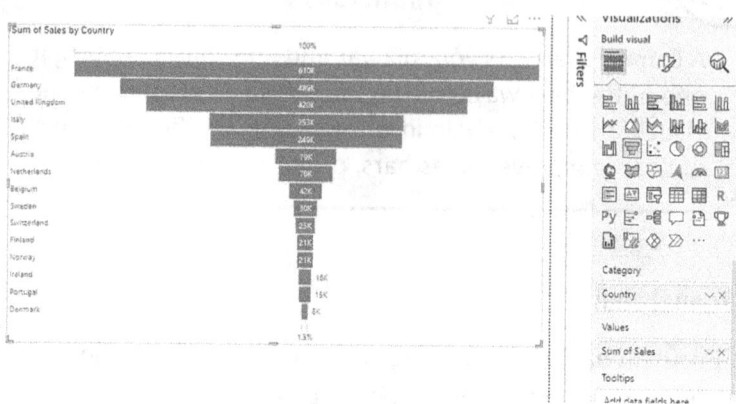

4. Ribbon charts

A ribbon chart is a visualization that displays rank change over time for categorical data. It is particularly helpful in demonstrating how the leading categories change between different periods. In this chart, the top-ranking category with the highest value is shown at the top, and ribbons join the values between periods so that it is simple to monitor changes in rank and value.

For instance, when monitoring sales performance of goods across many months, the ribbon chart points out which product was selling best each month, and how all products ranked each month, changed over time.

From the Visualizations pane, select the ribbon chart and resize it on the Report Canvas. From the Field pane, drag the segment of Sales Order to the X axis and the Total Sales or Sum of Sales to the Y axis or values bucket. The chart now looks like a column. Next, in the Legend bucket, drag country, we now see the ribbon chart showing the category value for each segment. Figure 4.48 represents the ribbon chart showing sales by segment and country.

Figure 4.48 Ribbon Chart

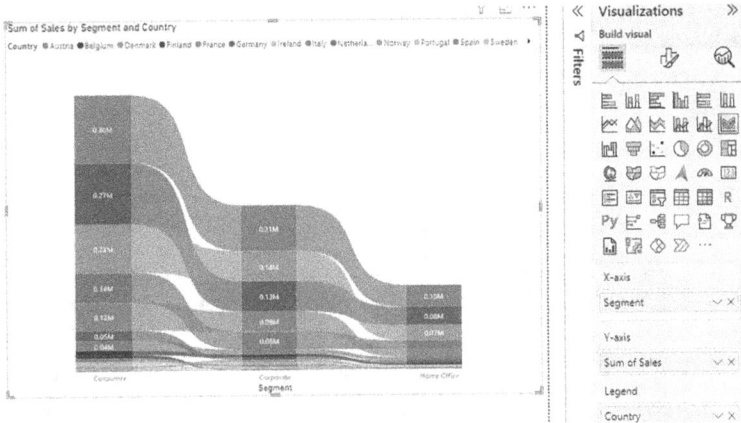

Data labels can be added for greater visibility. There is also a ranking feature in ribbon charts with lighter areas between each segment showing the value for the previous and upcoming segments.

5. Waterfall chart

A waterfall chart helps visualize the changes from the initial value and shows running values that have been added or removed. The breakdown option in the visual helps to identify whether each component contributes positively or negatively to the change between values.

To create the chart, select the waterfall chart from the Visualizations pane and reposition it according to the size required to create the chart. From the Field pane, drag the Region to the Category bucket and the Sum of Profit to the Values bucket. This will show how each region has contributed to the total profit. Again, from the Field pane, drag Country to the Breakdown bucket. In the waterfall chart, as shown in Figure 4.49, we can see each country's contribution to the regions.

Figure 4.49 Waterfall Chart

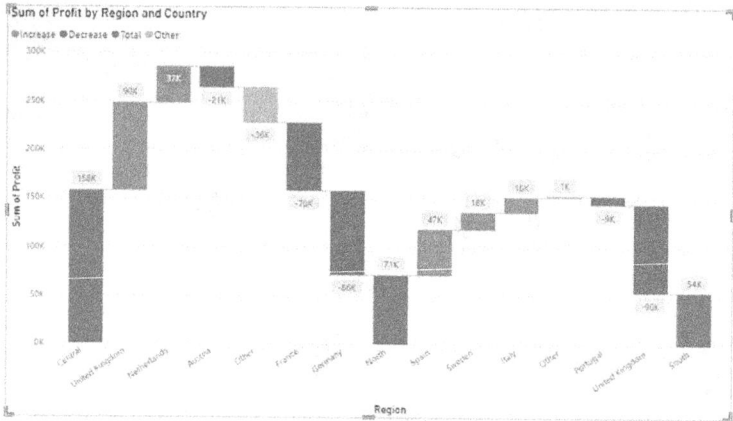

The green color in the waterfall chart shows positive changes, and the red color shows negative changes; this can be changed from the format section if required. The region-wise sum of profits is seen in blue. The data points as a table are shown in Figure 4.50.

Figure 4.50 Data Points as the Sum of Profits by Region and Country

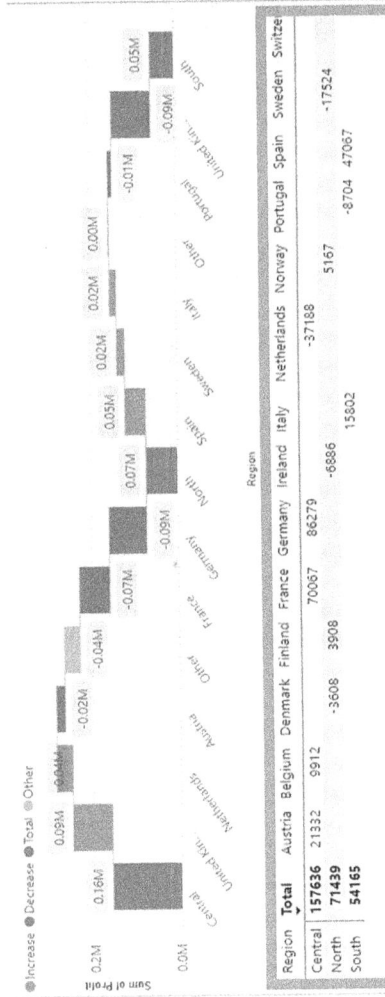

Enabling data labels in the visual brings more clarity, showing how much a particular category (country) contributes to the overall profit of each region.

FUN FACT

The Waterfall Chart is also known as the Flying Bricks Chart because its bars appear to float (Bouchefra, A., Jankov, T., James, H., & Antolovic, Z., 2018).

DISCUSSION QUESTIONS

1. How does the Report View in Power BI streamline the process of creating data visualizations?

2. Why is Report View preferred over Model View or Data View when designing reports?

3. How does a Line Chart help in identifying trends, and what additional insights can be gained when comparing multiple lines?

4. When is an Area Chart more effective than a Line Chart?

Chapter Summary

- There are around 27 visualization components in Power BI, but there is no reason to use them in a single report, as they can be confusing.

- The selection of visualization should be based on the specific requirements of the report for clarity and effectiveness in the presentation of data. And also, if a particular visualization type effectively displays the data, it can be used multiple times in the report.

- Color scheme in visualizations enhances the overall presentation of the report.

- Basic visual settings such as data labels, titles, and interactions should be customized to guide user focus and improve clarity.

- Overall, choosing the right visualization depends on the data and the insights you want to convey.

- Bar and column charts are suitable for comparing categories or trends over time, while line charts are ideal for showing continuous data patterns.

- Pie and donut charts work best when illustrating parts of a whole, but should be limited to a few categories to avoid confusion.

- Tables and matrices are used when detailed, structured data or exact values are needed.

- Scatter charts show relationships or distributions between two numeric variables.

- Slicers provide interactive filtering options for users. Custom visuals can be added when standard visuals are not sufficient, offering flexibility for specialized reporting needs.

QUIZ

1. **What is the primary purpose of using visualization components?**
   a. To store data
   b. To perform data calculations
   c. To enhance data interpretation and storytelling
   d. To export data

2. **A key feature of built-in visuals in Power BI:**
   a. Inability to filter data
   b. Pre-configured layouts for easy use
   c. Limited customization options
   d. Lack of cross-filtering and cross-highlighting

3. **Why should a user enable Preview Features in Power BI?**
   a. To access and experiment with upcoming or experimental features
   b. To view outdated features
   c. To remove visualizations from the report
   d. To export data into Excel

4. **Name the section that allows you to enable or disable Preview Features.**
   a. Home Tab
   b. Options and Settings
   c. Data View
   d. Visualizations Pane

5. **What is the advantage of using Visualizations in Report View?**
   a. They are static and non-interactive.
   b. They allow dynamic and interactive reporting.
   c. They limit data to tabular formats only.
   d. They do not support filtering.

6. **Which visualization is best suited for displaying categorical data?**
   a. Line chart
   b. Pie chart
   c. Table
   d. Scatter plot

7. **What is the difference between cross-highlighting and cross-filtering?**
   a. Cross-highlighting hides unrelated data.
   b. Cross-filtering removes data while cross-highlighting emphasizes relevant data.
   c. Cross-highlighting deletes data.
   d. Cross-filtering and cross-highlighting are the same.

8. **Which is not a function of cross-filtering?**
   a. Filtering data across multiple visuals
   b. Updating related visuals automatically
   c. Highlighting specific data within a single visual
   d. Applying filters to specific datasets

9. **Why is a Slicer Visual needed?**
   a. To perform calculations
   b. To allow users to filter data interactively
   c. To export data
   d. To store data

10. **Which type of data is most commonly used with a Slicer Visual?**
    a. Numerical data
    b. Text data
    c. Categorical data
    d. Date and time data

Answers

1 – c	2 – b	3 – a	4 – b	5 – b
6 – b	7 – b	8 – c	9 – b	10 – c

Case Study 2

(Chapters 3 and 4)

Improving Customer Experience Through Sentiment Analytics for a Telecom Company

Introduction:

Let's consider the case of a leading telecom service provider, offering broadband, mobile, and digital TV services. With a customer base of over four million, the company receives feedback through call centers, emails, social media, and app reviews.

Despite having abundant data, the company struggled to use this feedback effectively to improve customer satisfaction. In response, it initiated a Customer Sentiment Analytics project using Power BI. The objective was to integrate diverse feedback sources, analyze sentiment using DAX and text functions, and visually communicate customer pain points and satisfaction drivers to decision-makers. Through this case, we will understand how data modeling and advanced visualization techniques work in Power BI.

Challenges:

The service provider identified several challenges, including:

- **Fragmented feedback sources:** Data came from multiple platforms (Google reviews, customer emails, social media mentions), stored in different formats.

- **Unstructured text data:** Much of the feedback was in free-text format, lacking predefined structure for direct analysis.

- **No central data model:** There was no existing relationship between service data (plans, locations) and customer sentiment.

- **Limited visualization for actionable insights:** Management dashboards were basic and failed to reveal trends or root causes.

- **Poor performance with large datasets:** Previous dashboards lagged or crashed due to insufficient data modeling and large data volumes.

How Power BI implemented a Customer Sentiment Analytics project

Power BI was leveraged to implement a Customer Sentiment Analytics project, providing actionable insights for improved decision-making in the company. Here's how this project was executed.

Data modelling:

The company began building data relationships, importing data tables, enabling usability enhancements, performance optimization, and creating calculated columns with DAX.

Storytelling with visuals

It leveraged Power BI features such as Preview Features, Visualizations in Report View, Cross-filtering and Highlighting, Slicer Visuals, Categorical Data Visualizations, and Trend Visualizations.

As customer expectations rose, sentiment analytics supported by Power BI equipped the company to deliver a superior customer experience and maintain a competitive advantage in the sector.

Case assignment:

1. Create a data model by building relationships between customer feedback tables.

2. Use DAX expressions to calculate customer satisfaction scores.

3. Display the number of customers who have given a rating of more than 4.

4. Visualize sentiment trends using trend charts, category breakdowns, and slicers.

Sample datasets for reference: You can use these datasets in Excel/CSV formats for direct upload to Power BI.

Feedback ID	Cust ID	Feedback Text	Rating	Date	Channel
F001	C001	Excellent service, but poor network coverage in my area.	3	1/1/2024	Twitter
F002	C002	Great offers, but billing is confusing.	4	2/1/2024	Survey
F003	C003	Terrible customer support experience.	2	3/1/2024	Facebook
F004	C004	The network speed has improved significantly.	5	4/1/2024	Email Feedback

Case discussion questions:

You may address these descriptive and application-based case questions:

1. What type of data model was used in the case?

2. How were DAX functions used to classify and analyze unstructured customer feedback?

3. Explain the difference between calculated columns and measures in Power BI. Give examples from the case study where each was applied.

4. What types of visuals were used to represent sentiment trends and regional feedback differences?

5. How did features like cross-filtering and slicers enhance the interactivity and usability of the sentiment analytics dashboard?

6. Describe how Smart Narrative or Preview Features in Power BI were leveraged in the case study.

CHAPTER 5
KPI and Formatting Visuals

Key Learning Objectives

- Learn to create and interpret Gauge Visuals in Power BI.
- Understand the relevance of key performance indicators in measuring business performance and how Power BI can be leveraged for this purpose.
- Explore various techniques in Power BI to build visuals from geographical data using maps.
- Study various customization options available in ArcGIS and Azure Maps for enhanced data representation.

Key Performance Indicators (KPIs) are quantifiable metrics that guide managers to evaluate success by providing insights about organizational performance. Managers rely on KPIs t`o measure and identify how well the company is performing in relation to its overall objective and how well it is contributing to its mission and vision.

KPIs support in creating a connection between daily operational activity, short-term intermediate operational activities, and the long-term strategic goals across departments. Thus, managers can identify gaps and areas for business improvement and make informed decisions.

Some examples of KPIs in marketing include customer retention rate, website traffic, and Return on Investment (ROI); in finance, common parameters are revenue growth rate and profit margin, and in Human Resources, there are employee turnover rate, time to hire, training effectiveness, and so on.

Power BI enables managers to measure the progress of various business KPIs and assess the efficiency of operational processes. Using Power BI, managers can display key values and monitor their progress toward a specific goal.

This chapter offers a detailed view of the use of Gauge Visuals and KPI Visuals. It explains how these tools assist in evaluating business performance. It specifically explores building visuals from geographical data and features various types of maps representing data.

In the context of BI, maps are visual tools used to represent geographical data. Using maps, managers can analyze and interpret location-based trends and patterns to identify regional opportunities, challenges, if any, and growth areas. For example, maps can be used to plot data points, including sales value, distribution of customer segments, or supply chain operations on a geographical canvas. Managers can use this canvas for performing various spatial analyses, identifying high and low-performing regions, and optimizing resource allocation to enhance sales volumes.

When KPIs are combined in visuals, maps can provide more insights into region-wise customer segments. This helps make strategic decisions related to targeted marketing efforts, identifying opportunities for opening new stores or markets, and addressing challenges such as closures or operational/ logistical issues.

Some of the most commonly used mapping platforms are ArcGIS Maps and Azure Maps. Various customization options are available on these platforms, out of which some key options are discussed in this chapter.

5.1 Gauge Visuals

Gauge Visuals is a feature in Power BI that provides a clear and concise way to monitor KPIs against a defined target. For example, a retail business can track its monthly sales performance against a target revenue. The gauge visual shall display how much of the sales target has been achieved as a single value and its progress toward the target value, inside a circular arc.

As a result, a new calculated measure is created in the sheet. This will help sales managers quickly assess performance and make actionable decisions. For example, if the gauge displays low progress, then managers can take steps to boost sales through various marketing and operational methods.

To initiate this, select Gauge from the Visualizations pane and fit it to the required size in the Report Canvas. Drag the total sales value to the value bucket and drag the newly created measure, sales target, to the target value bucket. The gauge visual is displayed in the Report Canvas, as shown in Figure 5.1, with total sales and sales targets.

| Figure 5.1 | Gauge Visual |

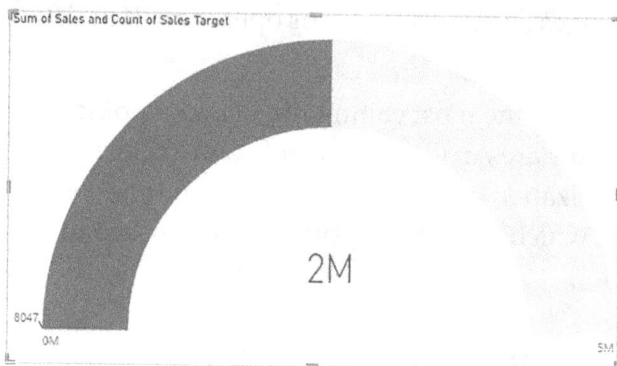

We can also use a Slicer Visual to filter data by year. By selecting a specific year, we can see changes in the values compared to the target and validate the total sales for each year. The gauge visual does not require a minimum, maximum, or target value, but including those would provide a more user-friendly visual.

5.2 KPI Visuals

KPI Visuals are similar to gauge visuals, but KPI visuals are more explicit, showing the values in plain text along with the goal. Color coding is a feature of KPI visuals that distinguishes them from other options. The value will be in red when the indicator value is lower than the goal, and when the indicator value surpasses the goal, the text will be in green color.

Select the KPI option shown in Figure 5.2 from the Visualizations pane and resize it to the required fit in the Report Canvas.

Figure 5.2 **KPI in the Visualizations Pane**

Drag the Sum of Sales from the Field pane to the Value axis, drag the count of Target Sales to the Target Goal bucket, and finally, drag the year to the Trend axis. Now, we can view the KPI visual in Figure 5.3, where values exceeding the target are displayed in figure value.

Figure 5.3	KPI Visual

Sum of Sales and Count of Sales Target by Order Date

2412
Goal: 9 (+26700%)

KPI visuals can be applied to track and improve metrics, and facilitate informed decisions in areas such as sales performance, operational efficiency, employee performance, employee engagement, financial performance, and so on.

POINT TO REMEMBER

KPI Visuals in Power BI can automatically change colors based on performance thresholds. You can set them to turn green for success, yellow for caution, and red for warning, just like a traffic light!

5.3 Visualization With Cards

Another visualization feature in Power BI to demonstrate KPIs is "Card Visualization." This tool aids in displaying a fundamental value as a visual when managers require one figure to represent the whole quantum of data.

Tables, bar charts, ribbon charts, etc., display large data quantities visually. However, managers often need to view just a single number, similar to a KPI visual, which we have seen in Section 5.2. While KPIs include target components, when those aren't needed, a single-value visual card is the best option to help managers make quick decisions.

Through the following figures in this section, we will understand how Card Visualization works. A card displays a single value of the dataset's most recent or oldest date, or critical numbers. The card is selected from the Visualizations pane, as shown in Figure 5.4, and adjusted to the required area to fit in the Report Canvas.

Figure 5.4   **Card in Visualizations Pane**

From the Field pane, drag the sum of profit to the field legend, and it gets displayed in the Report Canvas, as shown below in Figure 5.5.

Figure 5.5 Card Visual

As shown in Figure 5.5, the values are displayed in the thousands format by default, but we can change it to any other format or remove formatting altogether to display whole numbers.

Using the format option, the title text and display units can be switched. The Card Visual is not limited to displaying numeric values; it can also show text-based insights, such as the name of the top-selling product, the most profitable category, or the employee with the highest salary.

When the card requires a display of more data, we need to switch to a multi-row card that accepts multiple fields and automatically summarizes all fields as groups. Multi-row cards display data as visuals in separate sections for each group. This card is also present in the Visualizations pane and is highlighted in Figure 5.6. It can also be resized to the required fit in the canvas.

Figure 5.6 Multi-Row Card in Visualizations Pane

Consider you are a business analyst, and you are required to provide a quick overview of sales performance for specific categories of consumer goods across different countries. You can use multi-row cards in Power BI to display the required key metrics such as total sales, profit, and quantity sold from each country. For this, from the Field pane, add the items' country, the sum of total sales, the sum of profit, and the sum of quantity to the fields bucket.

We see the multi-row card, as shown in Figure 5.7, displaying more fields in the card in separate sections for each country. For example, adding fields like Country and Sales will display one row per country. When additional fields such as Profit and Quantity are included, each row will show grouped values accordingly, and the Color field can be used to represent the country.

Figure 5.7 **Multi-Row Card**

Austria		
79382	21332	973
Sum of Sales	Sum of Profit	Sum of Quantity
Belgium		
42320	9912	532
Sum of Sales	Sum of Profit	Sum of Quantity
Denmark		
7763	-3608	204
Sum of Sales	Sum of Profit	Sum of Quantity
Finland		
20702	3908	201
Sum of Sales	Sum of Profit	Sum of Quantity
France		
609683	70067	7329
Sum of Sales	Sum of Profit	Sum of Quantity
Germany		
488681	86279	6179
Sum of Sales	Sum of Profit	Sum of Quantity
Ireland		
15998	-6886	392
Sum of Sales	Sum of Profit	Sum of Quantity

Using the multi-row card, we can quickly compare the sum of sales, profit, and quantity sold across different countries in a structured format. This helps identify which countries are performing well in terms of sales and profit, and which ones may need improvement.

Having learned the different types of visualization tools for KPIs in Power BI, we will now get familiar with visualization capabilities for geographical data using maps.

5.4 Building Visuals for Geographical Data With Maps

Maps illustrate data concerning locations. More precisely, they are concerned with geographical locations. Maps are identified as one of the most interesting and exciting ways to represent data in BI reports to leverage the power of spatial analysis. They bridge the gap between data and information for actionable insights. They help to align business strategies with location-specific insights by interpreting location-based information.

Maps combine spatial and numerical data to identify patterns, trends, or anomalies. This feature of maps makes it different from the use of spreadsheets or charts.

Other essential benefits of Map Visualizations for organizations and managers include the following:

1. Maps help managers with market analysis by spotting high and low-performing regions to enable targeted marketing interventions and strategic planning.

2. They play a key role in enabling the visualization of various distribution networks to streamline logistical infrastructure. In this way, maps help to reduce costs and enhance efficiency in supply chain operations.

3. Maps allow segmenting customers region-wise to determine customer behavior. This enables managers to tailor services and match needs based on geographical preferences.

4. They also help in real-time monitoring to identify potential risks such as infrastructure failure, market instability, or natural disasters in specific regions, enabling proactive mitigation strategies.

In Power BI, maps like Shape Maps use latitude and longitude coordinates to accurately plot and verify geographic locations. Then, the visual information is given to Bing Maps to identify and verify the positioning on the map for desired results.

Power BI enables the provision of geographical data, which helps managers identify the type of data as a data category. Geographical data includes details about locations, which include countries/ country names, states, cities, or postal codes.

The Power BI platform treats each of these details as distinct data categories when assigning them for map visualizations. This capability is critical for the system to associate data points with geographic locations and visualize and analyze them on maps. Examples of mapping tools include ArcGIS or Azure Maps.

Example:

Let's assume a manager wants to identify and analyze sales performance across various states in a country. The geographical data category will be the name of the states, which will be the "State" column in the dataset.

On selecting the geographical data category, Power BI will plot sales data on a map. The manager using the map can now easily identify the most performing states and identify the states that are not performing well and need more attention. These insights will help in strategic decision-making for the business.

Maps are selected and created from the Visualizations pane, shown in Figure 5.8. It can also be resized to the required fit in the canvas.

Figure 5.8　Maps in Visualizations Pane

5.4.1 How geographical visualizations work in Power BI

Geo hierarchy is made from the geography table by dragging the region drill down from the geography table to the location bucket to ensure that locations are mapped correctly. Suppose you want to analyze the sales performance of your store situated across different cities. For this, let's see how we use Power BI to visualize the total sales data geographically.

Visualizations will assist you in identifying the cities where retail stores are performing well, which are not performing well, and which ones may need more attention. For this, drag and drop total sales to the Bubble Size bucket. This action will indicate each city's size as bubbles displayed on the map.

When the bubble size is large, it shows that the sales value is higher for those cities. Thus, large bubbles represent considerable sales value for that city and mean that they are performing well. Dragging and dropping segments to the legend bucket will make each bubble look like a pie chart, as depicted in Figure 5.9, and the total sales map for city and segment, as in Figure 5.10.

Figure 5.9 **Pie Chart Form of Bubbles**

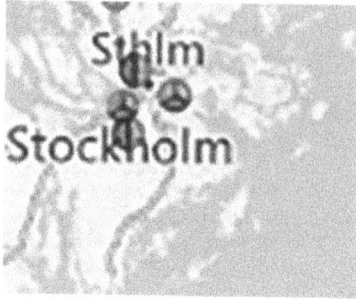

Figure 5.10 **Map Showing City Sales by Segment**

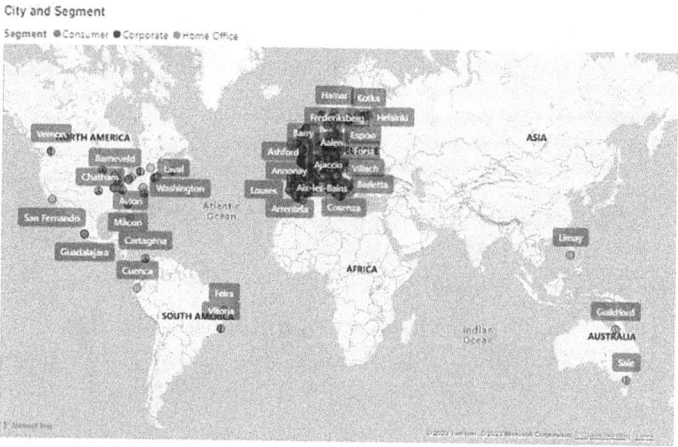

Check Figure 5.11, which represents the map showing city-wise profits based on a region-wise breakdown.

Figure 5.11 Map Showing City Sales by Segment

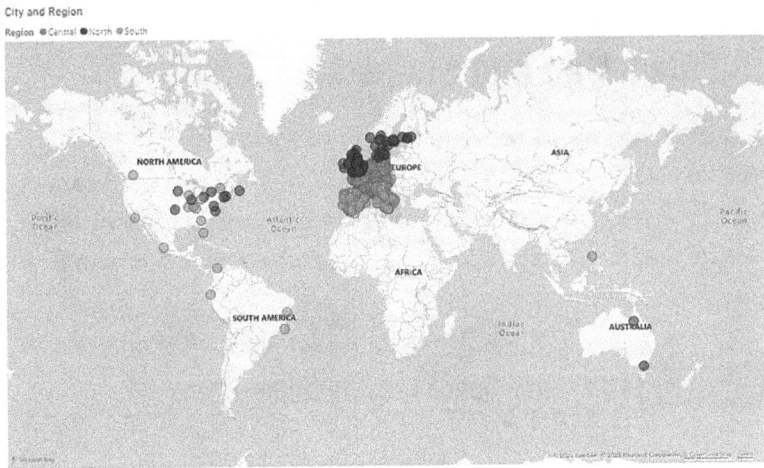

City and Region

Region ● Central ● North ● South

City and Profit are dragged and dropped to the Location bucket, and the Region breakup is dropped to the Legend bucket. Drill-down options can be enabled to make the visual more suitable and significant for exploring better views. This is how users can make informed decisions regarding resources, marketing strategies, and potential expansions to improve the sales value and performance.

If a city consistently shows low sales, the manager can consider investigating further details like local market conditions or even adjusting the sales strategy in that area. By effectively utilizing data visualizations using geographical maps, business managers can gain valuable insights into sales performance across locations and ensure factual analysis.

As seen in this section (Fig. 5.10 and 5.11), bubbles represent locations and are considered traditional visual representations. In the upcoming Sections 5.5, 5.6, and 5.7, we will explore other modern techniques for geographical visualizations in Power BI, which offer added functionalities and features.

5.5 Filled Map and Shape Map

A more detailed representation of location is enabled with the Filled Map Visual, which uses shading to display locations/ geographical data. Figure 5.12 shows the Filled Map in the Visualizations pane. It can be resized to the Report Canvas.

Figure 5.12 Filled Map Option in Visualizations Pane

The shading in Filled Maps shows data density and visually communicates the variations in data density across different regions. When the shading is lighter, it represents a lower presence, and if the shading is thicker, the contribution would be higher.

This enables users to quickly identify the impacted areas and get insights for actionable decisions. Various colors can be selected from the Format section for a pleasant appeal. Users can enhance visual appeal by customizing map colors, making the data more interpretable.

Next, drag the region drill down to the location bucket from the Field pane, switch to the Format section to expand the data color options, and click on the URL for conditional formatting, as shown in Figure 5.13.

Figure 5.13 Data Color Options in the Format Section

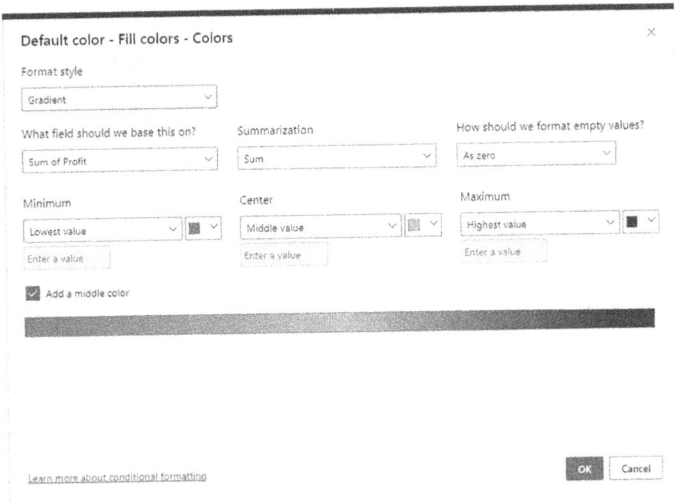

Modify the field by selecting Profit from the Field pane. To update the data visualizations again, check the box near the diverging option with OK. We can see that the Filled Map with city-based profit is based on category breakdown, as shown in Figure 5.14.

Figure 5.14 Filled Map

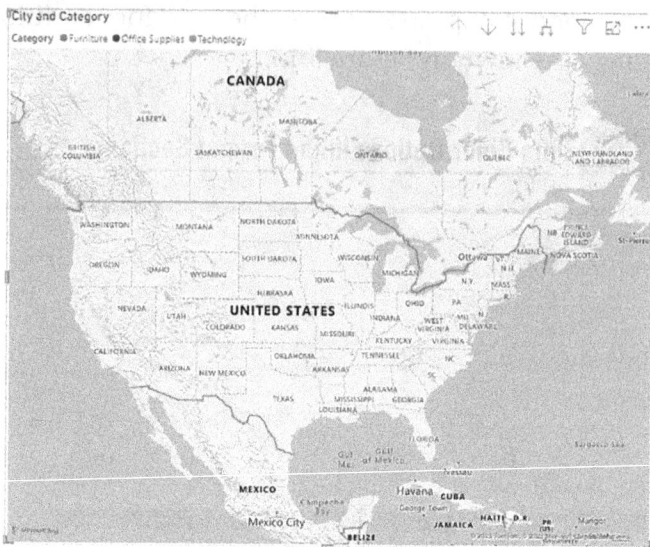

The Filled Map can also be edited based on a variety of themes, such as dark, light, road, aerial, and so on, to provide users with greater flexibility in using the visualizations. The themes improve the map's appearance, readability in various lighting conditions, and emphasize certain aspects of the data wherever required, according to the user's demand.

For example, a dark theme is ideal for presentations in dim-lit environments to offer better contrast for highlighted data points; a light theme is apt for printed reports or presentations in well-lit settings; the road theme is useful for presentations showing routes or locations that involve infrastructure like stores and the aerial theme is suited for satellite view or environmental studies.

Example for a Filled Map:

A retail company wants to analyze sales performance across different states. Using a Filled Map, they can color-code states based on total revenue, with darker shades indicating higher sales and lighter shades showing lower sales.

In Power BI, we also have the Shape Map, similar to a Filled Map in the Visualizations pane, representing geographical data as shown in Figure 5.15.

Figure 5.15 Shape Map in the Visualizations Pane

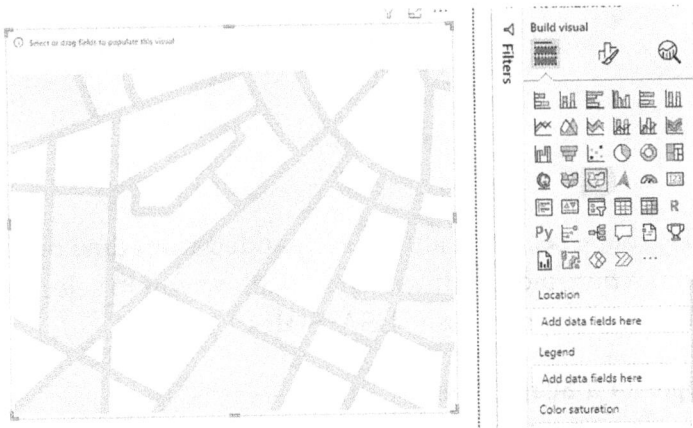

A Shape Map in Power BI allows managers or analysts to upload custom maps using a TopoJSON file containing the necessary geographical data. Moreover, Shape Maps are best for regional or country-level custom geographies and do not support global maps well due to projection limitations.

Figure 5.16 shows a Shape Map, where the City from the Field pane is dragged and dropped to the Location bucket, and the Sum of Sales is dragged to the Color Saturation bucket.

Figure 5.16 Shape Map Showing Sales by City

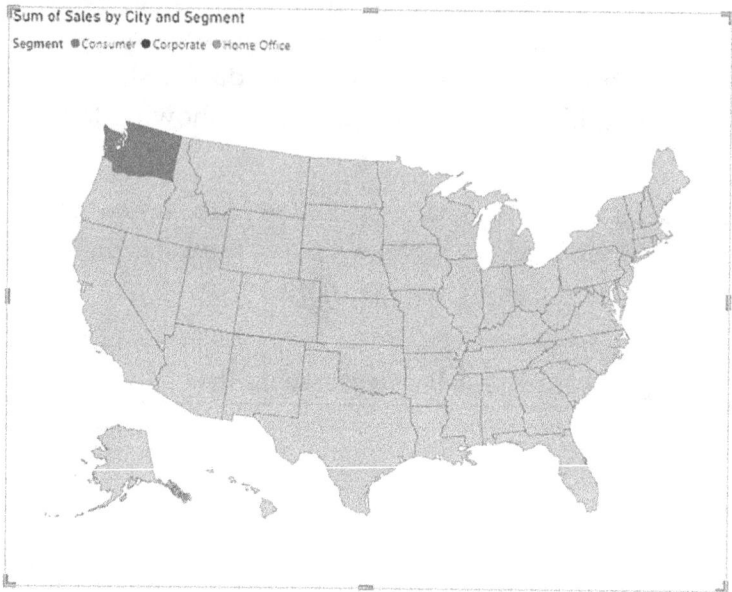

Sum of Sales by City and Segment
Segment ● Consumer ● Corporate ● Home Office

The Shape section should be expanded from the Format section, where a drop-down list will allow you to select a map category and choose "USA: States."

Example for a Shape Map:

A telecom company wants to visualize network coverage across different telecom zones instead of standard state boundaries. Using a Shape Map, they can upload a custom map of telecom regions, allowing them to analyze signal strength and customer distribution in each zone.

5.6 ArcGIS Map

ArcGIS Map, where GIS stands for Geographic Information System, is a geospatial analysis mapping platform that comes with advanced features in Power BI. Since Filled Maps or Shape Maps allow only for custom shapes to be displayed with limited analysis functions, users can leverage the ArcGIS Map to perform proximity analysis and spatial querying and gain deeper insights. ArcGIS Maps integrate a vast array of geospatial datasets, offer extensive customization options, and support advanced interactivity features, enabling users to engage with the map data dynamically.

Also, various visual changes can be made to the ArcGIS Map as it hosts diverse features. The map can be accessed from the Visualizations pane and resized in the Report Canvas. Let's walk through some of its functionalities with the help of the following figures.

From the Field pane, drag and drop City in the Location bucket and Total Sales in the Color bucket to create the ArcGIS Map, as shown in Figure 5.17, displaying the total Sum of Sales city-wise.

Figure 5.17 ArcGIS Map Displaying the Sum of Sales by City

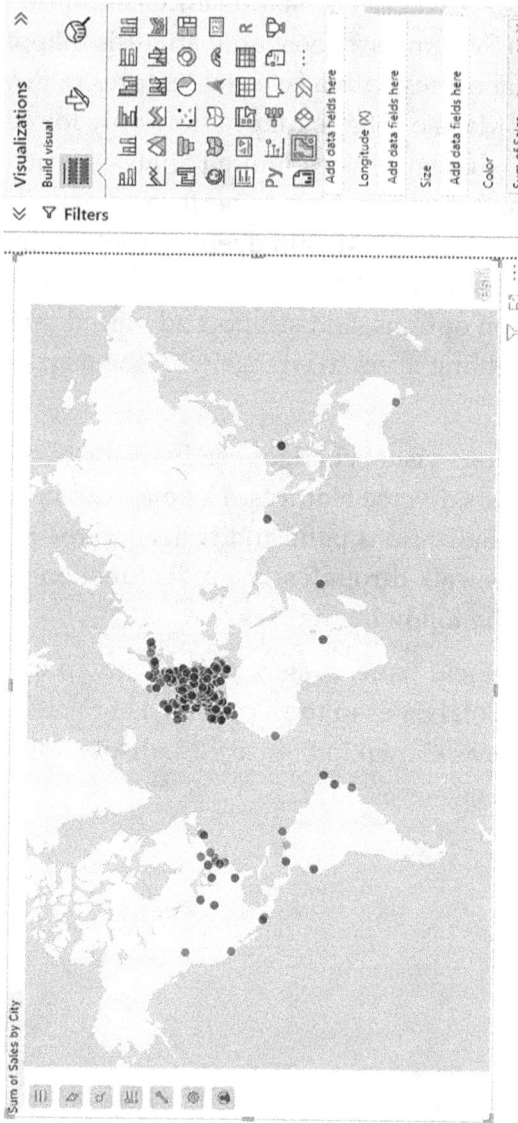

The visual can be customized using the ellipsis and choosing the edit option. Figure 5.18 shows various customization options available in ArcGIS Maps.

Figure 5.18 Options for Customization in ArcGIS Maps

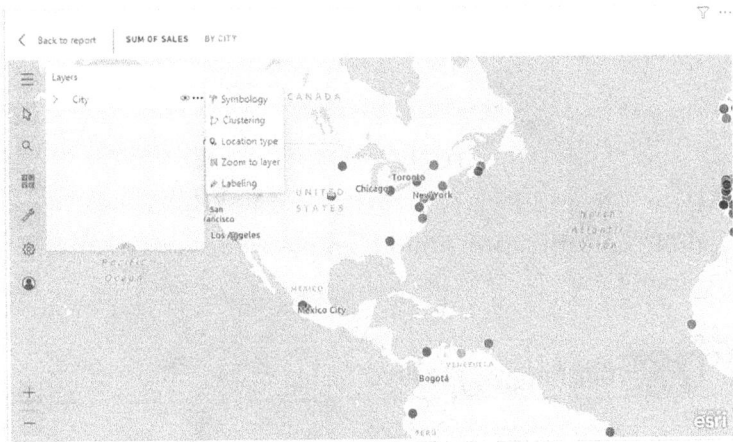

Symbology, Clustering, Location type, Zoom to Layer, and Labeling are some standard geographic customization options available. Figure 5.19 shows the Symbol Style option in the ArcGIS map.

Figure 5.19 Symbol Style Option in ArcGIS Maps

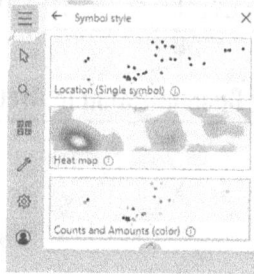

Figure 5.20 and Figure 5.21 display the Clustering option of customization and Labeling in the ArcGIS map, respectively.

Figure 5.20 Clustering in the ArcGIS Map

Figure 5.21 Labeling in the ArcGIS Map

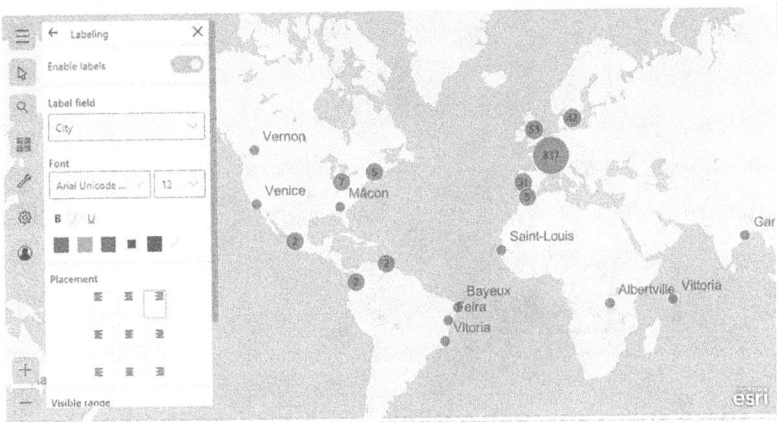

Basemap features and infographics are displayed in Figures 5.22 and 5.23, respectively.

Figure 5.22 Basemap Features in ArcGIS Maps

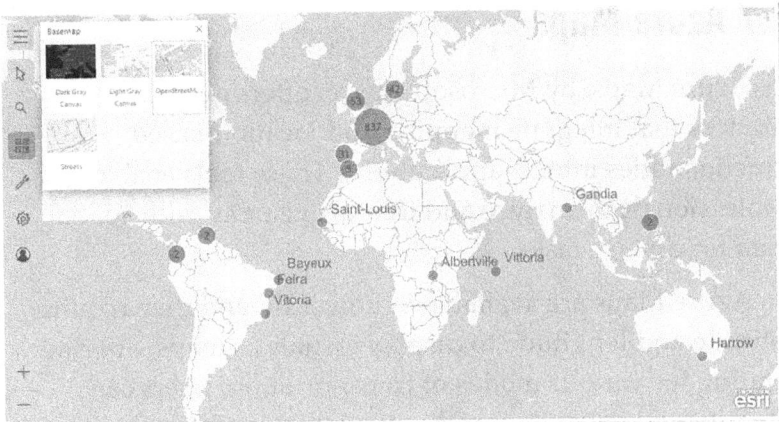

Figure 5.23 Infographics in ArcGIS Maps

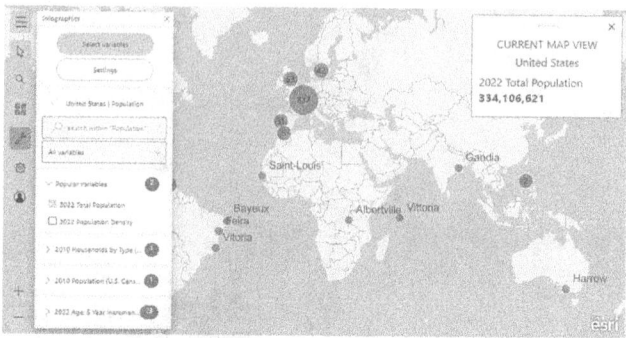

There are many such options available for visualization in this map type, including Map layers, Symbology Layers, Heat maps, Labels, Data-driven styling, Popups, amongst others. All these features in ArcGIS Maps make Power BI an effective tool for analyzing and interpreting geographical data visually.

5.7 Azure Maps

Azure Maps, by Microsoft Azure, offers geospatial services that integrate mapping and location-based functionalities into its applications. These tools enable professionals to analyze and interact visually with spatial data for diverse tasks.

Azure Maps are available in Power BI, and they require latitude and longitude to display visuals as maps, offering routing for various modes of transportation. Users can identify and generate routes, calculate their travel times, and find the optimal paths between two locations or across locations.

Another feature is that the Azure Map can add reference layers and display real-time traffic, providing location-based functionalities. But, one limitation of this map is that it does not accept locations or city/state/zip codes, although it can be adjusted using various other options such as satellite, hybrid, grey, or terrain formats.

Figure 5.24 Azure Map Showing Population by States

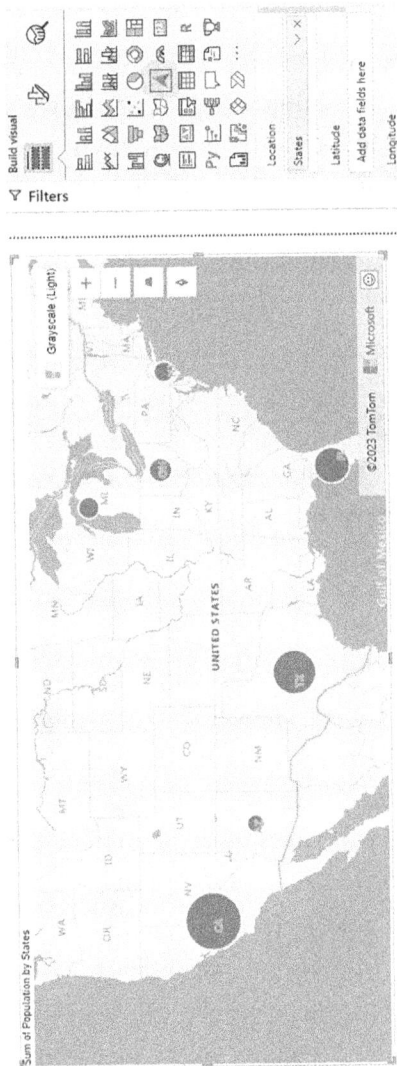

Even though all the maps covered by us so far: Filled Map, Shape Map, ArcGIS Map, and Azure Maps display similar visualizations, each one is different based on its specific functionality. Managers must identify the best map choice for visualization to illustrate the dataset better, compared to the other available options.

Example:

If a manager wants to display sales data across various regions, he can use a Filled Map. This allows sales performance in each area to be shown with color coding, making it easy to identify high and low-performing regions. Or, if the objective is to show the routes taken by various delivery trucks, a Route Map can clearly show the paths and distances travelled.

Using Route Maps, users can identify and generate routes, calculate their travel times, and find the optimal paths between two locations or across locations. Therefore, by choosing the right type of map, managers can even enhance the understanding of datasets and convey insights more effectively.

5.8 Q&A Visual

Sometimes, a dataset may not be complete or straightforward. However, Power BI is flexible enough to aid leaders and professionals by providing an array of options for cross-filtering and drilling down. This enables users to view the data behind the visualization.

In this context, Power BI is also equipped with a self-service Q&A feature that acts as a search engine for the data. Similar to a search engine, it allows managers to ask a question and get a visual as an answer to that question. Power BI also enables suggestions and autocomplete for data exploration, providing flexibility in searching for new answers.

Figure 5.25 shows the Q&A in the Report Canvas when Q&A is selected from the Visualizations pane and resized to fit the Report Canvas.

Figure 5.25 Q&A in Report Canvas

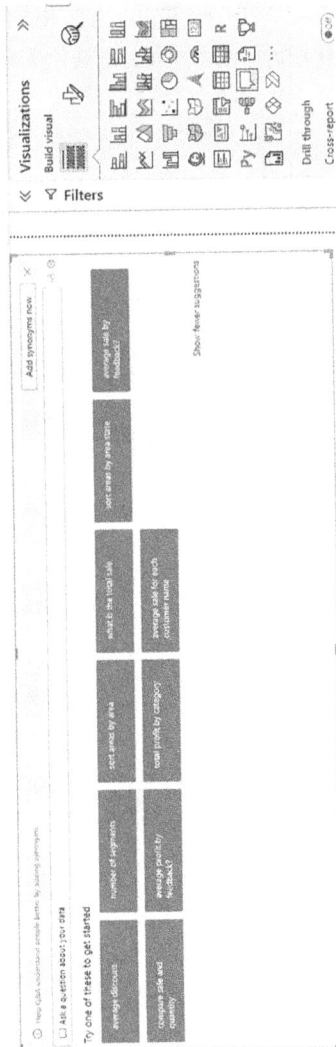

Power BI also provides a feature that allows users to ask questions directly. This feature is indicated by a text prompt, *"Ask a question about your data."* Apart from this feature, Power BI provides suggestions for potential questions, making it easier for users to interact and analyze their data.

Simply type "Total Profit by Category" and see that the visual is switched to display a bar chart showing total profit category-wise across office supplies, technology, and furniture, as shown in Figure 5.26. The length of the bar is proportional to the corresponding profit value for each category.

Figure 5.26 **Q&A Visual**

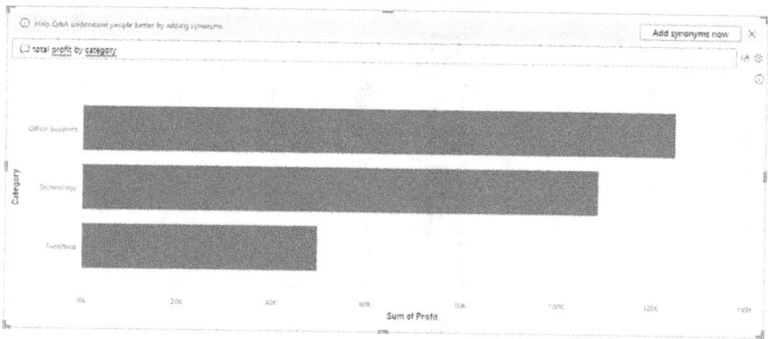

Figure 5.27 shows the Q&A result for Average Sales by Customer Name as a standard visual. This appears when clicking on the "Turn the Q&A result to a standard visual" button located on the right side of the query box. Refer to Figure 5.26 above, you will find two icons on the right side of the query box. The first icon allows you to turn a satisfactory answer into a standard visual.

Figure 5.27 Q&A Result Converted to Standard Visual

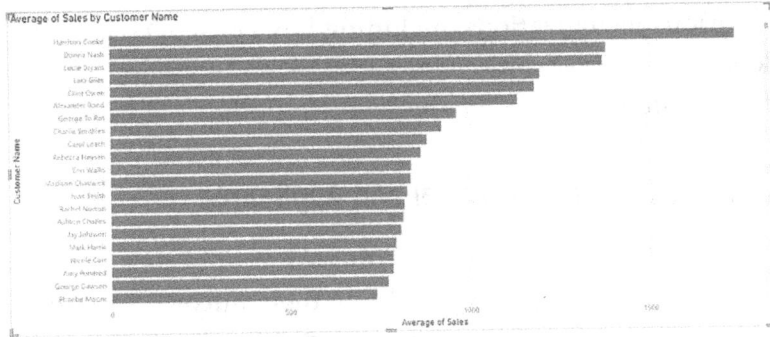

5.9 Power BI Visuals From Analytics

All the visuals discussed so far use data from a data model. However, in some cases, managers cannot get the required information from the visuals generated by transforming data. Such complex data may require advanced analytics to create meaningful visualizations.

In such cases, it is essential to leverage machine learning and other programming languages within Power BI. By doing so, managers can generate accurate visualizations from complex datasets.

The most commonly used programming languages are R and Python. But, before using Python or R visuals in Power BI, we have to install these tools and configure their path in Power BI Desktop. Go to File → Options and Settings → Options → Python scripting or R scripting.

Although Power BI offers a built-in visual for these languages, each of these requires local installation before use in Power BI. The codes associated with each programming language need to be selected in the fields bucket, and users must reference them by name in the code for generating visuals.

Various visualizations, including box plots, 3D scatter plots, etc., can be explored by adding R and Python in Power BI, providing additional value to the reports.

5.9.1 Key Influencers Visual and AppSource

Power BI empowers users with analytical visuals that go beyond standard reporting, helping them uncover insights, patterns, and drivers behind business outcomes. Key Influencers Visual is a tool that can determine which fields influence an outcome most significantly. Those fields must be analyzed, and for this purpose, they are added as influencers.

The result demonstrates how each field is influenced by ranking them. The resulting output ranks these fields based on their level of influence on the outcome. Additionally, it provides detailed metrics, highlighting the field with the highest influence and quantifying its impact in comparison to others.

Further, visualizations display data in bar charts; slicers can be applied to select bars to filter critical influencer visualizations. For example, if analyzing sales performance in Germany, the visual reveals that Customer Segment and Store Type are the top drivers of sales success. This not only adds strategic value but also encourages deeper exploration, isolating critical factors and refining the analysis for different customer groups, time periods, or geographies.

The Key Influencers Visual tool thus aids decision-makers in quickly identifying critical drivers behind key metrics, making the tool valuable for business strategy development.

To further extend the analytical and visualization capabilities in Power BI, users can explore AppSource through any web browser or by choosing the AppSource option from the "More Visuals" menu on the Power BI Desktop. AppSource is an online marketplace by Microsoft that offers a variety of custom visuals that can be integrated into Power BI to enhance reports and dashboards with an additional range of visualization options and tools.

By integrating tools like the Key Influencers Visual and leveraging the extended capabilities from AppSource, Power BI enables decision-makers to analyze data more effectively and present findings with compelling visualizations.

We have explored the Field section and the Format section in the Visualizations pane of Chapter Four, Section 4.2. We have also created a visualization as a line chart in that chapter. Here, we are going to use the Analytics section to add further analysis to the visuals.

For this, once we have the visual ready, like the line chart shown in Figure 5.28 below, navigate to the Analytics section.

Figure 5.28 Line Chart Showing the Sum of Sales by Segment and Sub-Category

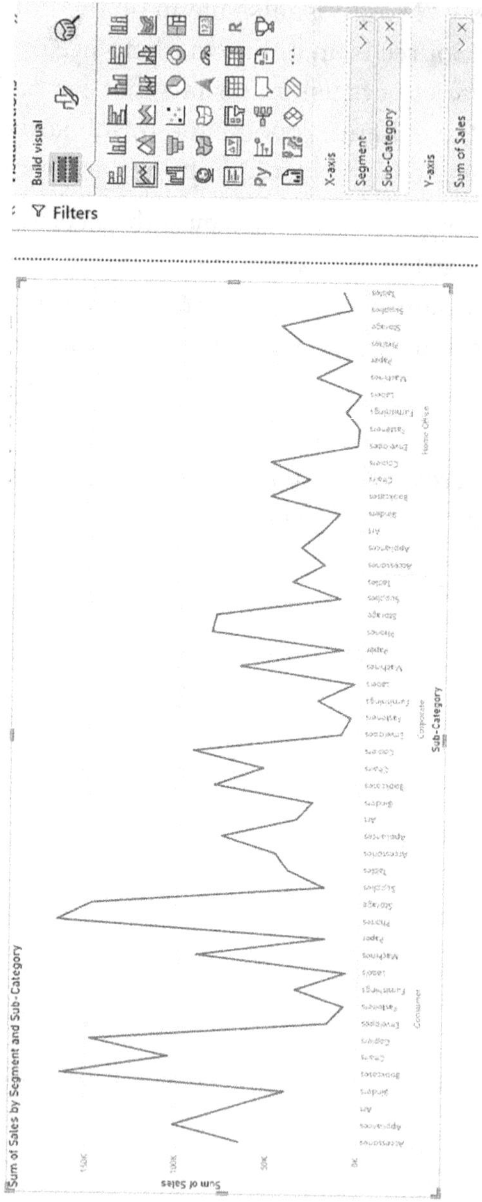

The Analytics section displays seven different lines: Y-axis constant line, Min line, Max line, Average line, Median line, Percentile line, and error bars as shown in Figure 5.29. These can be added to the visual and customized according to the required analysis.

Figure 5.29 **Analytics Section**

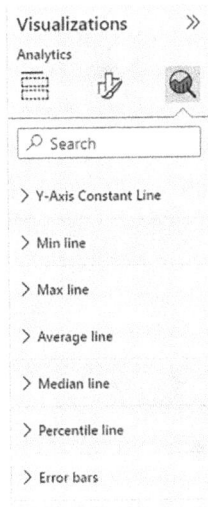

For the visual as shown in Figure 5.30, an Average line can be added by expanding that section and selecting the Add option. Further, the color, name, style as dashed, solid, and dotted, along with the position (in front and behind), can be changed as required. Min line and Max line are also added to the visual, as illustrated in Figure 5.30.

Figure 5.30 Reference Lines in the Analytics Section

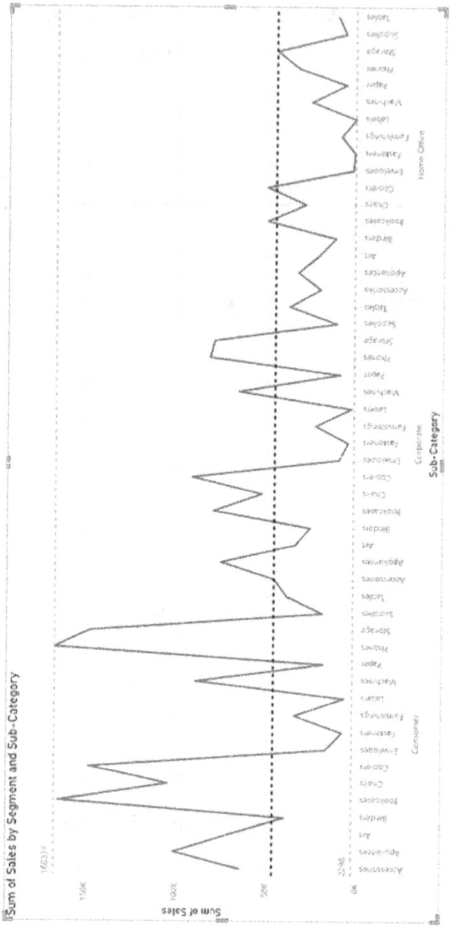

Power BI provides a Top N filter option that will show the visualization's top or bottom number of values. Country-wise total sales can be displayed with a visual, but if we need to display only the top 5 countries based on a chosen measure, we can use the Top N filter, input the value as "5," and apply the filter. The Top N filter can also be used for advanced and range filtering.

Follow these steps to apply the filter:

1. First, select the visual in the Visualizations pane and go to the Filters section.

2. Under the field which we want to filter (e.g., Country), click the drop-down arrow.

3. Then choose Filter type as Top N. Enter the number of items to display.

4. Drag and drop the measure we want to use for ranking (e.g., Sales) into the "By value" field. Click Apply Filter.

As we head towards the final two chapters, let's quickly glance through what we have studied so far across Chapters One to Five. We saw how Power BI can be leveraged for data analysis and visualizations. We explored data, sources of data, and the need to transform data into visualizations. We also understood how to connect Power BI with various data sources like Excel, SQL Server, and the Web.

We learnt how to use the Power BI Query Editor, a powerful tool in Power BI to perform transformations and data cleaning, and discussed various transformation processes, such as filtering, sorting, and merging, with examples.

Further, we learnt about the principles of data modeling and how to create data models that are scalable and flexible. We saw different forms of data visualizations available, and about 27 visualization tools represented with data and examples. We also gained insight into key performance indicators and various formatting options in visualizations, enabling the enrichment of business stories to track business performance, measures, and indicators.

In the upcoming chapter, we will explore how to customize visualizations on a larger scale and geographical context using spatial analysis and precise map visualizations. This is followed by the last chapter, which will introduce the Power BI Desktop, focusing on creating Power BI datasets, reports, and dashboards, and applying a managerial perspective to craft data storytelling with business acumen.

Discussion

- How can businesses use KPIs and formatted visualizations in Power BI to track performance and drive strategic decisions?

- Why is spatial analysis important in data visualization, and how can map-based visualizations help businesses make location-based decisions?

- Based on your learnings so far, what do you think are the most important skills needed to become proficient in Power BI? What areas would you like to explore further?

Chapter Summary

- KPIs are important in visual storytelling, helping business managers monitor and assess organizational performance. They provide a quick snapshot of progress toward strategic goals and highlight areas needing attention.

- Gauge Visuals and KPI Visuals are effective tools for representing performance metrics like targets, thresholds, and actual values. These visuals enhance understanding and make performance tracking intuitive.

- Card Visualization aids in displaying a fundamental value as a visual when managers require one figure to represent the whole quantum of data.

- The shading in Filled Maps shows data density and visually communicates the variations in data density across different regions.

- Shape Maps are best for regional or country-level custom geographies and do not support global maps well due to projection limitations.

- ArcGIS Maps offer rich mapping capabilities such as layers, basemaps, and demographic data. These features support detailed geographical analysis for location-based decision-making.

- The Azure Maps integration facilitates visualization of location intelligence using dynamic maps and real-time data. It supports heatmaps, clustering, and time-based animations for spatial insights and also introduces Q&A visuals, allowing users to ask natural language questions and get instant visual answers. This interactivity makes data exploration more accessible to non-technical users.

- The Analytics pane in Power BI allows users to add dynamic reference lines—such as average, median, trend, and forecast lines—to visuals like line and column charts. These lines help highlight key insights, trends, and thresholds directly within the visual. This enhances data interpretation and supports better decision-making by providing immediate context.

QUIZ

1. **What is the purpose of a Gauge Visual?**
   a. To display detailed tabular data
   b. To show progress toward a specific target or goal
   c. To visualize geographical data
   d. To create a trend line

2. **Which type of data is best suited for a Gauge Visual?**
   a. Time series data
   b. Categorical data
   c. Numerical data with a target value
   d. Textual data

3. **A key advantage of using the Q&A Visual:**
   a. Automates data entry
   b. Displays only tabular data
   c. Limits interaction with data
   d. Allows users to interact with data in a conversational manner

4. **What is a good KPI?**
   a. Specific, measurable, and aligned with goals
   b. Vague and subjective
   c. Based only on qualitative data
   d. Complex and difficult to measure

5. **A key feature of a KPI Visual is to:**
   a. Display the entire dataset in a table format.
   b. Show a comparison between actual performance and a target.
   c. Display multiple categories of data simultaneously.
   d. Visualize trends over time.

6. **Which visual is most commonly used to represent performance against a target?**
   a. KPI Visual
   b. Line Chart
   c. Scatter Plot
   d. Table Visual

7. **What is the application of a Card Visual?**
   a. To show geographical data
   b. To display a single data point or metric prominently
   c. To compare multiple categories
   d. To create trend lines

8. **Identify the advantage of a visual map for geographical data.**
   a. It provides a detailed textual analysis.
   b. It visually represents data distribution across different locations.
   c. It simplifies the data by removing details.
   d. It automatically calculates trends.

9. Select the map visual that displays data points as bubbles on a map.
   a. Filled Map
   b. Shape Map
   c. ArcGIS Map
   d. Bubble Map

10. What is the difference between a Filled Map and a Shape Map?
   a. A Filled Map is used for categorical data, while a Shape Map is for numerical data.
   b. The Filled Map is static, while the Shape Map is interactive.
   c. Filled Map displays regions with color fills, while Shape Map displays outlines of regions.
   d. There is no difference.

Answers

1 – b	2 – c	3 – d	4 – a	5 – b
6 – a	7 – b	8 – b	9 – d	10 – c

This page is intentionally left blank

CHAPTER 6

Tools for Digital Storytelling

Key Learning Objectives

- Explore various storytelling tools, such as Drill Through, Bookmarks, Selection Pane, and Spotlight features for storytelling.
- Gain proficiency in creating custom visualizations to enhance interactive data storytelling, leveraging Power BI.
- Learn how to leverage filters and other Power BI features to craft dynamic digital stories and uncover deeper insights from your data.

Chapters Four and Five explored various visualizations readily available in Power BI to represent and display data models. They explained how cross-filtering and cross-highlighting options make visuals work closely with each other. They presented visualizations using the drag-and-drop reporting system to represent data as pre-built visuals.

However, Power BI also provides features that support data storytelling. It allows managers to navigate multiple pages to explore the required level of detail from the data. Managers can take control of their data in the Power BI dashboard, generate reports and data summaries, and extract deeper insights.

Modern organizations produce massive volumes of data. Storytelling tools in Power BI bridge the gap between these huge volumes of data and actionable insights. They enable users to craft insightful narratives based on the analyses, transforming complex datasets into visually engaging reports and dashboards that are easier to understand and act upon.

In short, storytelling tools simplify data complexity by presenting data in a more structured, visually appealing format. Storytelling in Power BI, with interactive visuals, provides context behind numbers, connecting data trends with real-world implications. For example, linking sales trends to seasonal patterns or market events can drive strategic actions.

Let's explore the various storytelling tools in Power BI and their features that guide managers to create interactive data narratives.

6.1 Drill Through

We have seen how filtering provides different views on a single visual. A slicer can cross-filter a bar chart representing total sales country-wise. A pie chart with sales per country can be filtered, too. Similarly, Drill Through is another powerful and advanced exploration tool for data storytelling in Power BI.

Unlike standard filters, which provide different views within a single visual, Drill Through can be applied at the page level only. A Drill Through tool equips managers to navigate from one visual to another report page while maintaining the filter of the visual.

This tool cannot be used at the visualization or report level and operates exclusively at the page level, which permits managers to move between summary and detail page views. For example, a summary page shall present overall sales across countries. Using the Drill Through option in Power BI, managers can access a detailed breakdown of sales value country-wise. This capability in Power BI provides a focused and contextual view of the data.

Let's understand the Drill Through tool in Power BI with the help of an example:

We assume that a manager is particularly interested in finding the total sales of a specific country in detail. Figure 6.1 shows a pie chart with total sales across many countries and a summary page.

Figure 6.1 Pie Chart With Sum of Sales by Country

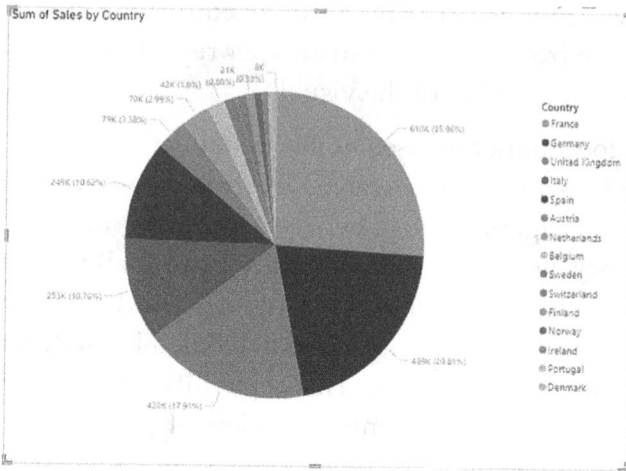

Sum of Sales by Country

Country
● France
● Germany
● United Kingdom
● Italy
● Spain
● Austria
● Netherlands
● Belgium
● Sweden
● Switzerland
● Finland
● Norway
● Ireland
● Portugal
● Denmark

As shown in Figure 6.2, the Drill Through option must be applied to get a detailed report showing sales of that particular country.

Figure 6.2 Drill Through Section

Drill through

Cross-report   ● Off

Keep all filters   On ●

Add drill-through fields here

A Drill Through section has three options:

1. **Cross report:** This option will drill through another report in the Power BI workspace.

2. **Keep all filters:** When this option is enabled, all filter contexts from the visual, along with fields listed in the

bucket list, will be applied; when disabled, only the fields listed in Drill Through will be applied.

3. **Add Drill Through fields here:** When fields are added to this bucket, the visualization will be enabled for a Drill Through automatically, any time on any other page within the same report.

To set up Drill Through in Power BI, you need two pages: a Summary Page (where users start) and a Drill Through Page (where detailed data is displayed). For example, on the Summary Page, you might have a pie chart showing Total Sales by Country.

To enable Drill Through, follow these steps:

1. **Create the Summary Page:** This is where your users will view high-level data, like the Total Sales by Country pie chart.

2. **Create the Drill Through Page:** This page will show more detailed data, such as Sales by City in France, when the user selects France from the pie chart. On this page, drag the Country field into the Drill Through field. This will ensure the page filters by the chosen country.

3. **Enable Drill Through:** On the Summary Page, when a user right-clicks on a country in the pie chart (e.g., France), the Drill Through option will appear. Clicking it will navigate the user to the detailed Drill Through Page, showing only data related to France.

4. **Back Navigation:** Power BI automatically adds a backward arrow to the top of the Drill Through Page, allowing users to return to the Summary Page.

For example, in Figure 6.3, the region is dragged and dropped in the Add drill through bucket. Now, there are three regions: Central, North, and South. Upon selecting South as shown below, the total sales of the South region, showing the sales per country, Italy, Spain, and Portugal, are displayed as a pie chart in the report. Figure 6.4 shows the map representing the city-wise sum of sales.

Figure 6.3 Drill Through for the South Region

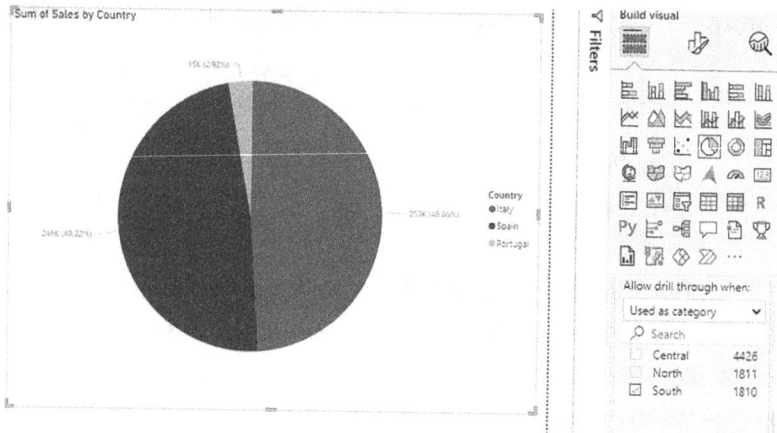

Figure 6.4 **Map Representing the Sum of Sales City-Wise**

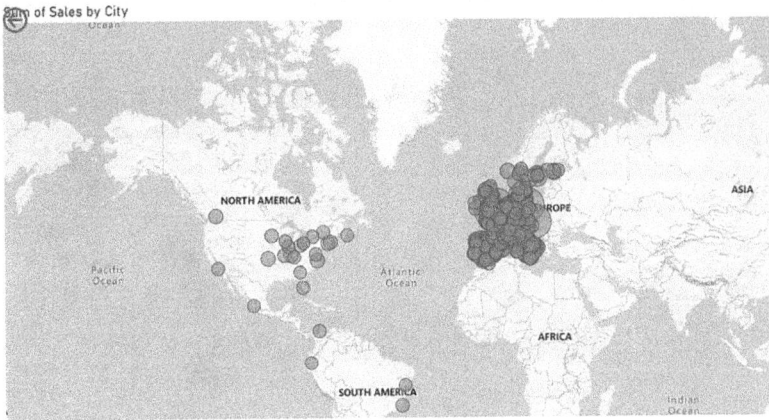

Sum of Sales by City

Now, in the Add drill through bucket shown in Figure 6.5, Country is applied to drill through for a specific country, for example, France.

Figure 6.5 **Drill Through for a Specific Country**

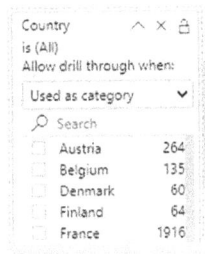

Country	∧ × 🔒
is (All)	
Allow drill through when:	
Used as category	∨
🔍 Search	
Austria	264
Belgium	135
Denmark	60
Finland	64
France	1916

The Sum of Sales in France is shown in Figure 6.6. The backwards arrow, which is automatically added to the page in the upper right-hand corner area, is highlighted in yellow in the figure.

Figure 6.6 Map Drilled Through to the Sum of Sales in France

Drill Through filters are applied at the page level only. They are configured in the Field Section of the Visualization pane. The back arrow at the top-left corner of the Drill Through page enables one to go back to the previous report page seamlessly. Additionally, the Format settings in Power BI offer various other customization options to enhance the visual appearance of the report.

For example, if a Drill Through action is performed in Germany, the detailed data view will appear, as shown in Figure 6.7.

Figure 6.7 Drill Through Field Enabled for Germany

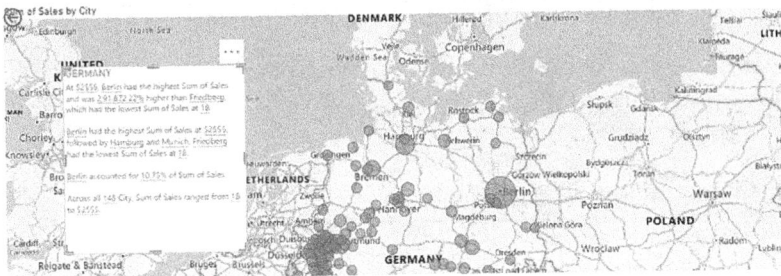

You can summarize the content by right-clicking on the visual and selecting the Summarize option. To view the detailed table, click on the three dots (ellipsis) on that specific visual and choose Show as a table, illustrated in Figure 6.8.

Figure 6.8 Table View for Drill Through

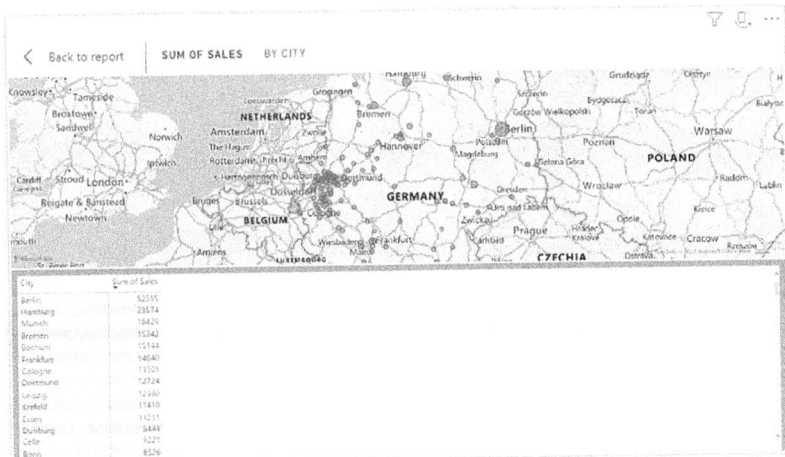

Figures 6.9 to 6.14 illustrate how different filters applied to the report can dynamically alter the sum of sales displayed country-wise. The filters include state, category, segment,

ship mode, subcategory, and feedback. These filters provide a powerful way to interact and drill into the data to uncover specific insights based on selected criteria.

Figure 6.9 focuses on sales within specific states, affecting the country-level totals accordingly.

Figure 6.9 **Sum of Sales by State**

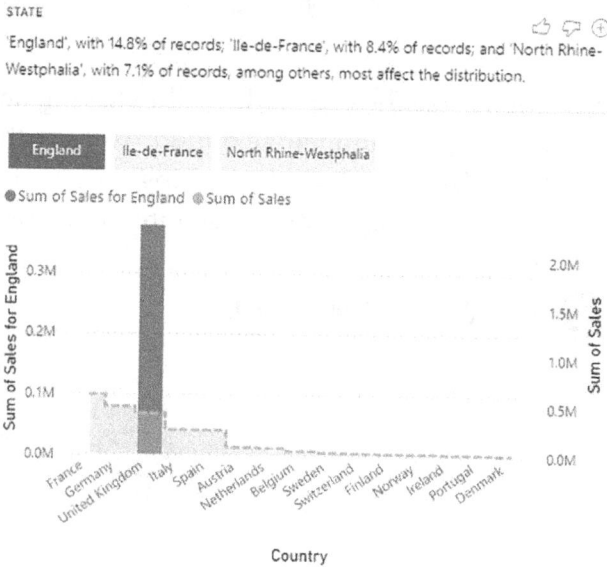

STATE

'England', with 14.8% of records; 'Ile-de-France', with 8.4% of records; and 'North Rhine-Westphalia', with 7.1% of records, among others, most affect the distribution.

Figure 6.10 filters sales data based on product categories such as Furniture, Office Supplies, or Technology.

Figure 6.10 Sum of Sales by Category

CATEGORY

'Office Supplies', with 65.7% of records; 'Furniture', with 15.4% of records; and 'Technology', with 18.9% of records, most affect the distribution.

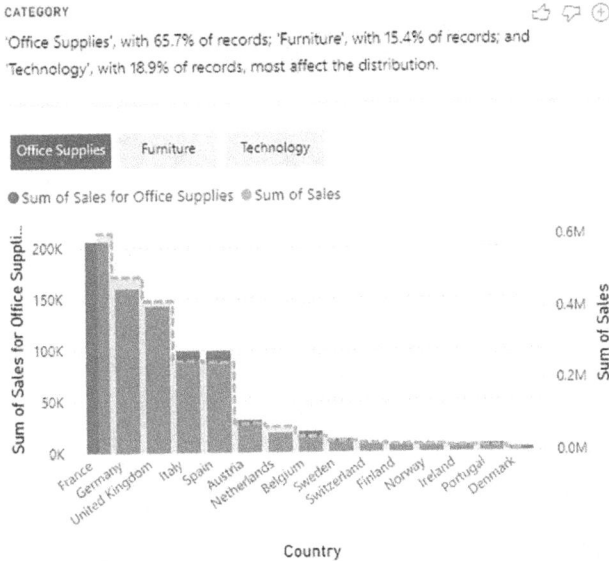

Figure 6.11 enables users to view data based on customer segments like Consumer, Corporate, or Home Office.

Figure 6.11 Sum of Sales by Segment

SEGMENT

'Corporate', with 31.2% of records; 'Consumer', with 51.9% of records; and 'Home Office', with 16.9% of records, most affect the distribution.

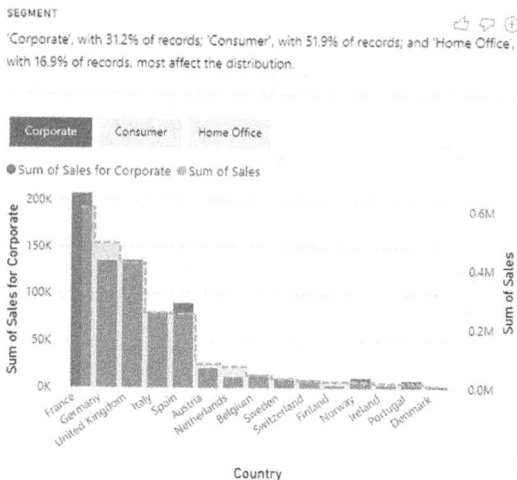

Figure 6.12 adjusts the sales data depending on the chosen delivery method, such as First Class or Standard Class.

Figure 6.12 Sum of Sales by Ship Mode

SHIP MODE

'Economy', with 60.4% of records; 'Economy Plus', with 19.8% of records; and 'Immediate', with 5.3% of records, among others, most affect the distribution.

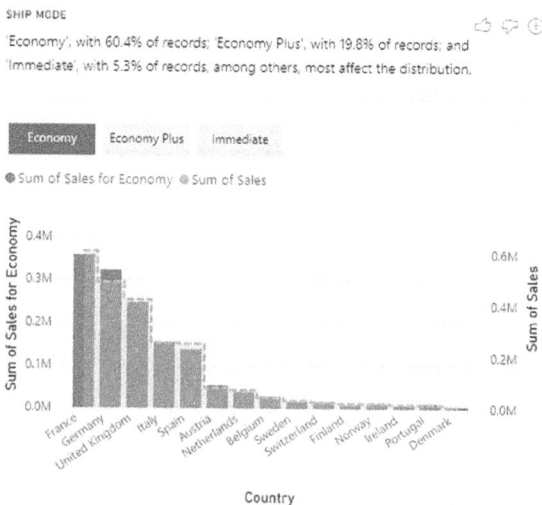

Figure 6.13 provides a more granular filter by focusing on specific sub-categories within each product category.

Figure 6.13 Sum of Sales by Sub-Category

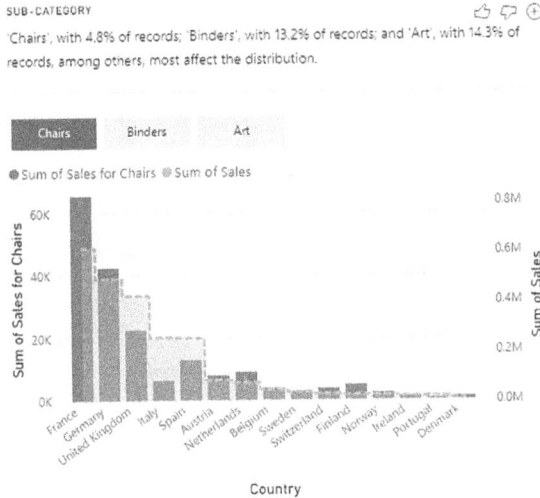

SUB-CATEGORY

'Chairs', with 4.8% of records; 'Binders', with 13.2% of records; and 'Art', with 14.3% of records, among others, most affect the distribution.

Figure 6.14 offers an additional layer of filtering based on customer feedback, helping to link qualitative input with sales performance.

Figure 6.14 Sum of Sales by Feedback

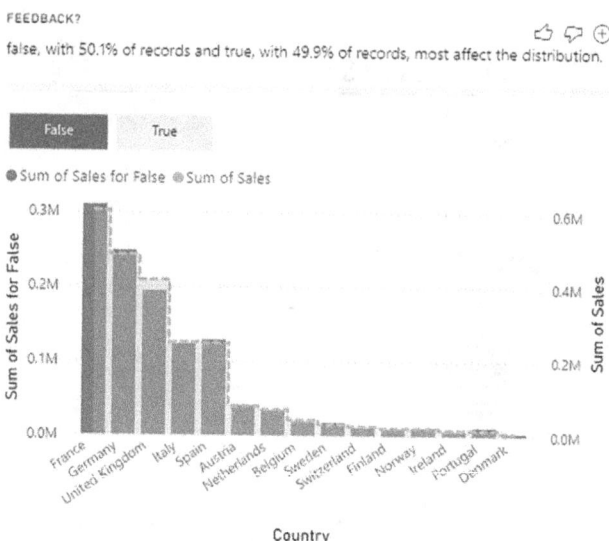

FEEDBACK?

false, with 50.1% of records and true, with 49.9% of records, most affect the distribution.

The Drill Through tool allows a deep dive into the data for more precise digital data storytelling. As more pages are added to the report, they can be connected to interact with one another. This is done by applying Drill Through filters across the report to provide greater clarity.

> **FUN FACT**
>
> Drill Through in Power BI is like a secret door unlocking deeper insights. Users can create a hidden report page that only appears when someone clicks on specific data points.

6.2 Curated Storytelling With Bookmarks

Another very interactive way to present data and visualizations in Power BI is through bookmarks. While Drill Through enables customizations in presenting data and visuals, bookmarks enable curated storytelling for when managers must see data in a particular way in a report. They provide many dimensions to how managers view the data.

Bookmarks save the current filters and spotlight visuals as they appear at the moment of creation.

Bookmarks represent the entire state of a report page, with all filters, and maintain the properties of the visual. The Bookmarks tool is in the View ribbon pane; see Figure 6.15.

Figure 6.15 Bookmarks in View Option

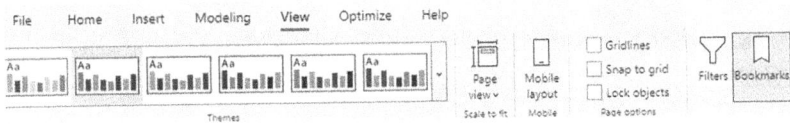

When selecting bookmarks, a new pane, as shown in Figure 6.16, will appear on the left side of the Visualizations pane.

Figure 6.16 Bookmarks Pane

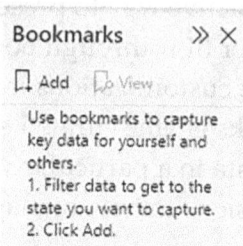

Bookmarks   » ✕

⬜ Add   ⬜ View

Use bookmarks to capture
key data for yourself and
others.
1. Filter data to get to the
state you want to capture.
2. Click Add.

Since bookmarks are not created, the only option is to add them via the Add button at the top of the Bookmarks pane. An analyst can develop the report page with all the filters and visuals and then click Add to save these settings as a bookmark. To start with, create a line chart showing the trend of profit and sales. Again, add a slicer using the region field from the Field pane.

The slicer then filters the bar and line chart using the cross-filtering option in Power BI. Figure 6.17 shows the slicer applied to the bar and line chart.

Figure 6.17 Slicer Applied to a Bar Chart and Line Chart

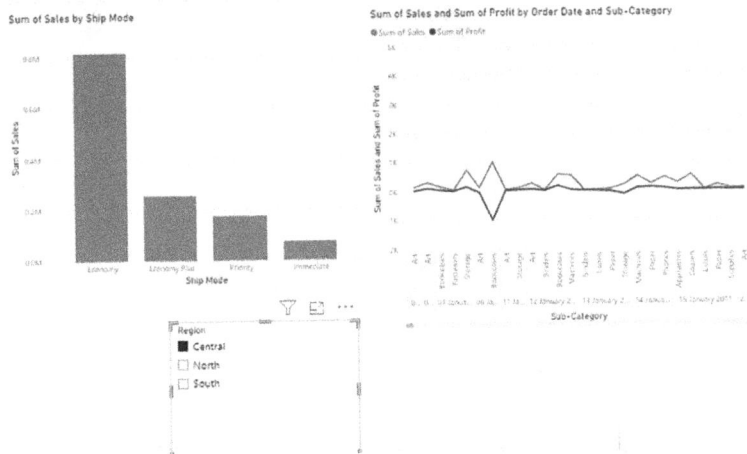

Sum of Sales by Ship Mode

Sum of Sales and Sum of Profit by Order Date and Sub-Category

---

POINT TO REMEMBER

Bookmarks in Power BI don't just save report views, but they let you create interactive presentations, switching between data insights.

When visuals are in place, bookmarks can be created in the Report Canvas. A straightforward option is to filter a specific country and select the Add option inside the Bookmarks pane. Figure 6.18 shows bookmarks applied to a particular country, for example, France.

Figure 6.18 Bookmark Options Filtering for Specific Country

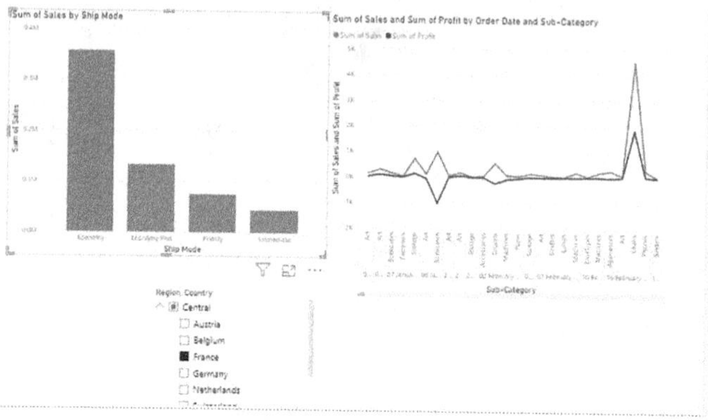

Similarly, bookmarks can be used for each report page. The filter options can be changed and switched within the bookmarks. Figure 6.19 shows the switching option region-wise to identify the sales and profit country-wise and the shipment mode. It also displays the page-level filters within bookmarks.

Figure 6.19 Page-Level Filter Option Within Bookmarks

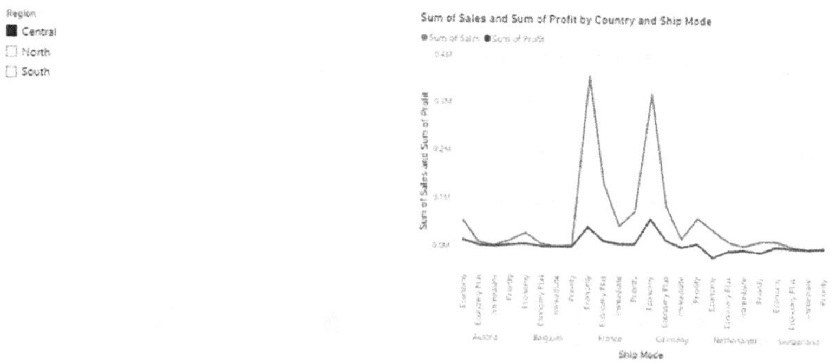

The Options menu in the Bookmarks pane includes options like "Update," which can overwrite bookmark settings, resetting to the current state of the report. The next option is "Rename," which would edit the bookmark's name.

Another option is the "Delete" option that enables removing a bookmark. Whereas, enabling the "Data" option aids in retaining the current state of the filter's pane and allows the selection of specific visuals.

The next option is the "Display" option, which, when enabled, supports the bookmark to retain the visual properties, especially the visibility and spotlight features, which will be discussed in the upcoming section.

Selecting the current page takes users to the page where the bookmark is created and applies data and display settings according to the bookmark. If the current page is disabled, the bookmark will only function when the user is already on the page where the bookmark was created.

When all visual options are selected, all visuals on the page will be included in the bookmark. When the "Selected Visuals" option is chosen, the bookmark will update only the selected visuals, whether visible or hidden. Only the visuals that are chosen will be stored. The options discussed above are listed in Figure 6.20 below:

Figure 6.20 Options Menu in Bookmark

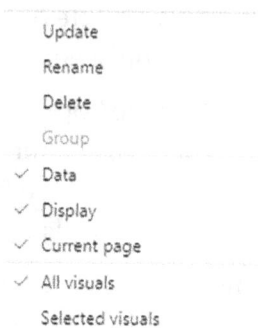

Update

Rename

Delete

Group

✓ Data

✓ Display

✓ Current page

✓ All visuals

Selected visuals

In short, a Bookmark in Power BI lets you capture and save a specific view of your report, including filters, visuals, and their visibility.

6.3 Digital Storytelling With Selection Pane and Spotlight Features

Selection pane and Spotlight features are the two properties of Bookmarks that are closely related. Let's look at their individual features.

6.3.1 Selection pane

The Selection pane is present in the View tab of the Report View. This pane enables certain textboxes to be kept hidden on the report page and, on the other hand, allows specific text boxes to be visible when associated with a bookmark. Figure 6.21 shows the selection pane and bookmarks pane in the Report View.

Figure 6.21 Selection and Bookmarks Pane

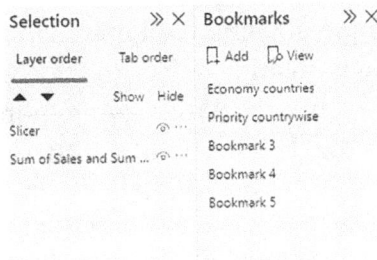

The Selection pane displays all objects on the report page; selecting an object from this pane provides access to the properties associated with that object. The same report page can be reused to display the same data with different visuals, making efficient use of limited space.

Refer to Figure 6.22, where two text boxes are created for the report page. One is visible for the bookmarks, and the other is hidden.

Figure 6.22 Selection Pane Showing Visibility and Hidden Layers

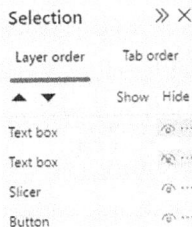

The icons near the objects can be toggled between visible options, shown as an eye symbol and hidden as a dash symbol. The Selection pane is commonly used with bookmarks to develop report pages. It permits specific features to be displayed as visuals when selecting properties from the Selection pane.

A simple example of using Bookmarks in Power BI with the Selection pane is creating a "Show/Hide Chart" button. Suppose you have a bar chart displaying monthly sales, and you want users to toggle its visibility with a click. Follow these steps:

1. Use the Selection pane to hide the chart for one view and show it for another.

2. Create two bookmarks: one with the chart visible and one with it hidden.

3. Add a button (like "Show Chart" or "Hide Chart") and link it to the corresponding bookmark.

When users click the button, the chart appears or disappears instantly, making your report cleaner and more interactive without having to switch pages.

6.3.2 Spotlight

The second feature associated with Bookmarks is the Spotlight option to highlight stories in data visualizations. The Spotlight option, as shown in Figure 6.23, is accessed through the ellipsis, a three-dot menu icon in the top right-hand corner of the visual. You can view the ellipsis in Figure 6.24 on the right side, where three dots are highlighted.

Figure 6.23 Spotlight Option

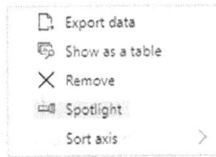

- Export data
- Show as a table
- ✕ Remove
- Spotlight
- Sort axis   >

Spotlight draws attention to critical insights by highlighting key visuals in a report. It brings attention to the specific visual by making all the other visuals fade into the background. Only the spotlighted visual is highlighted, and the rest fades. Figure 6.24 shows the highlighted visual on applying the spotlight, and the other visual is seen as faded.

Figure 6.24 Applying Spotlight to Highlight the Specific Visual

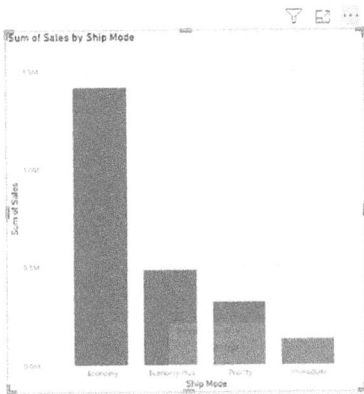

Focus mode is another option, and an alternative to the Spotlight for highlighting particular data details and curating stories from visualizations (refer to Fig. 6.25).

Figure 6.25 Focus Mode

The Focus mode can also be saved as a bookmark, and both horizontal and vertical layouts can be displayed as shown in Figures 6.26 and 6.27, respectively.

Figure 6.26 Horizontal Layout in Focus Mode

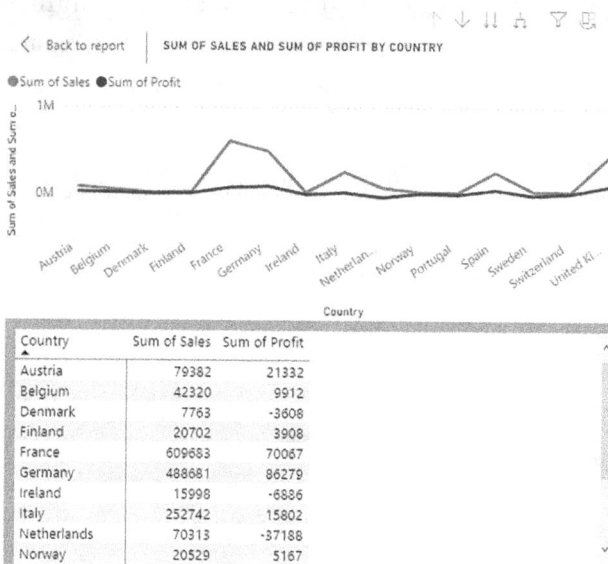

⟨ Back to report | SUM OF SALES AND SUM OF PROFIT BY COUNTRY

● Sum of Sales ● Sum of Profit

Country	Sum of Sales	Sum of Profit
Austria	79382	21332
Belgium	42320	9912
Denmark	7763	-3608
Finland	20702	3908
France	609683	70067
Germany	488681	86279
Ireland	15998	-6886
Italy	252742	15802
Netherlands	70313	-37188
Norway	20529	5167

Figure 6.27 Vertical Layout in Focus Mode

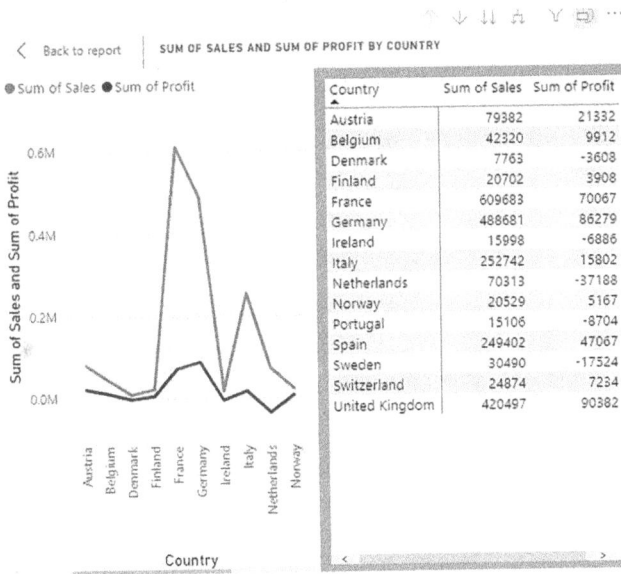

Country	Sum of Sales	Sum of Profit
Austria	79382	21332
Belgium	42320	9912
Denmark	7763	-3608
Finland	20702	3908
France	609683	70067
Germany	488681	86279
Ireland	15998	-6886
Italy	252742	15802
Netherlands	70313	-37188
Norway	20529	5167
Portugal	15106	-8704
Spain	249402	47067
Sweden	30490	-17524
Switzerland	24874	7234
United Kingdom	420497	90382

6.3.3 Other smart ways to view Bookmarks

Bookmarks can also be viewed in a slideshow mode. There is an option named View to the right of the Add button in the bookmark that puts up new icons at the bottom of the report page.

Figure 6.28 shows bookmarks 6 out of 8, which can be used to tailor stories about data. The order can be changed by dragging and dropping bookmarks into the desired order.

Figure 6.28 View Options in Available Bookmarks

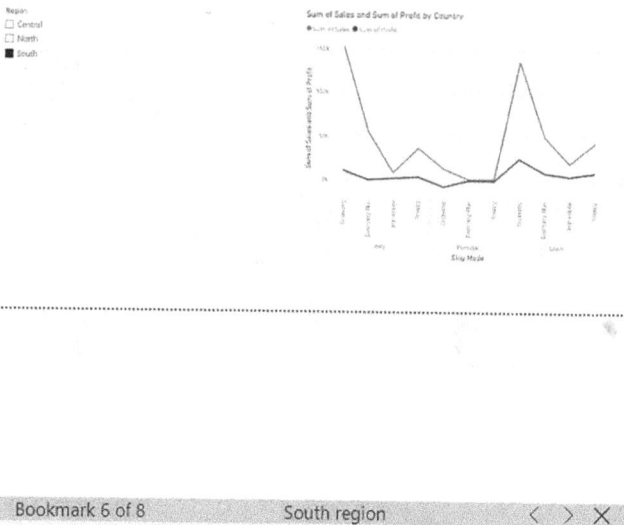

Bookmark 6 of 8   South region   < > X

Finally, click the Exit option icon shown in Figure 6.29 in the Bookmarks pane to exit.

Figure 6.29 Exit Option in Bookmarks

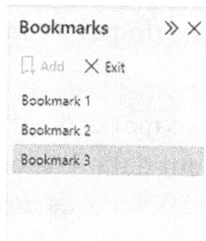

The same report page can be reused for the same data with different visuals when space is pressed. A chart and table can be created on the same page without creating new pages for the same data. Both visuals will be on the same page, and the required visual can be made accessible and visible by hiding the other visual.

6.3.4 Switching between Chart View and Table View

In this section, we will explore the process and advantages of switching between Table View and Chart View bookmarks for easy navigation. When different views of the same data need to be displayed, both a chart and a table can be displayed on the same report page, as shown in Figure 6.30.

Figure 6.30 Table and Bar Chart Displayed on the Same Report Page

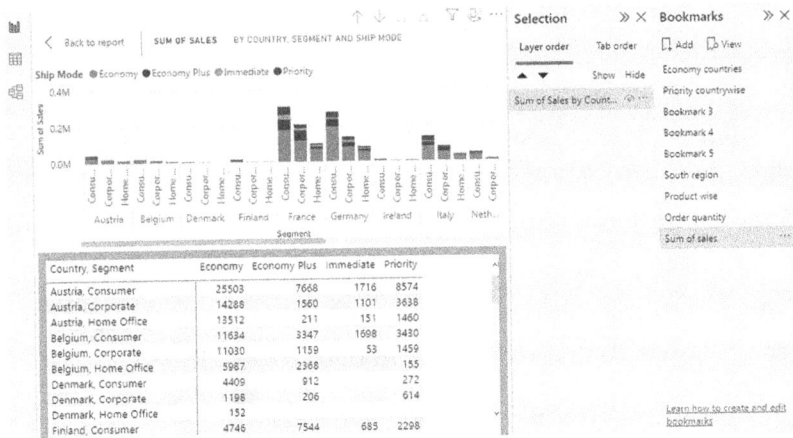

However, we can bookmark only the visual and not the data. For this, refer to the following steps:

Step 1: Create a new bookmark and rename it as Chart View. Ensure that the data option is not selected from the bookmarks option and only the visual is displayed (Fig. 6.31).

Figure 6.31 Chart View Bookmark With Data Option Removed

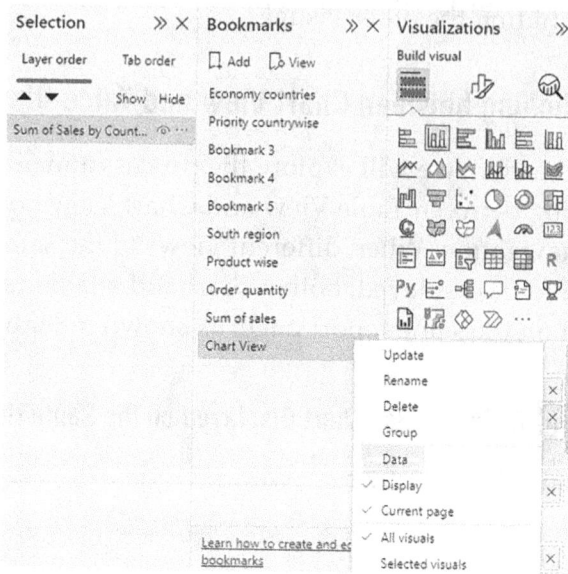

Step 2: Create another bookmark named Table View. Hide the stacked column chart and ensure the data option is disabled in the bookmark settings.

In this way, two different ways of displaying the same data within the same report page can be enabled to curate stories about data for managerial decision-making.

However, this requires switching between Table View and Chart View bookmarks. To make it more user-friendly, a clickable button option can be added to the report to enable easy switching between the bookmarks.

Step 3: Navigate to the Insert ribbon, as shown in Figure 6.32, and click Image in the Elements section. This will launch a file browser to select an image file that has to be added to the Report Canvas.

Figure 6.32 Image Button in the Elements Section of the Insert Ribbon

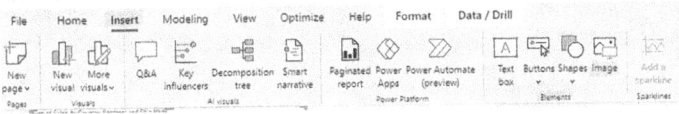

Step 4: In the Format section, turn the Title ON and rename the image to Chart Button for easy identification. Then turn the Title OFF to hide it from the Report View as displayed in Figure 6.33.

Figure 6.33 Title Disabled on the Chart Button

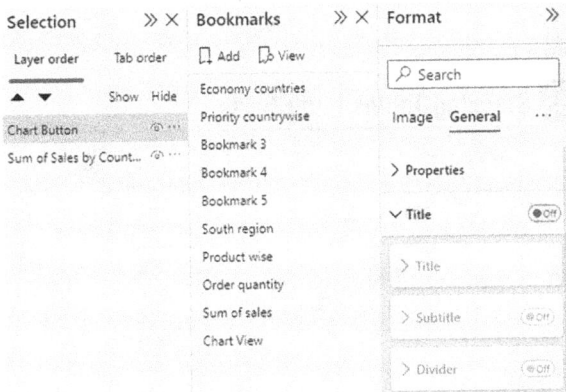

Step 5: Click the image button from the Insert ribbon to launch a file browser and select a table.

Step 6: From the Format section, turn the Title ON to rename the image as Table button and then turn the Title OFF, as shown in Figure 6.34. This helps to distinguish between the buttons.

Figure 6.34 Title Disabled on Table Button

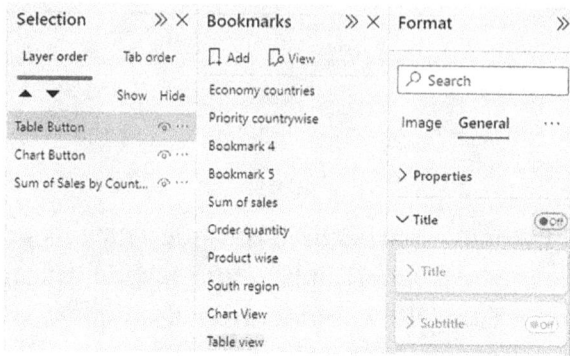

Step 7: The images/visuals need to be stacked by providing space for each visualization, as shown in Figure 6.35

Figure 6.35 Stacking Tables and Charts

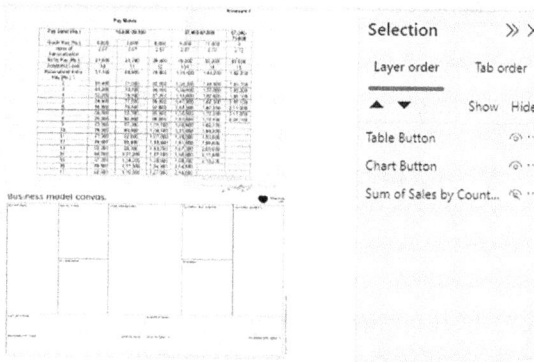

The images must be turned into buttons to enable easy toggling between the Chart View and Table View bookmarks.

Step 8: Select the Chart View bookmark and hide the table button in the Selection pane to do this. Again, select the ellipsis for the Chart View bookmark, as shown in Figure 6.36, and choose the update option.

Figure 6.36 **Update Option in Chart View, Turning Off the Table Button**

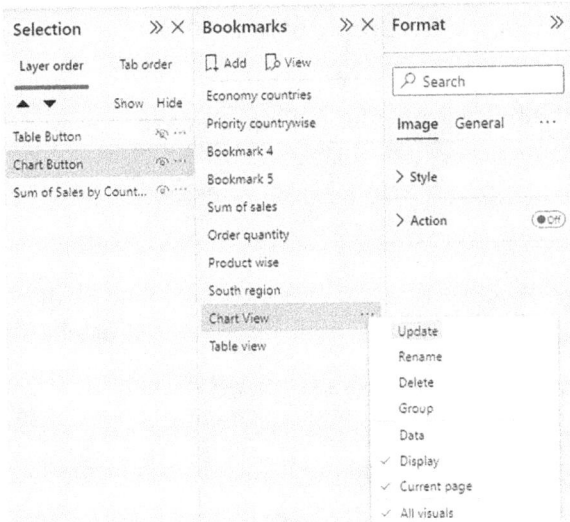

Similarly,

Step 9: The exact change has to be made to the Table View bookmark by selecting it and hiding the Chart button image in the Selection pane, then choosing the update option from the Bookmarks ellipsis of the Table View.

Step 10: Next, assign an action to the respective image within the bookmarks, allowing analysts to click on the chart button image, visible on the Chart View bookmark, and then toggle to the Table View bookmark.

Step 11: Click the Table button image, which is visible in the Table View bookmark. This will take you to the Chart

View bookmark. When the Table View bookmark is selected and the table button image is highlighted, the Visualizations pane will switch to the Format tab.

Step 12: Now, Action properties in the format image need to be expanded, and switched to ON mode from the top drop-down; select the bookmark and select Chart View against the Bookmark drop-down as shown in Figure 6.37.

Figure 6.37 Action Properties in Format Image

After enabling the Action properties, follow these steps:

Step 13: Click the Table button, and the image will be taken to the Chart View bookmark, making it look like a static image controlled with an interactive button.

Step 14: Holding the control key on the keyboard and clicking the image would then take you to the Chart View bookmark; left-click the image to move to the Chart View bookmark.

Figure 6.38 Chart View and Table View Bookmark

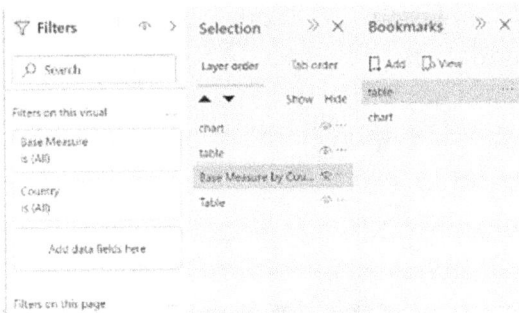

Step 15: Enabling Bookmarks and the Selection pane enhances digital storytelling. It allows users to switch between Chart View and Table View on the same report page, as shown in Figure 6.38 above. Using a single report page with these digital storytelling tools, managers can present data and visualizations to effectively curate stories for business thinking.

6.4 Tooltips as Tools for Storytelling

In Power BI, Tooltips serve as a powerful storytelling tool by offering contextual information when users move over a visual. They allow users to explore data more deeply and interpret insights with greater clarity. Complementing Tooltips are Value Labels that play an equally important role in storytelling.

Value labels are data points displayed directly on visualizations like bars, lines, or columns to enhance clarity. For example, consider a bar chart showing "Sales by Region." Value labels here would display the exact sales number on top of each bar, say, USD 1440.

Value labels facilitate easy and quick interpretation of data in charts, graphs, and maps. For example, in a bar chart, value labels display the exact sales figures country-wise or for each product category. In a line chart, they can show the exact values of profits over specific months, and in a pie chart, value labels display both the percentage share and the actual values for each slice.

Value labels are often kept in ON mode to display details in the visuals. Still, most of the time, it clutters the visual, especially when there are a lot of visuals on a single report page. The visual may seem smaller as it holds all the labels.

In such cases, Tooltips solve the problem of cluttering. Tooltips are a functionality in Power BI that enables managers to see precise information about a visual while moving the mouse around the Report Canvas. Tooltips are unique because they equip managers to see the information for only the datasets they are interested in. This is done by specifying a report page as a tooltip for a specific visual.

For example, in a Power BI report, you have a bar chart showing profit by country. When you hover over a bar representing a specific country, a tooltip appears displaying additional information such as total profit, segment-wise profits, category, sales value, and other associated fields for that country. This enables users to quickly access more detailed data without clicking, enhancing interactivity and providing more context on demand.

Such default Tooltips are automatically generated, making them a quick way to convey underlying data at a glance. While default tooltips provide quick insights, Power BI also allows you to design "custom report page tooltips" for more advanced, context-rich information.

Report page tooltips allow for more customized and detailed information, including visuals, filters, and can be formatted to suit specific user needs. The tooltip from the Format section needs to be switched to ON mode on the report page. In the tooltips section, as shown in Figure 6.39, there is an option as "Type," which needs to be set as Report Page.

Figure 6.39 Tooltips in the Format Visual

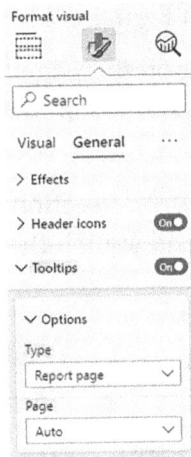

Further, to enable Power BI to choose the appropriate page, the setting has to be set to Auto.

In some reports, users may prefer to view data either in a tabular format or as a visual chart. To provide this flexibility, we can create two buttons in our Power BI report: the first button to switch from Chart View to Table View and the second button to switch from Table View to Chart View. This setup ensures users can toggle between views seamlessly without navigating away or manually changing visuals.

To implement this, bookmarks are used in Power BI. As learnt in Section 6.2, Bookmarks capture the current state of a report page, including visible visuals, filters, and selections. By assigning a bookmark to each button, we can enable users to switch views with a single click. This interactivity improves user experience and makes the report more dynamic and user-friendly.

Let's follow this step-by-step guide to enable Tooltips:

Step 1: Create a new page in the Report Canvas, and name it as Tooltip as shown in Figure 6.40.

Step 2: Right-clicking on the page name and selecting the "hidden" option blocks users from navigating to that page directly.

Step 3: Now, in the Format section, expand the page information properties and switch the Tooltip to ON mode as shown in Figure 6.40.

Figure 6.40 Page Information Property

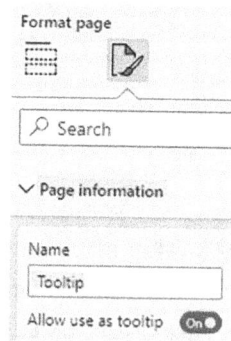

Step 4: Also, expand page size properties and change the type to Tooltip. The size of the Report Canvas is smaller now due to the scaling applied.

Step 5: If actual size is required, the View ribbon on the page view option, as shown in Figure 6.41, must change to Actual size.

Figure 6.41 Actual Size Fitting in Page View

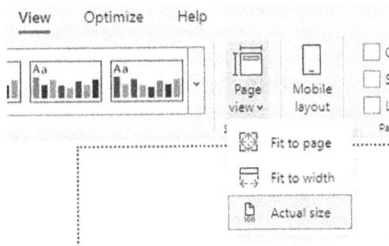

Step 6: On top of the Report Canvas page, create a card showing the sum of profits based on the store data sheet.

Step 7: At the bottom of the canvas, make a pie chart showing the sum of earnings by dragging the segment to the legend bucket to display the sum of the sales segment-wise. Figure 6.42 shows the card and pie chart visuals.

Figure 6.42 Adding a Tooltip for Visualization to a Report Page

Step 8: To add a filter based on location, deselect both visuals by clicking on the blank space and adding Country from the Field to the Tooltip bucket in the Visualizations pane.

Step 9: The sum of profit for the country Germany is shown in Figure 6.43 by applying the tooltip country-wise.

Figure 6.43 Tooltip Applied to the Visualization for a Specific Country

Step 10: Take the summary page from the Report Canvas.

Step 11: Select the stacked column chart.

Step 12: Move to the Format section in the Visualizations pane to locate the tooltip as shown in Figure 6.44 to switch it to ON mode.

Figure 6.44 Tooltip Properties

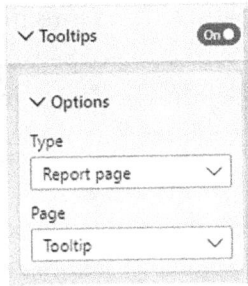

Step 13: Select the Report page in Type and Tooltip in the Page property. After enabling this, when the cursor is taken to the stacked column chart, the visual tooltip created will appear as shown in Figure 6.45, with the country passed as a filter to the tooltip. The settings of the tooltip can be modified to provide relevant information, extending the Tooltip functionality.

Figure 6.45 Getting a Visual Tooltip as a Filter for a Visualization

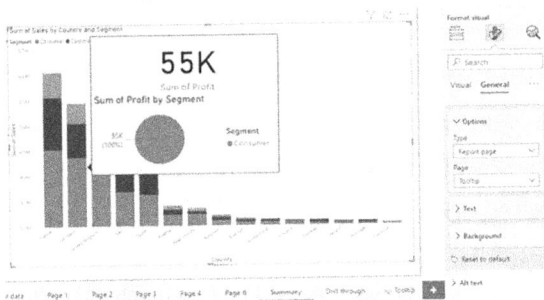

Tooltips in Power BI are a valuable tool to highlight important details and improve readability and focus. They help users streamline complex information and highlight essential details with ease.

In this chapter, we explored digital storytelling tools in Power BI, which add depth and clarity to data visualizations. These capabilities transform data into more than static visuals—they create a narrative experience. By using them, users can tailor reports and presentations to convey interactive insights.

In the final chapter of this book, we will explore "Reporting," which is the cornerstone of Power BI and one of the most critical components of business decision-making.

DISCUSSION QUESTIONS

1. In what situations would you use Bookmarks versus the Selection pane?

2. How can the Spotlight feature be used to present insights to stakeholders?

3. What challenges may arise when using filters and custom visuals, and how can they be addressed?

Chapter Summary

- Power BI offers features that enable managers to take control of data and generate comprehensive reports in the form of stories.

- Drill Through allows users to view detailed information related to a specific data point on another page.

- Bookmarks help capture and return to specific views for storytelling.

- The Selection pane manages visibility and layering of visuals, while Spotlight highlights a chosen visual to focus audience attention.

- The use of custom visualizations, along with filters and visuals, enables deeper insights into selected data and facilitates impactful communication within organizations.

- By leveraging visuals and filters, more data can be used to provide vast insights for dynamic and interactive digital storytelling.

- The Tooltips feature allows users to hover over data points and instantly view additional information, enhancing interactivity. This feature provides detailed context without cluttering the main report, making it easier for users to explore specific data points, such as sales or order totals, on demand.

QUIZ

1. The purpose of the Drill Through feature is:

   a. To export data to Excel
   b. To allow users to navigate to a detailed report from a summarized view
   c. To create a new dataset
   d. To highlight specific data points

2. Drill Through is most beneficial when:

   a. Displaying time series data
   b. Providing users with a detailed view of a specific data category
   c. Comparing two datasets
   d. Visualizing geographical data

3. Which of the following needs to be created in a Power BI report to use the Drill Through feature?

   a. A separate dataset
   b. A dedicated Drill Through page
   c. A new Power BI workspace
   d. A static table

4. Why do we use Bookmarks in Power BI?

   a. To save specific views of reports for later use
   b. To share reports via email
   c. To export data to a CSV file
   d. To create a static visual

5. **How do Bookmarks enhance storytelling in reports?**
    a. By allowing users to toggle between different report states and views
    b. By removing unnecessary data points
    c. By exporting data to Excel
    d. By limiting interactivity in reports

6. **Bookmarks create a guided storytelling experience by:**
    a. Linking a series of Bookmarks to create a narrative flow through the report
    b. Disabling user interaction
    c. Displaying all data on one page
    d. Exporting the report as a PDF

7. **What is the function of the Selection pane?**
    a. To filter data within a report
    b. To manage the visibility of report elements
    c. To import data from Excel
    d. To create new visuals

8. **What is the Spotlight feature in Power BI?**
    a. A tool to export data
    b. A feature that highlights a specific visual or object
    c. A method for creating new data columns
    d. A technique for importing data from the Web

9. **How is the Spotlight feature used in a Power BI presentation?**

   a. By focusing the audience's attention on key visuals during a presentation
   b. By hiding all data
   c. By creating a new report
   d. By exporting the report to PDF

10. **What is the purpose of Tooltips?**

    a. To display additional information
    b. To create a new data model
    c. To export data
    d. To remove data from the report

Answers

1 – b	2 – b	3 – b	4 – a	5 – a
6 – a	7 – b	8 – b	9 – a	10 – a

CHAPTER 7

Deploying Reports in Power BI

Key Learning Objectives

- Learn how to deploy reports from Power BI Desktop to the Power BI Service.
- Understand how to pin elements to the dashboard with real-time data and Q&A features to generate reports.
- Explore managing dashboards on mobile devices and setting up dashboard subscriptions.
- Learn to view and manage datasets, workbooks, dashboards, and reports in My Workspace.

Power BI follows a freemium model, offering most features in its free version, but when it comes to sharing data, it requires an update to the Power BI Pro edition. The previous chapters provided detailed guidance on creating visualizations for digital storytelling within report pages. The next step is to share these reports with stakeholders.

This chapter discusses deploying reports from the Power BI Desktop to the Power BI Service. Pinning elements to the dashboard to generate reports, adding real-time data, and adding a Q&A feature in the dashboard are also detailed in the chapter.

It introduces the application of workspaces in managing and delivering content to users in the Power BI Service. Enabling dashboards in mobile devices and options for dashboard subscriptions are also highlighted. Viewing reports, datasets, workbooks, and dashboards in My Workspace, along with managing security issues, will also be covered in the chapter.

7.1 Deploying Reports Using Power BI Desktop

Power BI supports a wide range of data sources such as Excel, SQL databases, and the Web, allowing users to consolidate information from multiple platforms into a single report. Power BI simplifies report creation to build and deploy dashboards and visuals through Power BI Desktop.

It also allows users to share reports with collaborators through Power BI Service, and its scalability supports both small and large organizations. In this section, let's understand how to deploy reports in Power BI.

A simple method to deploy reports from the Power BI Desktop to the Power BI Service is to click the Publish button in the desktop application, as shown in Figure 7.1. This requires signing in with an existing account if not previously done.

Figure 7.1   Sign-in Option to Publish a Report

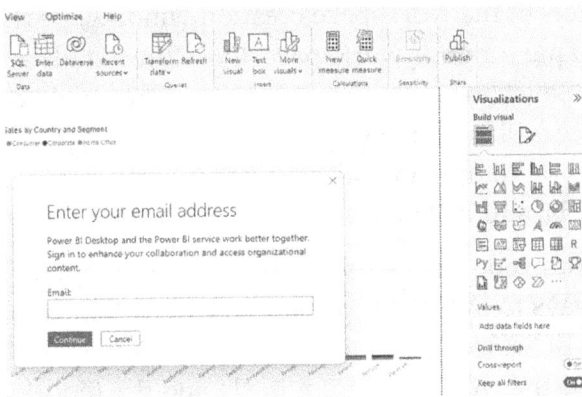

Power BI Service includes a prominently highlighted feature, My Workspace, consisting of dashboards, reports, and datasets. We will explore My Workspace in detail in Section 7.2. The Workspace is an area in the Power BI Service that is like a folder and can bundle reports, datasets, and dashboards, as shown in Figure 7.2. It can also assign security to the workspace to secure the data.

Figure 7.2   My Workspace View of Report and Data

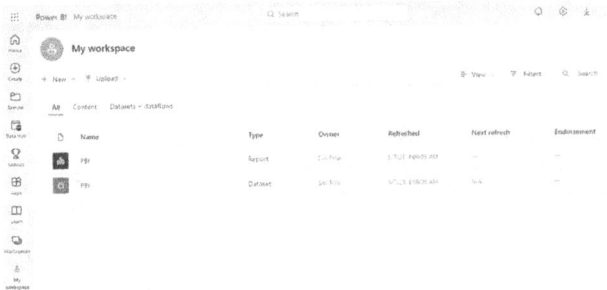

To create a workspace, on the left-hand navigation pane, click on "Workspaces," and then select Create → New Workspace. In the workspace creation window, provide a unique name for your workspace. Once the details are filled in, click "Save" to create the workspace. The newly created workspace will now be listed under your workspaces, allowing you to upload and organize reports, datasets, dashboards, and collaborate with team members seamlessly.

Once our report is ready in Power BI Desktop, there are several ways to publish and share it. One option is to publish to Power BI Service. For this, click File → Publish → Power BI. Choose the workspace to publish, and the report is now available on the Power BI web platform.

| Figure 7.3 | Publishing Report to Power BI |

Publishing to Power BI   ✕

✓ Success!

Open 'PBI.pbix' in Power BI

Get Quick Insights

Did you know?
You can create a portrait view of your report, tailored for mobile phones.
On the **View** tab, select **Mobile Layout**. Learn more

Got it

For example, if one selects My Workspace, it will send the report and its data to the personal workspace. The Upload time here depends on how large the dataset is. Next, there are two options: Open the report and get quick insights. The "Open the report" option lets you view and interact with the report in the Power BI Service, while "Get quick insights" runs AI-generated analysis to highlight key patterns in your data.

Before we understand the creation of reports through dashboards further, let's learn how dashboards work in Power BI through the following section:

7.1.1 Dashboards functionality in Power BI

A dashboard is a single-page canvas that uses visualizations to tell a story. Limited to just one page, a dashboard is well-designed to contain only the most important elements of that story. It is a high-level summary of business metrics or KPIs.

The dashboard brings together all elements and variables, such as total sales quantity, discount, total products, and customer satisfaction, onto a single canvas.

Dashboards are best for quick insights and summaries, whereas reports are best for in-depth analysis. An example of a dashboard is shown in Figure 7.4 below.

Figure 7.4   Pinning Elements to the Dashboard

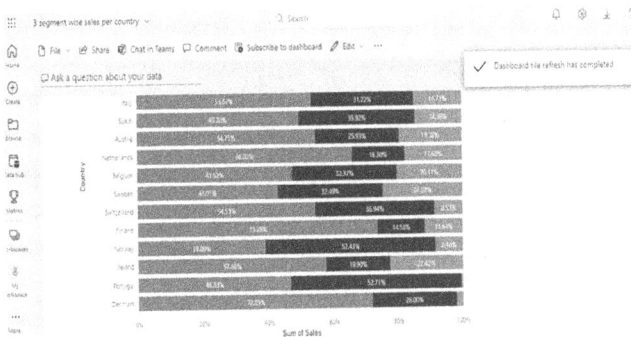

Next, let's explore the various common features of dashboards in Power BI for reporting:

1. Pin to Dashboard

The most important information from various report pages can be displayed using dashboards in a single space. And if deeper insights are required, it's possible to click on any dashboard item and immediately return to the report that was the source of information.

On each visual of the report, there is a pin icon on the top right side of the object. Upon clicking the pin, a few options appear, asking to choose an existing dashboard or create a new one (Fig. 7.5).

Figure 7.5 **Pinning a Visual to an Existing Dashboard**

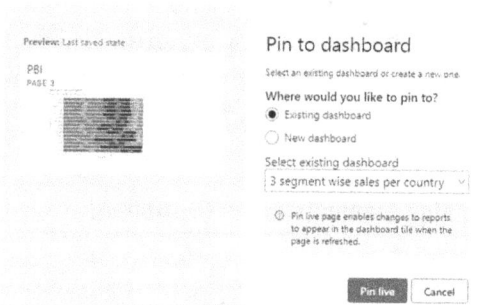

If an existing dashboard is available, select the one you need; otherwise, create and name a new dashboard, then click the pin. Most importantly, using this function, any data from a functional department, be it sales, operations, or finance, can be pinned to a single dashboard. It also enables resizing visuals and allows them to be displayed for additional information.

> ### POINT TO REMEMBER
>
> In Power BI, you can pin visuals from multiple reports within the same workspace to a dashboard. However, you cannot pin visuals from reports that belong to different workspaces to the same dashboard.

2. Quick Insights

Power BI automatically runs an analysis when opening a report. The Quick Insights feature helps explore new trends in the data and automatically notifies of interesting, unnoticed insights with explanations across the report. For getting quick insights, select More Options (...) in the upper-right corner of the visual and click on "Get insights" to see insights about just that visual, as shown in Figure 7.6(A).

Figure 7.6 **(A) Quick Insights Feature**

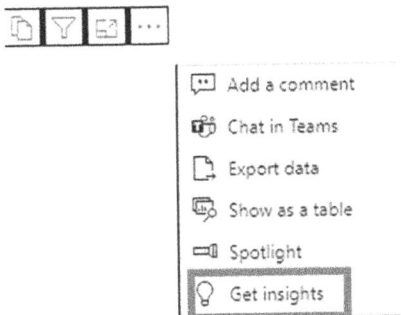

Usually, a narrative will be provided on the right side of the visualization. Clicking the pushpin at the top right of the visual will save the insight/ narrative into the dashboard, which is the first thing most users will interact with.

Power BI can use AI to analyze data and develop exciting patterns; for smaller datasets, such analysis can be done quickly.

3. Add Tile

Managers can add interesting and relevant data, such as video, web content, images, and text, to the dashboard using the Add Tile option in the upper right corner, as displayed in Figure 7.6(B). This option equips them to curate stories for their business with better clarity.

Figure 7.6 **(B) Add Tile Option in Dashboards**

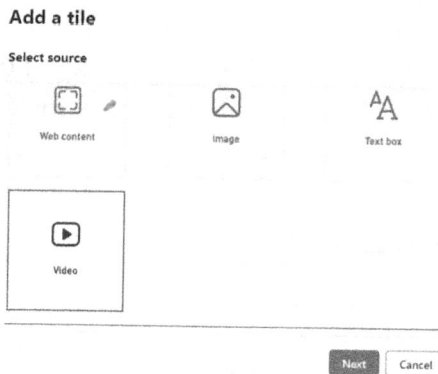

Professionals and organizations can use this feature to add their company logos or even a short video of the team to the dashboard. This can enable an effective curation of stories that hold the attention of all stakeholders while presenting data in the form of visualizations.

4. Streaming Data

Even real-time data can be added as a tile to show live streaming data (Fig. 7.7). There are three methods to do this.

Figure 7.7	Adding Real-Time Data in the Dashboard

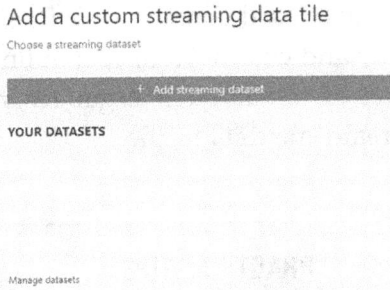

A. Azure Stream Analytics

Once users click a custom streaming dataset, they can add a new dataset to push data into the dashboard. Azure Stream Analytics is the most commonly used dataset for live data streams in Power BI. Live records in the cloud are aggregated by Azure Stream Analytics. The visualizations can be shown second-by-second in Power BI as a line chart or a moving needle on a gauge.

B. API

Once they click a custom streaming dataset, managers can add a new dataset to push data into the dashboard using the Power BI REST API. This method allows developers to send real-time data from their applications or services directly into Power BI. With the API-based push, data is sent as soon as it is generated, and visuals in the dashboard, such as line charts or KPI indicators, update in near real-time, typically second-by-second.

C. PubNub Streaming

Once they click a custom streaming dataset, users can integrate real-time data into Power BI dashboards using

PubNub, a real-time data streaming network. PubNub allows live data to be pushed from IoT devices, apps, or systems.

The Power BI dashboard connects to a PubNub data stream using a key and channel name, enabling second-by-second updates of visuals such as gauges, maps, or line charts based on real-time data traffic.

PRACTICAL TIPS

- Use Live Pinning to keep dashboards updated with real-time data.

- Leverage the Q&A Feature and quickly analyze trends without manual filtering.

- Test mobile dashboards before deploying to ensure they display correctly on smaller screens.

- Set up Dashboard Subscriptions for important stakeholders to automate report sharing.

- Organize My Workspace efficiently by using folders and naming conventions for easy access.

5. Natural-Language Queries

Dashboards facilitate asking questions about the data, and Power BI provides answers as if you were consulting a colleague or friend. This feature is termed natural-language queries. Refer to the area above the dashboard for the Q&A box (Fig. 7.8).

Figure 7.8 Asking Questions in Dashboards

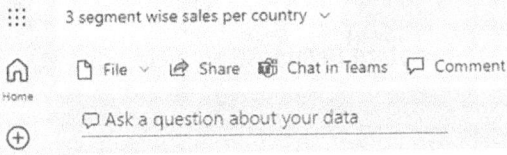

3 segment wise sales per country

Home   File   Share   Chat in Teams   Comment

Ask a question about your data

For example, the visual for the question *"What is the maximum profit by product-name?"* is shown in Figure 7.9 as a bar chart.

Figure 7.9 Q&A Feature as a Bar Chart Response in the Dashboard

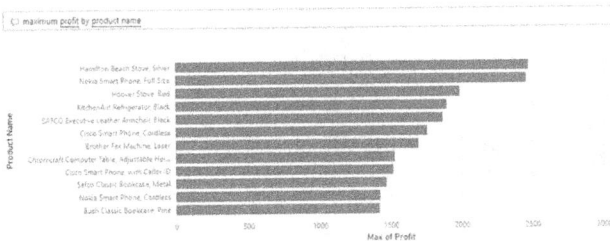

maximum profit by product name

Dashboards will understand the query and present the right visualizations. After analyzing the dataset, they also suggest other valid or alternate queries in a list that appear as one begins to input the question.

Featured questions can also be created with linguistic models. Moreover, Cortana integration enabled in the Settings tab allows managers to ask questions using voice-operated assistants. If the visual/ response of the Q&A is required to be saved and pinned to the dashboard, then click the Pin Visual at the extreme top right side.

This is shown in Figure 7.10 below, which demonstrates the visual for the metric, Total Sales Over Time, as a line chart over the years. Additional filters and visualizations can also be expanded using the report item.

Figure 7.10 Q&A Feature Response as a Line Chart

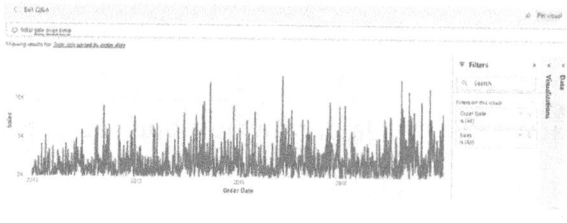

Dashboards can also be enabled on mobile devices, as managers usually log in to their mobile devices to get a quick view of the numbers. Figure 7.11 displays the mobile view similar to that of the desktop view.

Figure 7.11 Power BI Mobile View

6. Subscription

Most of the time, it is discouraged to print the dashboard directly as it can lead to poor formatting, minimize interactivity, and lead to the sharing of outdated, static data. The most preferred option is to subscribe to dashboards as it ensures secure and interactive insights. Power BI sends email notifications to the manager with updated dashboard snapshots based on the selected date and time schedule, such as daily or weekly.

Figure 7.12 Subscribing to Dashboards and Reports

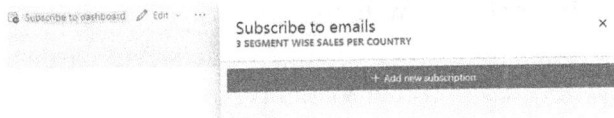

A Subscribe feature, as displayed in Figure 7.12 above, is available in the upper ribbon area to enable this subscribe option. Power BI allows users to add recipients while setting up a subscription. For dashboards, the entire dashboard is emailed to the specified recipients.

> **PRACTICAL TIP**
>
> If you need a weekly sales update in your inbox without manually opening Power BI, you can set up a Power BI subscription. This will automatically email a report every Monday with weekly sales trends, customer acquisition statistics, and revenue insights. So, without logging into Power BI, you can get the report to your email inbox and act accordingly.

7. Alerts

Both Subscriptions and Alerts are useful tools; Subscriptions for consistency, and Alerts for critical actions. Subscriptions allow users to receive email snapshots of a report or dashboard on a regular schedule.

Alerts are triggered when a data threshold is met for a particular visual on a dashboard. These alerts are interactive and conditional, designed to notify users only when data crosses defined limits. Alerts provide interactive notifications, preferably via email, and users can even choose whether the alert should trigger every time or just once until reset. It is important to note that alerts apply only to specific visuals—namely KPI cards, gauge visuals, and cards—and are not supported on other visual types such as tables, matrices, or charts.

To create an Alert, navigate to the desired dashboard in the Power BI Service (alerts cannot be created in Power BI Desktop). Hover over the supported visual (KPI, card, or gauge), click on the ellipsis (...) menu in the upper-right corner of the visual, and select Manage alerts.

In the Alerts pane, click Add alert rule, define the threshold value, set the alert condition (above, below, equal to), choose whether the alert should trigger every time the condition is met or only once until reset, and enable email notifications. Once configured, Power BI will monitor the visual and automatically notify users when key data crosses defined limits.

Figure 7.13 shows the frequency of alerts (hourly, daily, weekly, and monthly) with specified periods and times, along with the mobile alerts available in More options.

Figure 7.13 **Options in Subscription Management**

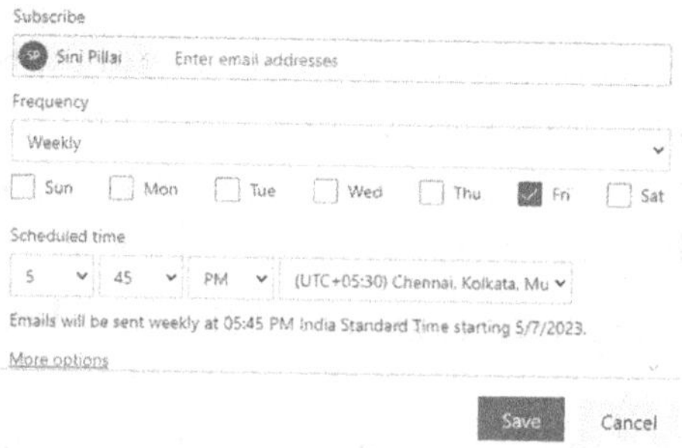

8. Sharing Dashboards

Dashboards can also be shared by clicking the Share button of any dashboard that needs to be shared with a user. The email ID needs to be used for sharing the dashboards, and the type of access has to be given. Similarly, the dashboard creator can also see various dashboards shared with them by clicking "Shared with me" from the left menu of the service page. Figure 7.14 shows sharing options in dashboards.

Figure 7.14 Sharing of Dashboards via Email

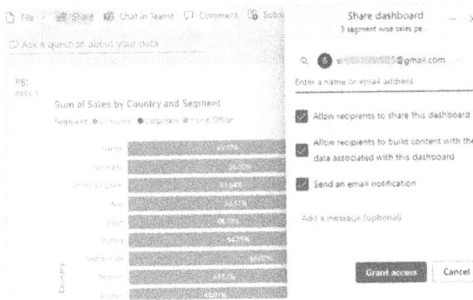

7.2 Managing Datasets, Workbooks, Reports, Security, and Dashboards in My Workspace

Learning how to organize, secure, and maintain assets such as datasets, workbooks, reports, and dashboards, along with handling security aspects, is essential for ensuring sustained data accuracy and user accessibility in your Power BI environment. Whether building reports for personal use or preparing them for broader distribution, mastering these management practices will help you maintain a well-structured and secure workspace.

7.2.1 Managing datasets

Excel workbooks can be uploaded to My Workspace and used as workbooks pinned to the dashboard or simply as datasets. When there are any updates, workbooks can be updated by refreshing manually. Raw data imported into the Power BI Desktop is used to create datasets, and new reports can be built based on these datasets. Figure 7.15 displays a workbook and dataset uploaded in MyWorkspace.

Figure 7.15 Workbook and Datasets in My Workspace

7.2.2 Managing reports

The reports made in Power BI can be modified or downloaded to the reports section. To save a report, click the file option and save the report by providing a name. This feature appears in the Myspace pane and can be accessed anytime when logging into Power BI.

When the saved report is opened, it remains read-only until it is activated for editing. This feature is enabled to prevent unintentional editing of the report. Additionally, to enable filtering, it must be activated through the edit option.

The user interface of a report is powerful. It combines multiple features in a single window and is organized to communicate insights about data. This makes it possible to annotate reports with remarks. For instance, you can add text inside a shape and use arrows to highlight or point to specific remarks.

Figure 7.16 displays the Workspace with reports and various other available options.

Figure 7.16 **Report Generated in Power BI With Editing Options**

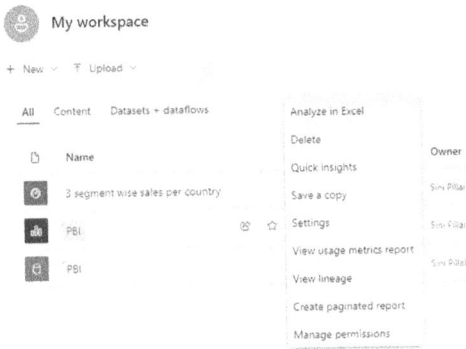

My workspace

+ New ∨   ⊤ Upload ∨

All	Content	Datasets + dataflows		Analyze in Excel	
	Name			Delete	Owner
				Quick insights	
	3 segment wise sales per country			Save a copy	Sm Pilla
	PBI		⊠ ☆	Settings	Sm Pilla
				View usage metrics report	
	PBI			View lineage	Sm Pilla
				Create paginated report	
				Manage permissions	

7.2.3 Dataflow and datasets in Power BI

Dataflow is a new feature in Power BI that helps extract, transform, and load data from various sources and make it available for processing. It ultimately enables publishing and serves as a central data source for managers to view in Power BI. This is shown in Figure 7.17 below.

Figure 7.17 **Dataflow in My Workspace**

All	Content	Datasets + dataflows	
	Name		Type
	PBI		Dataset

Datasets, on the other hand, hold raw data used to build reports; upon left-clicking the datasets, even new reports can be created from the data. However, managers will not be able to model data relationships or make any measures of calculated columns again here.

The most significant advantage is that the entire organization will have a central dataset, and the IT team will be able to own it. Different options available in datasets are shown in Figure 7.18 below.

Figure 7.18 **Exploring Options in Datasets**

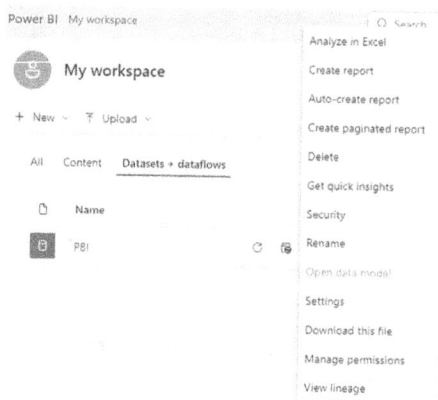

7.2.4 Ways to share reports

Once our report is ready in Power BI Desktop, there are several ways to publish and share it.

Option 1: Publish to the Power BI Service. For this, click File → Publish → Power BI. Choose the workspace to publish, and the report will be available on the Power BI web platform. You can directly share a report with individuals or groups by selecting the "Share" button within the Report View.

Option 2: Publish to the Web. For this, generate a public URL or embed code for websites or blogs.

Option 3: Export in PDF/PPT format for offline sharing.

Option 4: Bundle dashboards and reports into a Power BI app and share them among users via workspace or app distribution.

Option 5: Use the Subscription feature in the Power BI Service to email report snapshots to stakeholders on a schedule.

7.2.5 Sharing workspaces

Workspaces are collaborative environments where we can manage and publish datasets, reports, and dashboards. We can invite users to a workspace and assign roles depending on the level of access we require to provide.

The Admin will have full control over the workspace. They can add or remove members, publish, edit, delete content, and also assign roles. One of the roles is a Member who can edit and publish reports, dashboards, and datasets. However, the members cannot manage permissions.

Another role that can be assigned by the Admin is that of a Contributor. Contributors can create and edit content, but cannot publish or update content for others. There is also a Viewer role, where they can only view content, and they have no permission to make changes or share with others.

Follow these steps to add members to a workspace:

Step 1: Navigate to the workspace in Power BI Service

Step 2: Click on "Settings" → "Permissions."

Step 3: Click "Add people."

Step 4: Enter the user's email address and assign an appropriate role.

Step 5: Click "Add" to complete the process.

7.3 Data Governance Strategy and Row Level Security

A data governance strategy is implemented to deploy Power BI reports. Data governance includes tasks such as identification of all data sources, classification of data (confidential or organizational), assignment of data to dashboards, and identification of critical data sources using deployment models hosted on-premises or on the cloud. It also involves defining who can access the data by managing security groups, as well as developing audit and monitoring solutions, and so on.

Row-Level Security (RLS) is a feature that restricts access to data at the row level based on user roles. By enabling RLS, users only see the data that is relevant to them, maintaining data privacy within organizations.

In Power BI, we can define roles and specify rules to filter rows of data. For example, a role for Cluster Managers might allow each manager to view only the sales data for their respective cluster. We can also use DAX expressions to create dynamic security filters, which adjust data visibility based on the respective user's email or login credentials.

Let's see how to incorporate row-level security using DAX expressions:

Data Analysis Expressions (DAX) is a formula language used in Excel and Power BI to create dynamic, automated filters and security options that control the data behind the scenes. DAX acts as automated rules that evaluate which rows of data are visible to specific users.

To enable row-level security using DAX, follow these steps:

Step 1: Open Manage roles from the Modelling ribbon as shown in Figure 7.19 and click to create a new manager role.

Figure 7.19 Manage Roles for Row-Level Security

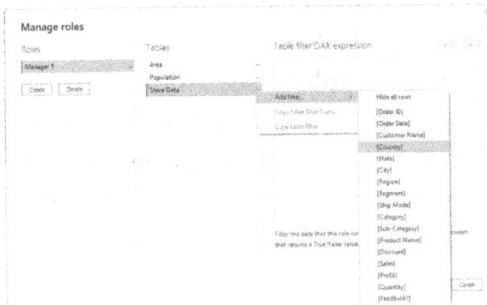

Step 2: Once roles and DAX filters are set, create a visualization using the required fields. Power BI automatically filters data based on the viewer's assigned role. In Figure 7.20, the role of "Manager" is assigned for row-level security.

Figure 7.20 Assigning Row-Level Security in Power BI Service

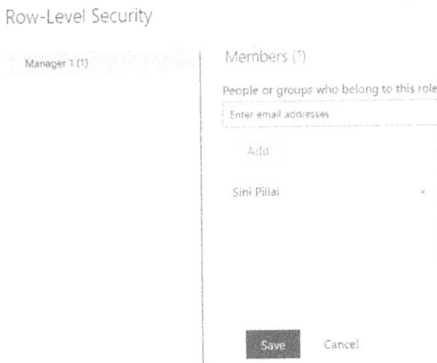

Step 3: Test the role by clicking "View As" in the Modeling tab and choosing a specific role to preview how the report appears with those security filters applied.

Step 4: Again, to publish the report in the Power BI account, select the security option when opening the dataset.

Step 5: Click Add and Save to start using the role.

If a manager has edit permissions in the Power BI workspace, Row-Level Security (RLS) will not be enforced for them. They will be able to see all the data, regardless of assigned roles. RLS roles are only effective in view mode or when the report is accessed through the Power BI Service without edit rights. Additionally, the Q&A feature does not function when RLS is enabled.

7.4 Data Refresh

In Power BI, you can refresh your dataset using Refresh Now or Schedule Refresh, from the More options menu (...) next to your dataset. If your data is stored in the cloud, refreshing is straightforward. However, if your data is stored in files on your local computer or server, you need to install an on-premises data gateway to allow Power BI to access and refresh the data.

A download icon is on the top right of Power BI when signing in to the account; refer to Figure 7.21.

Figure 7.21 Downloading Data Gateway

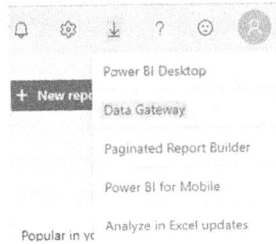

You can download the free Power BI gateway to connect to on-premises data sources. Here, there are two options: either to download the standard mode or to download the personal mode, as shown in Figure 7.22.

Figure 7.22 Download Options for On-Premises Data Source

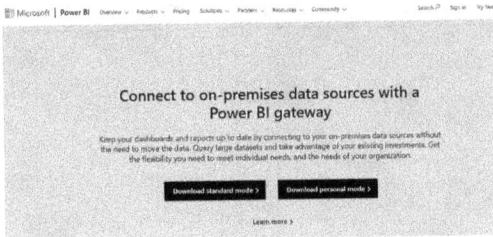

The on-premises personal mode gateway runs as a local application, risking the data becoming stale if the application is not open while starting the system. As a result, data cannot be refreshed when the system is turned off.

The on-premises data gateway in standard mode works in the Windows service, as shown in Figure 7.23, which makes it reliable and manageable.

Figure 7.23 Installing On-Premises Data Gateway

Users are encouraged to download the gateway and configure it by providing their Power BI credentials, as shown in Figure 7.24

Figure 7.24 Configuring the On-Premises Data Gateway

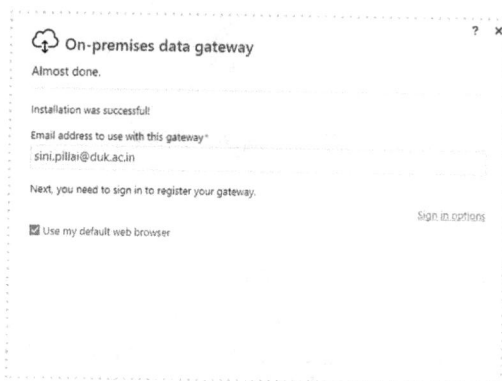

The gateway must be renamed, and a recovery key must be provided to encrypt the connection strings and configuration. The on-premises data gateway configuration is complete now.

From Settings, which is on the top right side, select Manage Connections and Gateways. This is shown in Figure 7.25.

Figure 7.25 Manage Connections and Gateways From Settings Gearbox

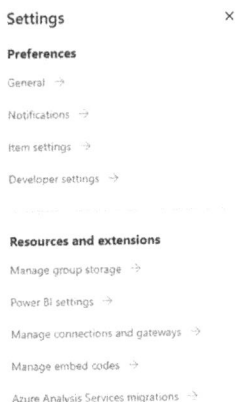

More administrators with the power to add data sources can be added to the administrator's tab, and the gateway can be tested before proceeding.

The on-premises data gateway serves as a connector, enabling fast and secure transmission of data between on-premises data and Power BI. The virtual network data gateway offers fast and secure data transfer between a virtual network and the service.

The following steps enable the user to connect to each file or database in the report that is on-premises:

Step 1

Click the "New" button at the extreme left top-side corner. On clicking, it opens a window to input a new data source. Naming it helps to identify the source later; the name should match the file name or database name to assist with debugging later on.

Step 2

The file can be selected from the Data source type drop-down box. Input the full path for the file name, and provide Windows credentials to access the shared file or folder.

Step 3

After selecting the Add option, click on Test all connections to ensure proper connection to configure files/databases and on-premises data gateways. The Users tab also enables controlling the accessibility of data sources. All these options are to be saved in Settings.

Step 4

To refresh data stored in on-premises files using an on-premises gateway, click the ellipsis button near the dataset and select 'Refresh Now.'

Step 5

Expand the Gateway connection to select the On-Premises data gateway and click Apply. The gateway name will be seen with the status as online.

Step 6

Again, if required to schedule a refresh later, click on Schedule Refresh in the Datasets tab, which will take you to the dataset configuration screen. Here, you can define the refresh frequency (daily, weekly, etc.), set time zones, and choose preferred refresh times.

This feature helps automate data updates without manual intervention. The refresh history tab is also available to identify and check whether data is successfully refreshed. Email notifications of refreshes can also be enabled in the Power BI Service.

Step 7

The Usage Metrics Report in Power BI Service can be checked by clicking the ellipsis near the edit button on the top right side. Refer to Figure 7.26, which displays an option to open usage metrics.

Figure 7.26 Checking the Usage Metrics Report

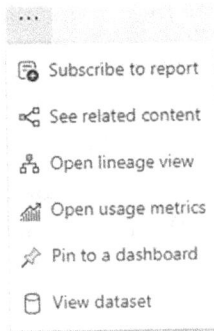

After this step, a Power BI report with usage metrics will be displayed, which includes total views, total viewers, views by user table, etc. Even a dashboard, with Usage Metric Reports, can provide accurate insights for the workspace.

The Power BI Premium solution would be the best-fit enterprise solution to scale Power BI, support enhanced user adoption, and manage massive datasets. Power BI Premium offers more customized features to deploy reports and dashboards with enterprise BI tools and controls. It is better suited for larger organizations with thousands of users.

7.5 Data Security in Power BI Reports

Before we dive into this section, it's important to understand why security is a critical aspect of Power BI report management. Power BI reports often contain sensitive or business-critical data, and without proper security measures, there is a risk of unauthorized access, data breaches, and potential compliance violations.

Ensuring that the right users have access to the right data and only that data helps protect organizational assets, maintain trust, and comply with data privacy regulations. As we discussed in the Row-Level Security (RLS) section, we can restrict users to view only their respective data within a report.

Additionally, to control broader access to reports, we explored workspace access management, where we can limit users to specific permission levels (such as viewer, contributor, or member) to ensure they can only perform permitted actions within the workspace.

Further, BI teams can track the usage and performance of the content deployed to the Power BI report server. In Power BI, several built-in security roles can be assigned to various users or groups of users. You may go to the Manage page to configure the security for both reports and folders. By default, the BUILTIN\Administrators group is assigned to the System Administrator role, and the Content Manager role is assigned to the Home folder.

SQL Server Management Studio, which is a tool provided by Microsoft to manage and configure SQL Server databases, can also create and assign security roles in Power BI. Reports and folders can be customized using the View Report options, and users can also modify them to edit or manage comments on the report content. Based on the type of users, the report server administrator can assign various tasks, allowing users to create, view, or manage comments.

7.6 Power BI Apps in Power BI Services

Power BI Apps offer a powerful way to distribute insights at scale in a structured and secure manner. A Power BI App is a packaged collection of reports bundled together. They are distributed to a specific group of users or the entire organization through the Power BI Service.

This tool simplifies access to content by providing a single interface, allowing users to explore data without dealing with complex navigation or permissions setup for each report.

Power BI Apps are particularly useful for sharing content across departments and creating a central hub for data analytics and visualizations. Also, Apps enable non-technical users to interact with data easily.

To create and share a Power BI App, follow the steps given below:

Step 1: Create and publish reports and dashboards within a Power BI workspace.

Step 2: Go to the workspace and click the Create app button in the top-right corner.

Step 3: Configure App Details with name, description, and then select which reports/ dashboards to include.

Step 4: Set permissions by defining who can access the app.

Step 5: Publish the App by clicking "Publish." The users will receive a link or can access it from the "Apps" section in the Power BI Service.

Step 6: Once published, share the app link directly with users.

Alternatively, users can go to Apps > Get apps > My organization, search for the app, and install it themselves.

Key features of Power BI Apps are:

- Users get all reports in one place.

- Whenever the underlying content is updated in the workspace, users automatically see the latest version in the app.

- It facilitates role-based access control over who can view what.

- It is designed for users to consume insights without access to the full Power BI workspace.

- An App can include multiple reports from the same workspace only.

- If any updates are made to a report other than just data refreshes, the App must be updated to reflect those changes.

7.7 Power BI Content Distribution

One of the key advantages of using Power BI is that it allows users to access content in a format and context that is suited to their needs. For instance, most read-only users log in to view dashboards or reports specific to their role; some receive snapshot images of reports and dashboards through an email subscription.

Certain users may also analyze datasets directly from the Excel workbook, which is hosted in Power BI. On the other hand, other users may prefer to view reports embedded in the SharePoint site, a collaborative platform by Microsoft, for document management and content sharing. Power BI can be integrated with SharePoint to create interactive reports. This leverages its capability of data storage and collaboration features.

Based on the specific needs of users, organizations can choose from various distribution methods or a combination of multiple techniques to host Power BI content in the Power BI Service. The most commonly used distribution options include Power BI Service, share dashboards and reports, SharePoint, Email subscriptions, datasets, directly publishing to the Web, analyzing in Excel, or live connections directly to Power BI Desktop.

Access to shared Power BI content requires users to have a valid Power BI account and appropriate permissions. Content such as dashboards, reports, and apps shared within an organization can only be viewed by licensed users.

For Pro features like sharing and collaboration, users must have a Power BI Pro license or the content must be stored in a premium capacity workspace. Without the necessary access, users will not be able to view or interact with the shared content. Power BI Premium and Pro differ in pricing and features. Pro is suitable for small teams and premium for larger organizations. Power BI Premium offers additional features, including AI capabilities.

Alternatively, reports can be shared by generating a public web link using the "Publish to web" option. This allows anyone on the internet to view the report without needing a Power BI account. However, this method is not secure and should only be used for non-sensitive or publicly intended data, as anyone with the link can access the content.

Even though there are various methods to distribute content, the most commonly used method in organizations is Power BI Service. It supports a large number of users, embedding the content into custom applications. Options such as data alerts, email subscriptions, analysis in Excel, and embedding options also streamline the data analysis process.

The Power BI mobile application also supports and aligns various distribution methods, including Power BI apps, data alerts, and sharing of reports and dashboards.

7.8 Power BI Usage Metrics Report

Power BI Service provides Usage Metrics Reports for dashboards and reports that allow users to monitor and analyze the usage and performance within an organization. To access usage metrics, navigate to your workspace, then select the desired dashboard or report. Click on "More options" (...), and choose "View usage metrics report." This opens a pre-built report showing views, shares, viewers, and performance trends.

The reports are automatically pre-built, providing detailed information about the usage of dashboards and reports as to how many times they have been viewed, who is engaged in the dashboard, who viewed them, and what actions were taken. Thus, these metrics offer valuable insights about user engagement, helping the report administrators understand the impact and reach of the content.

The Usage Metrics Reports offer key insights on total view counts, unique viewers, viewer details, interaction patterns like filtering or exporting data, distribution of views across day, week, or month, frequency of access, load times of reports, dashboards, and data on device and browser usages.

The benefits of usage metrics are not only limited to understanding which dashboards and reports are most often opened and edited, identifying power users, and how they interact with data, but also in providing a feedback loop, facilitating better decisions about report development and deployment in the future.

FUN FACT

Power BI Usage Metrics Reports can spy on the most popular reports in your organization. You can see who's viewing, sharing, and interacting with dashboards.

7.9 Real-World Applications, Challenges, and Future of Power BI

Let's explore two practical scenarios where Power BI delivered measurable business value:

1. Walmart's inventory management mechanism

Walmart, one of the world's largest retail chains, leveraged Power BI to optimize its inventory operations. It utilized Power BI visualizations and dashboards to monitor stock levels of various product categories across thousands of stores in real time.

Initial integration with legacy systems and data standardization for seamless reporting were some challenges Walmart faced while adopting Power BI in its inventory management process. However, with time, Walmart overcame these challenges and achieved a significant reduction in stockouts thanks to Power BI. It was able to boost customer satisfaction and operational efficiency through the power of Power BI analytics and visualizations (Lin, 2019).

2. Patient insights at Providence Health

Providence Health used Power BI to analyze patient records and improve patient care. They relied on visualizations from Power BI, identified high-risk patients, and optimized resources accordingly.

They faced challenges in managing sensitive patient data in the process of adhering to compliance regulations as they used Power BI for data insights. Upon overcoming these challenges, they achieved better patient outcomes through targeted care plans and optimized the application of medical resources (Annapurani et al., 2021).

7.9.1 Challenges

Even though Power BI is a powerful tool for data visualizations and storytelling, there are a few challenges. Some of the challenges in Power BI adoption are as follows:

1. Companies often face challenges in preparing data for analysis. Managing data cleaning and transformation processes may become a tiresome task.

2. Integrating Power BI with old, outdated systems is complex and time-consuming.

3. Users/ managers require significant training to fully understand Power BI.

4. As the volume of data increases, maintaining performance is a challenge.

5. Infrastructure costs are an obstacle while scaling Power BI in larger organizations.

Users can take a structured approach to overcome these challenges and successfully adopt Power BI. Leveraging Power Query for automated data cleaning can significantly reduce the manual effort. Providing regular, hands-on training sessions and creating self-service learning resources can help companies become proficient and faster.

Finally, conducting a cost-benefit analysis and scaling the Power BI infrastructure, starting with Power BI Pro and moving to Premium as needed, will surely help. With the right planning and support, Power BI adoption can become a powerful enabler of data-driven decision-making in business.

7.9.2 The future ahead with Power BI

Power BI continues to enhance its natural language processing and machine learning capabilities. This enables predictive analytics, intuitive data interactions, and automated insights for data-backed decision-making.

In the coming years, organizations will continue using Power BI for real-time, data-driven execution and develop tailored analytic solutions, especially in industries like IoT and supply chain management. The Power BI solution is also expected to roll out more robust features for compliance and governance. It will evolve as a forward-looking tool that supports fact-based insights for smarter business intelligence.

As we bring this book to a close, I do so with the hope that it has equipped you with a strong foundation in the capabilities of Power BI. From data preparation and modeling to the creation of impactful visualizations and dashboards, Power BI has emerged as an indispensable tool for modern organizations.

While the journey of learning Power BI may come with its challenges, the rewards it offers through its interactive, automated, and user-friendly features are truly transformative. As the platform continues to evolve, staying curious, consistently practicing, and diving deeper into its advanced features will help professionals and organizations stay ahead in the dynamic landscape of data analytics and visualization.

Chapter Summary

- Power BI Desktop is designed for advanced tasks. It provides tools to analyze data and derive insights from a managerial perspective by curating stories through visualizations.

- The three major elements of Power BI include datasets, which are the source of data; reports, which create visualizations with interactive capabilities; and dashboards, which are a collection of visualizations and/ or reports.

- Users can build dashboards directly on the Web using the Power BI Service and access interactive reports on both Web and mobile platforms. Power BI Service also provides the same type of interactivity, similar to the Power BI Desktop.

- Row-level security allows organizations to control who will access specific data within a report. By assigning roles, users can view only the data that is relevant to their role to ensure data privacy and prevent unauthorized access.

- Once a report is published in the Power BI Service, row-level security can be applied to view data, even at a granular level. The data can be refreshed now or scheduled for later by configuring on-premises data gateways to bring data from on-premises to the cloud.

- Configuring data gateways for on-premises sources in Power BI enables automatic data refresh, ensuring reports and dashboards stay up-to-date with the latest real-time data for accurate analysis.

- Power BI dashboards support subscriptions and alerts to keep users informed and proactive.

- Subscriptions deliver scheduled email snapshots of dashboards, ensuring regular access to updated insights.

- Alerts notify users when data crosses defined thresholds, enabling timely actions based on real-time changes. Together, they enhance data-driven decision-making and monitoring.

- Power BI enables efficient content distribution through workspaces, sharing, and subscriptions, ensuring reports reach the right audience.

- Usage Metrics Reports provide insights into how content is consumed, tracking views, shares, and user engagement. Together, these features help organizations monitor, report performance, and optimize content delivery strategies.

- Despite its strengths in data visualization and storytelling, Power BI adoption can be hindered by data preparation issues, integration complexity, training needs, performance limitations, and scaling costs. Users can take a structured and strategic approach to overcome these challenges and successfully adopt Power BI.

- In the coming years, Power BI is expected to add stronger compliance features and continue evolving to support smarter, insight-driven decisions.

QUIZ

1. **What is the primary use of Power BI Desktop?**
    a. To browse the web
    b. To create and deploy reports
    c. To edit videos
    d. To play music

2. **Identify the element that is not part of the three major elements of Power BI.**
    a. Datasets
    b. Reports
    c. Dashboards
    d. Forms

3. **What is the first step in deploying a report?**
    a. Saving the report
    b. Exporting to Excel
    c. Connecting to data sources
    d. Sending an email

4. **Which tool is used for deploying reports?**
    a. Power BI Mobile
    b. Power BI Desktop
    c. PowerPoint
    d. Excel

5. **Where are reports created in Power BI Desktop deployed?**
    a. Power BI Service
    b. Microsoft Word
    c. Google Drive
    d. Dropbox

6. **Which elements can be managed within "My Workspace"?**
   a. Data models only
   b. Datasets, reports, dashboards, and workbooks
   c. Emails
   d. Web pages

7. **Identify which element is not managed in My Workspace.**
   a. Workbooks
   b. Emails
   c. Reports
   d. Dashboards

8. **How do I access "My Workspace" in Power BI?**
   a. Through Power BI Service
   b. By downloading it
   c. By signing up for Google Analytics
   d. Through Excel

9. **Which element in My Workspace allows us to visualize data?**
   a. Datasets
   b. Emails
   c. Dashboards
   d. Workbooks

10. Which feature in Power BI enables real-time collaboration through shared access and permission controls?

    a. Power BI Gateway
    b. Power BI Desktop
    c. SharePoint Integration
    d. Power BI Service

Answers

1 – b	2 – d	3 – c	4 – b	5 – a
6 – b	7 – b	8 – a	9 – c	10 – d

Case Study 3

(Chapters 5, 6, and 7)

Analyzing Geographical Sales Performance for a Global Enterprise

Introduction:

XYZ International, a multinational consumer electronics enterprise, operates across 15 countries. The company faced difficulties understanding regional sales trends, comparing KPIs across geographies, and delivering real-time sales insights to executives. Intending to create a unified and interactive dashboard for geographical sales performance, XYZ International adopted Power BI. It sought to visualize, analyze, and share critical sales data globally. This case study will help us understand geographical visualizations, storytelling, and report deployment functions.

Let's discuss the challenges faced by the company and the solutions adopted to address them.

Challenges:

1. Sales data was dispersed across regional databases with inconsistent formats.
2. The company had limited capabilities to visualize sales by location or region dynamically.
3. Executives lacked a clear view of KPIs like sales targets, growth rates, and customer acquisition in each market.

4. Reports were Excel-based, lacked interactivity, and were not scalable across the organization.

5. There was a need for role-based access to sales performance data while deploying the data globally.

Solutions:

- **Gauge and KPI Visuals:** The company created KPIs for revenue, market share, and year-on-year growth using Power BI KPI visuals.

- **Card Visuals:** Used to highlight regional performance at a glance.

- **Maps:**

  a. Filled Map and Shape Map provided continent- and country-level heat maps.

  b. ArcGIS Maps integrated demographic overlays like population density and spending capacity.

  c. Azure Maps enabled real-time tracking of supply chain issues.

- **Q&A Visuals:** Allowed executives to type natural language queries.

- **Visual Analytics:** Trend lines, forecasts, and decomposition trees helped in in-depth market analysis.

- **Drill Through:** Enabled users to drill from the global view into country and city-level data.

- **Bookmarks and Selection pane:** Used for guided story presentations highlighting best-performing regions.

- **Spotlight and Tooltips:** Spotlighted underperforming regions; dynamic Tooltips showed contextual insights (e.g., top product sold in a country).

- **Power BI Desktop to Service:** Reports were created in Power BI Desktop and published to the cloud.
- **Workspaces and Row-Level Security (RLS):** Used My Workspace and shared workspaces for collaboration. RLS ensured that regional managers could only see their own data.
- **Scheduled Data Refresh and Security:** Daily auto-refreshes pulled from cloud-based Enterprise Resource Planning (ERP) systems with secure data pipelines.
- **The Usage Metrics Report tracked engagement and feature usage.**

By leveraging Power BI capabilities from KPI Visuals to ArcGIS mapping and curated storytelling, the company transformed its sales performance analysis. This case highlights the value of integrating visual analytics, geospatial insights, and secure deployment for scalable and impactful decision support in a global enterprise setting.

Case assignment:

Let's assume XYZ International wants to track and present its regional sales performance to stakeholders engagingly.

1. Create geographical maps (e.g., ArcGIS and Azure Maps) to visualize regional sales.
2. Use KPIs and Gauge Visuals to track regional targets.
3. Enhance storytelling with Bookmarks, Drill Throughs, and Tooltips.
4. Deploy a Power BI report and set up row-level security to restrict data access based on user roles.

These datasets can be used in Excel/ CSV formats for direct upload to Power BI.

Region	Country	City	Sales Amount	Units sold	Target sales	Sales Manager
North America	USA	New York	500000	500	600000	John
Europe	Germany	Berlin	350000	400	400000	Anna
Asia	India	Bangalore	200000	300	250000	Ravi
Africa	South Africa	Cape Town	150000	200	200000	Thabo

Case discussion questions:

1. How did the use of different KPI visuals (Gauge, Card, KPI) help the company monitor sales performance effectively across regions?

2. What considerations should be made when choosing between a Filled Map, Shape Map, ArcGIS Map, and Azure Maps for geographical visualizations?

3. In what ways did features like Drill Through, Bookmarks, and Tooltips enhance the storytelling experience for executive users?

4. Why was Row-Level Security critical, and how does it support data governance in global organizations?

5. What are the potential challenges in managing data refresh schedules and user access when deploying Power BI reports at an enterprise level?

6. If you were the BI manager, how would you measure the success of this Power BI implementation project?

Glossary

ArcGIS Map: is a geospatial analysis mapping platform that offers advanced features in Power BI. Users can perform proximity analysis and spatial querying to gain deeper insights, as filled maps or shape maps allow only for custom shapes to be displayed, with limited analysis functions.

Azure Maps: Provided by Microsoft Azure, used in geospatial services to integrate mapping and location-based functionalities into user applications.

Bookmark: A tool to save report views, filter states, and visuals, allowing users to quickly return to a specific view and navigate, with the same filters and spotlighted visuals as when the bookmark was created.

Calculated Column: A custom column is created within a data table using DAX for additional analysis.

Cross-Filtering: A feature in Power BI that allows users to interact with the visualization and filter the visuals on the page, so that particular questions about the data can be answered.

Cross-Highlighting: Cross-highlighting is the default interaction between two visuals, which offers flexibility in deciding which visuals should be incorporated in a report.

Custom Visuals: Non-standard visuals created or imported into Power BI to meet specific business needs.

Dashboard: A dashboard is an assortment of visualizations on a single page that can be shared with other users or multiple users, wherein they can interact with the data offered in the dashboard.

Data Model: A structured representation of data that defines relationships, tables, and calculations for analysis.

Data Source: The origin of data imported into Power BI, such as Excel sheets, databases, cloud platforms, or APIs.

Data Analysis Expressions (DAX): DAX is a formula language similar to Excel functions for creating calculations and computations for information and insights.

DirectQuery: is applied in query performance when the dataset is too large to import to Power BI.

Drill-Through: Drill Through is a powerful and advanced data exploration tool that provides different views within a single visual. A drill-through tool would allow managers to navigate from one visual to another report page while maintaining the filter of the visual.

Drill-Down: Drill Down enables exploring data hierarchically, such as moving from a yearly summary to monthly data.

Key Performance Indicator (KPI): A measurable value that indicates success in achieving objectives.

Power BI: is one of the most vital tools developed by Microsoft to manage datasets and create visualizations that bridge raw data and business intelligence for data-driven decision-making.

Power BI Desktop: A free Windows application used to create, edit, and design reports and data models.

Power BI Mobile: A mobile app that enables users to view and interact with Power BI reports and dashboards on the go.

Power BI Service: The cloud-based platform where Power BI reports and dashboards are published, shared, and accessed.

Power Query Editor (Power Query): Power Query Editor is an interface for data cleaning and transformation in Power BI before loading data into reports.

Q&A Visual: A feature that allows users to ask questions in natural language and automatically generates visuals in response.

Relationships: Connections between tables in the data model that allow analysis across multiple datasets.

Report: A report is a collection of visualizations on one or multiple pages, usually comprising several charts, pie, line, or bar charts, maps, and graphs that convey the information.

Row-Level Security (RLS): A data governance strategy with a security feature that restricts access to specific rows of data based on user roles.

Slicer: A visual element that allows users to filter data interactively in reports and dashboards.

Visualization: is a visual representation of data in a chart, graph, map, or any other interactive graphic representing the data.

External Reading Resources

References Books

Deckler, G., Powell, B., & Gordon, L. (2022). Mastering Microsoft Power BI: Expert techniques to create interactive insights for effective data analytics and business intelligence. Packt Publishing Ltd.

Knaflic, C. N. (2015). Storytelling with data: A data visualization guide for business professionals. John Wiley & Sons.

Videos and Articles

(Links also available in Online Resources)

1. Microsoft Power BI Documentation
   http://bit.ly/41Q2oiJ
2. Power BI Learning Blog
   http://bit.ly/3VKZKHm
3. Power BI YouTube Channel
   http://bit.ly/461mxox
4. LinkedIn Learning: Power BI for Business Professionals
   http://bit.ly/3VbUw7y

References

1. Annapurani, K., Poovammal, E., Ruvinga, C., & Venkat, I. (2021). Healthcare data analytics using business intelligence tool. In *Machine Learning and Analytics in Healthcare Systems* (pp. 191-212). CRC Press.

2. Bouchefra, A., Jankov, T., James, H., & Antolovic, Z. (2018). *Performance tools.* SitePoint Pty Ltd.

3. Guo, X., Grushka-Cockayne, Y., & De Reyck, B. (2020). *London Heathrow Airport uses real-time analytics for improving operations.* INFORMS Journal on Applied Analytics, 50(5), 325-339.

4. Lin, R. (2019). The importance of successful inventory management to enterprises: A case study of Wal-Mart. In *The 2019 international conference on management, finance and social sciences research (MFSR 2019).* London: Francis Academic Press.

5. Lu, Y., & Wang, Y. C. (2025). Online hosts' storytelling strategies: A narrative analysis of mindfulness-themed Airbnb online experiences. *Journal of Travel Research, 64(5),* 1226-1243.

6. Mullan, M. (2019). *The data-driven airport: How daa created data and analytics capabilities to drive business growth, improve the passenger experience, and deliver operational efficiency. Journal of Airport Management, 13(4),* 361-379.

7. Sinthong, P., & Carey, M. J. (2021, December). *Exploratory data analysis with database-backed dataframes: A case study on Airbnb data. In 2021 IEEE international conference on big data (Big Data)* (pp. 3119-3129). IEEE.

8. Spence, I., & Wainer, H. (2017). William Playfair and the invention of statistical graphs. In Information design (pp. 59–76). Routledge.

9. Von Hoffen, M., Hagge, M., Betzing, J. H., & Chasin, F. (2018). Leveraging social media to gain insights into service delivery: a study on Airbnb. *Information Systems and e-Business Management, 16,* 247-269.

Bibliography

1. Aspin, A. (2016). *High impact data visualization in Excel with Power View, 3D maps, Get & Transform, and Power BI.* Berkeley: Apress.

2. Becker, L. T., & Gould, E. M. (2019). *Microsoft Power BI: Extending Excel to manipulate, analyze, and visualize diverse data. Serials Review,* 45(3), 184-188.

3. Ferrari, A., & Russo, M. (2015). *The definitive guide to DAX: Business intelligence with Microsoft Excel, SQL Server Analysis Services, and Power BI.* Microsoft Press.

4. Ferrari, A., & Russo, M. (2016). *Introducing Microsoft Power BI.* Microsoft Press.

5. Knight, D., Ostrowsky, E., Pearson, M., & Schacht, B. (2022). *Microsoft Power BI quick start guide: The ultimate beginner's guide to data modeling, visualization, digital storytelling, and more.* Packt Publishing Ltd.

6. Libby, T., Schwebke, J. M., & Goldwater, P. M. (2022). *Using data analytics to evaluate the drivers of revenue: An introductory case study using Microsoft Power Pivot and Power BI. Issues in Accounting Education,* 37(4), 97-105.

7. Nabil, D. H., Rahman, M. H., Chowdhury, A. H., & Menezes, B. C. (2023). Managing supply chain performance using a real-time Microsoft Power BI dashboard by action design research (ADR) method. *Cogent Engineering,* 10(2), 2257924.

8. Powell, B. (2017). *Microsoft Power BI cookbook: Creating business intelligence solutions of analytical data models, reports, and dashboards.* Packt Publishing Ltd.

9. Powell, B. (2018). *Mastering Microsoft Power BI: Expert techniques for effective data analytics and business intelligence.* Packt Publishing Ltd.